The Autobiography of My Mother

Books by Rosellen Brown

STREET GAMES

SOME DEATHS IN THE DELTA AND OTHER POEMS
(National Council on the Arts Selection)

THE AUTOBIOGRAPHY OF MY MOTHER

the autobiography of my mother

by rosellen brown

Doubleday & Company, Inc., Garden City, New York, 1976

Library of Congress Cataloging in Publication Data
Brown, Rosellen.
The autobiography of my mother.
I. Title.
PZ4.B87992Au [PS3552.R7] 813'.5'4
ISBN 0-385-09896-0
Library of Congress Catalog Card Number 73-36581

for Adina, for Elana

I am indebted to the Radcliffe Institute and
to the National Endowment for the Arts for
their very necessary support, financial and
psychological.

"Neutrality. Diverse neutralities. The even hand."

(Gerda Stein:
Journal of Family Court Proceedings)

you fit into me
like a hook into an eye

a fish hook
an open eye

(Margaret Atwood:
Power Politics)

The Autobiography of My Mother

one

RENATA

My mother called and informed me we were going on a picnic.

I am having a hard time figuring out where we should go. She said, "You choose, I do not know such things." Vermont's too far and I want water anyway; not Rockaway, or Fire Island with its housefuls of hopeful secretaries and well-married faggots. It's finally full summer, warm for too many days without breaking. I'm unbearably hot every morning by the time Tippy gets me up for breakfast; now she's sleeping with her legs straight up the wall where her calves can stay cool. The Cape, the Jersey shore, north on the Hudson? Montauk? No long hot drive anyway, especially with Tippy in the car, barfing.

Tippy will sit against my arm while I drive, she still has that irritating habit of piling on when you can least take it. There'll be a great wet spot above my elbow where the two of us sweat. She'll sing "The sow took the measles (and she died in the spring)" in her up-and-down approximation of a melody—"Skeetles or beetles or any such thing!"—and at some point in the trip when I suggest some practical business that has to be done, she'll kick and flail dangerously in her little stony red shoes, and cuddle in all her grandma's empty spaces, sweetly, sourly, for spite. Having a grandmother, in the absence of a father, especially that professional *competer*, encourages wiles and coyness. I had neither wiles nor father nor grandparents, only my mother, against whom, god knows, I couldn't curl, straight as a board. But Tippy's her own tight curl. And I'll be a yoke of shoulders to ride on, a nest of light hair to diddle fingers in. The laughing will be drunken. For an hour at a time we will guzzle each other down like bubbly water.

Then a split second, one lunge or laugh or question with no sane answer to finish it—"Why is this a car? Mommy. Come on." —and in a quick move she will knock against me, bare something like fangs, and I will have had more than enough. I will feel my child climb onto my shoulders and squat on my head, clutching, her knees spurs against my cheek. Or she'll ride under me, fiercely, like a rider whose stirrups have snapped, caught under the horse's belly, dragging, her teeth closed hard against her own unwelcomeness. She will not let go until the ride is truly over. I will walk away foot after foot, deliberate, weightless, dizzy with anger. Or sit huddled in silence. Poor Tippy, I think then, where can she go? I dream of going away, dream of escape. What is there for a child to dream, whose only friends are her grandmother who loves her just to leave me out, and her mother as unreliable as she is?

I choose Torora for the picnic. It has a game preserve with foxes and things in cages. I went once when I was in college, I remember seeing a bear cooling his ass off in the water. It was a leafy place, and cool.

What does my mother have up her sleeve, taking a Thursday off? Things are slow in summer but she just grinds on, forever indispensable. It's going to be a sour day and she has some ultimatum in her head.

two

GERDA

Monday, 6/16, my life in its seventy-second year:

In the law offices—one could never, seeing them, describe them as "chambers"—of Stein, Weisbacher, Tenney and Balch, Monday morning is filled with routines so enervating one wonders if the week ought not to be ending, rather than beginning. Our agendas are carefully checked against the court calendars; the law journals are combed in search of useful cases at all levels; we, my partners and I, sit down with our small research staff to outline the work that must be done; discuss that which has been done, like doctors reviewing cases for their residents. I am committed to the education of our apprentices. Our children, they shall succeed us, bearing the best and the worst of us into another generation.

It happens that of our current crop of three young lawyers and one law student, two are immensely irritating for listening like little tape machines themselves blank until I fill them up with words —and the young woman among them, who miraculously appears to have graduated near the top of her class at Penn, is practicing a sort of mean-spirited and small-eyed radicalism upon me which makes me into a witch of the bourgeois establishment because I do not divide the world bilaterally by sexes but search for overarching principles that apply to any and all comers. (Has it ever occurred to any of the great dichotomizers that there are, once and for all, only two kinds of people in the world—I mean the ultimate two: those who divide the world into two kinds of people and those who do not?) Her gold glasses glint at me coldly. She is more severe than my grandmother, and her lips are made for uninterrupted perturbation, of which she has no difficulty finding her fill. A lemon-sucker, my mother would have said of her and her *fercrimpte* mouth. "Why are you here, Miss Wachter?" "To learn your tricks." "But if the tricks are so ignoble—" "No, only your ends. Your means are brilliant and I intend to have them." "And having them will not change you?" Oh, the very suggestion. "No, they will not change me. Only you make oppressive law and I'll have to spend the first hundred years undoing it. It's like building ugly houses out of good wood." Her eyes slash at the air before her, seeing barricades, herself at the top, looking over into my eyes. I shall not bother to point out the rudimentary fact that never in my life have I made a law. "Good law favors no one unjustly." "Bullshit," she whispers sweetly. "Some small vestige of decorum if you please, Miss Wachter." She arches her chin up at me, a very small and frail chin really, like a horse nodding and thinking of shying, and flounces out of the office as well as one may flounce in flaccid dungarees, holding a clipboard.

Later, after this absurd confrontation, I go out of the office to see to the finishing touches of a miserable no-win affair. This is one of those dry victories of the civil rights of the insane above the intuition, probably correct, of the doctors who feel he will use his rights of freedom as license to jump off the closest bridge to hand. I shall sit clenched from now on for the telephone to bring bad news. It will be now or in a week or a year that John Tavistock may rebuke me with his life for having been convinced one time too many—of course, of course I have such doubts—that a principle was sufficiently urgent to find its containment in a particularly weak vessel. I speak of John Tavistock of the bled gray eyes and emaciated institutional white arms always showing out from the abrupt sleeves of his uniform, committed against his will, released as per mine so that he can be incarcerated again only after a hearing; and though I may have the ultimate decision in this case, I shall perhaps have the ashes of my victory in a box. This is one of those cases that leaves me standing, wanting not to be touched by comforters, in the long long empty hall of the Law: I have done an abstract duty. It is done for the sake of a few strong enough to benefit and for the health of a principle which is itself, of course, nerveless but which connects with, is part of, the body of our laws.

But how is one to leave such a case alone when it has been brought to one's doorstep? This kind of litigation is like a drug— let us say one of those broad-spectrum antibiotics: it saves lives, it overcures, it does not touch. Depending. Applied insensitively, in spite of contraindications, applied even with all due care, some- times it kills. Remember my sister, my dear sister Esther, who died of the drug that saved her. (DO NOT PRESCRIBE, said the label, WHERE ANY OTHER DRUG CAN BE SUBSTI- TUTED. CAN CAUSE ACUTE ANEMIA, CYANOSIS AND LEUKEMIA. And did. The odds! I said. Esther, the odds are with you. Well. Any card player knows, my father, her father knew, they do not bend and love us, the odds.) Not to mention my friend Amalie's little sister Sophie when we were very young, dead of the prevention of diphtheria, choked on a horse's dose of live vaccine. ("She is a large child," the doctor had assured her mother, "she can tolerate a serum for two.")

Just so, I go to claim like a lost package no one wants my client John Tavistock, who like many another paranoid had awareness enough of the legal machinations which paralleled those of his own head to call upon me more than a year ago. With me when I arrive is a small knot of newspaper photographers, swinging cam- eras that look like third arms, comfortable hard-shelled append- ages. I was informed that NBC-TV was sending a mobile unit; thus, a good hour on the phone when I can least afford it, plead- ing with them to keep their equipment away from my man. I am forced, ludicrously, to parry with the producer of the six o'clock news, attempting to explain to him that the sight of the smallest of those huge cameras, like undersea apparatus, those sneakered young men standing behind them zooming their lenses, running this way and that, would undoubtedly upset Mr. Tavistock at a time when he shall feel threatened quite sufficiently by the need to place one foot before the other and walk to freedom.

"But come on, is this man still paranoid?" asks the TV man,

laughing, with a sort of mock outrage; or perhaps it is not so very mock.

And so I must begin again—hardly the first time—to explain. "Yes, if he was in the first place, then still he is, yes, paranoid. The point of this exercise of liberty has not been to grant freedom to a cured man nor even to a man falsely incarcerated so much as—"

"Well, what are we there for?" Time is money; tape is time. But who, after all, invited them in the first place?

"Mr. Evans. If that is your name." A pause in which to match indignation for indignation. Let him spend a hundred-dollar minute in silence. "I should like to know why it is you are so hasty to send your infernal cameras to track the spoor of this poor being" (I hear him breathe heavily his exasperation) "if you do not so much as appreciate the significance of his release, which has entirely to do with a process, a constitutional guarantee not even that something shall happen to a man but that *nothing* shall happen to him. This is the essence of the fourteenth amendment, if you have ever taken the trouble to read it. And process is, I am afraid, not your most photogenic or visually comprehensible object—"

"Good Christ." I hear his weak sputter of comprehension, and then a long yawn of finality. There will be no morally certifiable image to be made of John Tavistock as he leaves the asylum. The viewer will be confused: here is a loony, a man who is mad, for all anyone cares to make distinctions between molesters who menace them and have designs on their children in the school playground and paranoids who walk in fear of *them*—and the victory in this case has been to set him free on one of those damned communist-plot softy technicalities on whose rock this country was so inconveniently builded. Now he will perhaps be re-committed under more precise and irreversible auspices, so it is not even his final deliverance we are fortunate enough to be seeing with our TV dinner. What the hell, one can hear them ask in their living rooms in all five boroughs, what is this due process anyway? What does it have to do with nuts roaming the streets?

And so the hounds of instant publicity have been put off our trail. I travel to Creedmoor, John Tavistock's most uncongenial temporary home, by dirty gray subway and green bus streaked with silver to suggest speed. This is a most inauspicious entrance to make but I have arranged to take him away by taxicab and there is no way to subsidize this long trip comfortably in both directions. My particular brand of justice, Brand X, is marginal. His family will not be there, since they are firmly opposed to all this "tampering," they call it, as if with divine right or nature taking its course. (It was, of course, their signatures on the commitment papers that secured him his little bed in the midst of nowhere.) He is not going home to them. He is going to live in one of those wretched hotels in Long Beach where released mental patients have founded a sort of leper's colony of shared abandonment, while all humanity (read the state agencies) looks the other way. I am happy to have reading on the subway because when I stop to reflect on what I am about to do I feel unclean.

It is a long slow walk from the bus stop up to the barred doors of the hospital. Why will grass not grow in this kind of graveyard, what does it know? Perhaps it is only that they are forever putting up new buildings, annihilating the lawns, infesting the air with bulldozed dust. It is like living forever on the wrong side of the tracks, in spite of the pretty plastic and the little knock-kneed trees. More graves, more and more, they are forever dying into this infinity of bricks and bars. If ever I were to go mad I would find a way to die before humiliation killed me.

I sign a great many papers in quadruplicate, as though I am co-signing the deed for a house, then I wait in the brightly lit lobby —dull and cheerful it is, the last outpost of sanity and a desperate inoffensiveness, and it reminds me of the newer sort of subway stations in our more enlightened smaller cities—until a young nurse approaches holding John Tavistock's arm firmly. She appears to feel the need to support him exactly as though it were his legs and not his will that was broken. In the hard light of the entrance to the cave, she drops his arm to pat her hair vaguely, whereupon, just in the nick of time, the first photographer moves toward her. She turns and gives a full gay smile to the camera and then, turning back to John, rising to an occasion of which she clearly disapproves, stiffly she shakes his hand and murmurs, per instructions, "Good luck." Roughly I am moved into sight of the camera with the white-faced John, whose every newly honed whisker hole seems a moon pock, the mark of unfillable darkness.

From here on the arrangement is that Legal Aid is going to do this work, you see; the routine cultivation after I have coaxed up the first hard yield. But where are they today, those young journeymen? What I mean is that I should like to have given up the privilege of settling this young man into his hotel. I shall not describe it, only say that I recall one hotel I lived in as a law clerk newly moved from home, until I discovered the uses to which it was put at night when a young man attempted to gain entrance to my room already removing his belt before he had so much as crossed the threshold. This place I had found for John was nearly as bleak: across the lintel a nonsensical name, the proprietor's spelled backward, I would guess: RENREL—and the dark lobby full of abandoned chicken parts: legs, arms, heads. Baggy dresses, collapsed spines in starched sport shirts. Newsprint over faces. The tall-ceilinged room is very brown-yellow, as though a hundred shades have been pulled against the summer light. The lobby is a rock and they are hiding under it, every one of them under his own. Slumped and stretched and curled they live on tranquilizers, and this nothingness, this holding of the body until a genuine death overtakes it, is the price of freedom from coercion. They live here halfway between the barred windows they abhor and the families that abhor and will not keep them. If this hotel is like the one I remember they must do battle with cockroaches every time they step into their crumb-strewn kitchens. They must stamp powerless feet. What does an army of roaches look like to a paranoid schizophrenic? Christ. The only thing they are missing here, by the looks of the occupants, who might wish it were otherwise, is the absurd racket of men who have bought the occasion to groan and chuff like locomotives and handsaws, and women who calculate the charm of singing out beneath them like distracted cats. Once I read in some fiction how a man suffered his most profound throes of passion vicariously listening to lovers in the room next door; but what I heard while I did my homework would not have interested any creature of two legs, I swear it, and perhaps in fact convinced me of the absurdity of dignity exchanged for a moment of high adrenalin.

At the front desk, one island of light in the back-bedroom dark, John Tavistock stops. He is not looking at them, he is staring at his feet in unpolished shoes and tears are at the corners of his eyes, stopped there. He has, can one blame him, the look of—how do I say this? I believe that in the freshest of clothes he would smell of unaired bedclothes, of undershirts slept in amid much tossing, for a month or two. An unwell cold sweat stands bead by bead on his neck, above the line of shirt collar. Something about him makes me think of a seasick sailor, perhaps his tight rolling walk is that of a man attempting to stay upright upon a tossing deck. His bones are well-knit, beneath the flab of starch food and inertia; somewhere very deep in, the healthy man hides out.

I must here take a deep breath. "John, you do not need to stay here, I am sure I can find some place in the city that is less—" I rub my fingers together suggesting either dirt or money, which-ever way your mind inclines. This man is thirty-two years old; he is afraid of women, he is afraid of men, afraid of himself and, needless to say, of me. When he was committed he had spent three months at the main post office where he worked tearing open letters on the sly, all those addressed to "John," insofar as anyone could determine, in search of letter bombs on their way to him. "I can take you somewhere else."

"Oh no." He says this gently, his voice bends at the center under the weight of such certainty. Never be vague with a man, a child, or an animal who does not trust you: somewhere? God knows where he thinks I may take him. His eyes dart forward, back, they remind me in their quickness of the red fangs of a harmless snake.

But of course it is of no use, John Tavistock *wishes* to disappear into the nothingness of this place, he prays that he may live drugged and submerged, safe. This shall be the nearest thing to happiness for him. He has learned from his doctors to call this "responsibility" and "facing up" when in fact it is nothing but going out from a ward full of others into a single room without bath where he may pretend there is no one in the world but him-self. Facing up to nought. He is opaque to me. Coming out of the hospital he paid attention to nothing, not to the insistence of the heat nor the distant smell of the trees. He bent his neck over and hung his head. Perhaps he thinks he does not truly deserve to be on this side of the bars, or perhaps it is simply no use to him. Here, a few blocks from the sea, he does not register the wholly different smell and feel of the air. I should actually find myself depressed, in time, as though waterlogged, by this dampness, I find it a kind of saddening weight. Salt begets salt tears, just so. But John is in a kingdom of his own, locked in his tower, and barely registers such subtleties. If he were acted upon perhaps he would act; only perhaps. Meteorological phenomena, I should suppose, are not useful to him at this moment. They tell him nothing, give him no warnings or clues to the kind of danger he sniffs for. But if it should develop that he needs a way out, one may be certain that he knows all he must about the steady rolling of those waves: John knows front and back entrances, skylights and trap doors with the precision of a cat burglar. What a bit of geography this is, on which to maroon these hopeless . . .

"I'll be all right." He touches my arm reassuringly, and then leaves his fingers there. We are standing in the doorway to his room, which is very dark and which he has not looked at. "It doesn't matter," he says quietly. "I'm going back to sleep." He has such very tiny eyes, over which puffy creases sag, no doubt drug-induced. If he were to laugh—very suddenly he may and then as suddenly chop it off and frown as though someone else had burst out with an indiscretion—his eyes would disappear, like a Chinese baby's. His cheeks are long and gray. If I pinched them I fear they would not snap back and color again for days.

"What have I done to you, John, getting you out and bringing you here?" Does sympathy seep through congenital terror? Can it mass and become tangible for him, or is it dangerous for me to doubt? I do wish I had more background in the needs of the deranged.

"Grandma" (for so he has always called me, most matter-of-factly, with what I hope is a small smile at the rear of his straightforward eyes) "you did OK, you got me out on my own, I don't care where. I asked you, didn't I? They can't hold me is all I care, you know I can't take that. Nobody ever did nothing for me," he says by way of thank-you, and the tears begin again at the infinitesimal arrow-points of his eyes. "I gotta go throw up," he tells me, so calmly. "The junk I take. You go." He is pointing down the stairs. "Go on. You don't have to see me puke," and I am ashamed that I do go. How awful. I have simply never been good at others' humiliations; could never stand my own daughter's diapers, let alone a stranger's vomit. This poor man with his stomach full of instant mashed potatoes thrashed about by a beaker of Thorazine. . . . And so I hear that delayed reaction like something shattered on the floor, a vast thing because it spills on and on, and know that white-faced John with his vestige of pride and his one clean shirt is bending over the landing, he does not yet know where the bathroom is. Well, he had better begin to cope right now, there, on the spot. I tell this to myself, sternly, fleeing at his order. I am so happy to be out in the open air, which smells of laundry starch, alkaline, bleached. One would think I had had a noseful of John's returned lunch. I am hurrying with my head down, chop-legged, thinking, Gerda, you are walking like your client, you are hoping no one will see you. I am chilled utterly, escaping.

So. If John is terrified, I am, far more. This is a beastly bit of law I barely believe in; by my teeth I did the work. I have won a dangerous landmark victory and I pray the defendant survives to thank me. Does it matter that he does not now realize that what I have done was in fact not for him? That it was in service of a general principle and that he might even suffer for it? The RENREL, like the law, only seems to offer shelter to a soul as lost as John. Grandma, who so bitterly retreated through that waiting room full of other grandmas who have gone mad or speechless or merely to sleep, never turned at the sound of his retching. What an auspicious beginning of his freedom, and an ending to my responsibility for him. That slow spilling, like rain from a gutter, I take with me all the way home to the office, and also my final view of the RENREL as I opened the heavy front door with its crosswise crack—I do hope it was not smashed by an aged inhabitant falling through, or lunging, or trying to die.

Well, if I am weak and overly frightened by the weakness of others, I must say that I have picked a profession for myself that will support whosoever leans against it, and never buckle, and never show pain. *Amen, selah.*

❀ ❀ ❀

Later in the day, some minor strains, internecine squabbles between the partners, all of whom have different feelings for our firm's priorities these days, what time, what energies shall be outlaid in getting as opposed to spending hard cash in the stewardship of the causes for which we exist. Sam dreams of his political career—all dreams at this juncture but I object to the manner in which they preoccupy his concentration. He is interested in defending a mayoral assistant against charges of graft, bribetaking in the granting of certain licenses; he dredges up arcane principles, which he swears are "under such heavy fire" one would think the constitutional crisis of the age upon us. When I deride this as *pilpul,* a kind of Talmudic nit-picking, he fumes at me like a small boy above the broad modish lapels of his suit-with-vest. (Sam is cultivating, these days, the looks of an ecumenical Abe Lincoln: he too is long and dark, though hardly self-educated; he is wishing he could find a legitimate justification for sounding like Sam Ervin's nephew.) Meanwhile, Stan Balch dreams of soft work so he can bring in commercial customers, with whom he has always been at home. And Jack is exalted by detente with Peking, certain possibilities there, *und so weiter.* At this rate our firm shall fly apart into a thousand pieces and never be found again. . . . "Fine," say I. "Let Stan pay our way, for the political education, especially, of Sam Eisenstadt while he toadies up to the mayor's man. Is that not what you both prefer?" No, no, not put quite like that, insist the two of them; they offer cleaner alternatives. "All right, Stan, you are the patron of our art, our philanthropy. You may defend corporations so that we may defend principles."

"Why do you have to go out of your way to make me feel crass, Gerda? We've always welcomed as much commercial business as we could find to support our other—"

"As much as we had time for without encroaching on our other work, dear. You are trying to raise your take-home, you want a yearly increment like some second-grade schoolteacher."

"Well, what in the bloody hell's the matter with that, Gerda, do we all have to crawl into that hair shirt of yours and die scratching? Goddamn. . . ."

"All right, Stan, you are not crass, you are necessary, does it make you feel better to think that? You are certainly more necessary to us than you would be to Arnold and Porter, where you are wishing you sat at this very moment. Here you are the only fiddle who plays a tune that can wheedle pennies for our supper, I don't mean to seem ungrateful."

"Well, you do a good job of seeming, Gerda. It's too easy for you to forget how the rent gets paid around here."

"Granted. Yet you are here. And you are here because we pay the rent, as it were, on your principles, and your moral satisfaction."

"Jesus," Sam mutters, "nothing that goes on in the mayor's sub-basement could get as seamy as this, you two."

Which leaves only Loren to chide awhile, to grind his newest ax. Loren is a gentle man who has always had a mustache, in fashion and out, and quizzical eyes set deep in lined, leathery furrows. He has rarely tried to make a ripple; will seldom make a direct accusation of stupidity or incompetence; has therefore, at times, had a limited usefulness at some of the more strenuous parts of this business: one has always had to go fishing with Loren as though he were a diffident witness, to find out what he wanted to say. But something has happened, perhaps middle age is upon him and he has grown, like a third set of teeth, a whole new mouthful of scruples. Loren's new *shtik*—Sam's word, not mine—is the changing of laws and the locking of horns with every lawyers' guild and bar association he can find if they object. New priorities, no more of this asinine housewifery, cleaning up here and there, emptying ashtrays down at the circuit court of appeals. We have been doing this for weeks now: sweetly we accuse each other of ill faith, which neither of us precisely believes. Then we do our dance of apology, and we get back to the work we have been doing for twenty years. In spite of their age, which after all increases as does mine, I feel I have here in the office a half-dozen young horses who need their exercise and must be free to run wildly in the pasture bucking at each other and leaping at shadows. It keeps them diligent when they are in the traces.

※ ※ ※

Now. I sit on my tall kitchen stool, putting Ac'cent on my dinner, also rosemary and some scattering of curry. Lovely colors all: who says that a solitary woman's meals must be ugly and plain. They are only a reflection of what she judges herself to be and I see mine blessedly uninhibited by the tastes and abhorrences of others. Adaptation is an overpraised virtue; if it is meant, like other genuflections to the superego, to be self-fulfilling, let me say that I have not often found it so. My husband, for example, short though his tenure in my kitchen may have been, demanded of me the least palatable of Yankee cooking: congealed sauces the color of school paste and meats with their death juices running in their parsley beds, and an atrocious sweet that sets my teeth on edge at the very memory, "hard sauce" for gingerbread. To what lengths must one go to be a fully assimilated American?

I eat my chop. Dinner music on the radio, or endless news, around and around on a Möbius strip, have your pick. The greatest American city and this is all they will provide, marching music, tubas and piccolos, or this monstrous rock, roll, whatever, grown men imploring the microphone, "Take me, kill me!" I do wish someone would oblige and protect a few of the remaining soft mucous linings of the world. And so I turn it off and confront my plate and the relatively varied typefaces of the New York *Times*.

After dinner, some cognac. I have work—always work, my husband, my companion, the soothing assurance that there is at least another day on which again to try reason in the world—but I sit in my old dog of an armchair first. I have my books, my pictures— Emma Goldman, whom I defended once, at the very end, so badly I deserved to lose (and lose I did), von Neumann, Kafka, Rilke, my old friend Lev Borowitz and his wife, the cellist Cora Schoenkopf, who live in Israel now, withered with age and illness. My heroes these, if you will. Gunnar Myrdal at my right, C. Wright Mills at my left, taken somewhere at a conference on law and ideology in North Carolina one time—silly Gerda with a hat over one eye looking very nearly rakish. I have my one glass of hot water in the morning, and the general air of busyness in the corners, independent life, no slackness, no emptiness, no rest, except insofar as the sense of time, slowly ticking, breathes out of the small carpets, the glassed bookcases, speaking of someplace else. My room, my mind are intended to be well beyond the reach of dusting. *Horror vacui?* Love of engagement? Merely a European tic to those so accustomed? You may rely on it: when I lose something in this old flat of mine, it stays lost. That comforts me.

Sleepy I let the words troop through my head. You see I can still play English like a rare music to myself. It is not my language. The measure of my true grief is that: fifty years, no, sixty, and then some, and still if I cross my eyes, in a manner of speaking, it all goes out of focus. It is abstract, it takes an effort at bad moments, I cannot lean on it, only suck on words, listen to them, bathe in them.

Revenant, dreaming? Revenant a nun on her knees humble and beseeching? Revenant, plundered, ravished by a man, but dreamily? A day like a Monet, shimmering in light?

I shall *stiffen* the language for myself only in time to die.

RENATA

As soon as I left the house I knew I had one suitcase more than I had a hand for. I carry the baby in one of those corduroy tie-on things, a neck-breaker, and even though it's supposed to leave your hands free I always find myself sort of keeping them at the ready, just in case the knot comes undone. So I took a cab to the airport, but there was this feeling I had that people must take to the gallows, you know? That they're about to die so it doesn't matter what they squander, really. The driver was lovely, he kept smiling at me in the rearview mirror, he knew I needed cheering up and his face was enough to do it: absurd mustache with little waxed-up points to keep him from taking himself too seriously. He looked like an Oakland A. I had the distinct feeling he'd pull over someplace if I gave him any encouragement—I think I have to be careful not to—and put the flag up for a while, but you'd better believe I'm into chastity belts these days, not quick trips in the back seat.

When we got on the plane the baby began to shriek, and then went and—extravagantly, stinkingly—did in three diapers, like some animal in terror. I read magazines and slept and changed her and slept and then I have to say I think I discovered a desperate sort of laughter that must have been cowering in a corner my whole self-pitying life. It was just at the point when the landing gear bumped down, but, you see, it was an hour later than the one on my watch—I had changed my time once, in Chicago—and so when I felt this thunk, like a boulder falling out of the plane's belly, I was sure we were lurching into a crash. All the stewardesses were hurrying around and the NO SMOKING sign was on for no discernible reason (except, I figured, to keep from exploding at the first spark). I opened my eyes wide out of a deep confusing sleep and declared to myself—almost in words, like a big cross-stitch on the wall inside my head—I said, "Don't let me die, dear Lord, I will never take myself seriously again and/or bother you if you just let me live." Picture me with a waxed mustache, smiling, smiling. Who could believe how old I was? With my baby-blond hair, weightless, and no character lines on my face, high-waisted and bony-kneed, twenty-nine, unaccomplished, unmarried, unemployed, ungood, unclean, not much more than a vapor of lazy habits and withered flower-child whims, passive to the point of an endless drowsiness, and suppressed perspective on it all. For those few minutes, I had more than enough perspective; it was like I was in the plane making passes over the head of a naked skinny girl who was waving and stamping and shouting Stop! Eight years in San Francisco at the end of the whole continent of possibilities: dropout from art school, for which I wasn't patient or talented enough; nursing school, for which I wasn't anywhere near strong enough; fashion design school, for which I wasn't frivolous or vain or in love with order enough; my left breast and thigh photographed at $2.50 an hour, my wispy hair in a TV commercial—"before"—mostly my skinny thighs met at the crossroads by dozens of hairy imbeciles. Also I did an Eastern trip for a while but, I don't know: I liked learning to sit still, I liked swallowing down that silence by the gallon, the non-rational would turn on anyone whose mother was the rationalist of the century. But still, it wasn't mine and I always felt too desperate, too fake and hungry meditating. You need to be calm to live in nothing happily.

I had wanted to fly out of that accidental life but who could believe it was this easy, getting on a plane and seeing it all dwindle and disappear? Well, now I could see it wasn't. The plane was quivering after that dreadful pounding in its underbelly, and retribution was at hand. The punishment begun in labor was about to be completed, and again I was going to smash to smithereens, but this time in earnest, and all these other poor good people would burn for me. What could I do but laugh or cry? I decided to laugh, with an option to cry later, it would be nearer the estimate everybody held of me (except my mother, who does not laugh, on principle). But it was too late for either: the plane vibrated with indecision.

I reached for the baby—she was half-propped up between ash-tray-arm and back—and clutched her to me, wide-eyed. She howled and thrashed at me. Then the plane's thumping settled and stopped. That stewardess twinkled over to my seat to ask if I was all right, we were about to land so would I please buckle my seat belt with the child outside it. "Lots of babies have trouble with these landings," she smiled, pointing to her ear like somebody calling herself crazy.

Not the least of whom is this baby, I thought. So much washed off me in that sauce of sweat I felt like I'd lost thirty pounds. I was to be let live in return for a smile, so I smiled at my, 100 per cent my, daughter. A manic-depressive going into an all-time high. Stan Belsky had given me this extraordinary gift and wanted nothing in return except to know I'd accepted. From each according to his ability. It was the only one he appeared to have. To each according to her need, whether she knew it was her need or not. The poetry of it, the symmetry, moved me deeply and suddenly I could see what he must have loved about the whole thing: how much easier it was to create, to make real flesh and matter, than not to. What did all our words make besides trouble? All our joint stupidities and ill will and irrelevant politics bypassed, unconsulted. It made me wonder why I didn't have a whole shoeful of children. The lovely irony, the reward of it is that when I stopped taking myself seriously—when I practically signed an oath against making piecemeal suicide out of all the toxins of self-loathing—I think that's when I became, finally, eligible for seriousness.

Maybe it was my reward for having made the decision to leave and keeping it. Joe wasn't even the baby's father but he was the only one there for me to leave. God knows he had given me cause. Way back in my mind Joe was Joe-Joe-How-do-*you*-know? because of the way he loved to put me down. (In retrospect I see he had plenty of reason, doing what I'd otherwise have done to myself, but I never spell out indictments against myself and he put words to them with a cruel delight.) And Stan, who *was* Tippy's father, was Stan-I'm-a-man because he turned out in fact to be a brainless stud who counted up the kids he had made the way murderers chip nicks on their guns for every hit. I didn't know that at the time we sort of drifted together, he had been living in San Jose, and I didn't know anything about him. That turned out to be his only recommendation. He had a kind of respectable cover, he was very political when everyone else was into speed and music, he spent all his time fiercely arguing with people who never even bothered to argue back. I don't think he noticed. He was playing back ancient tapes of the year he was at Berkeley—he was no kid. But then, neither was I, with the beginning of my sad crow's-feet. (Sometimes I reminded myself of Geraldine Fitzgerald or one of those other slightly aging stars who play sexpots against the grain of their talent.) And everybody he knew was really too young to recognize the cracked voice of a dead movement when he harangued them. So he was one of those people who's professionally out of phase, you know, martyred by indifference. Poor Stan. Destined to be rare forever. Somehow I think I got involved with him thinking he was serious—didn't Mother always want me to be serious? I mocked the question—and that his seriousness would rub off on me if I got close enough and pressed tight, like those rub-off tattoos that come in cereal boxes.

All that happened, of course, was that I started falling asleep while he talked, and then waking up sick in the mornings. That was serious, if seriousness was what I wanted. He was living with me in this big sunny room somebody had lent me in Sausalito, which had a terrific unreal view sort of pasted up there against the windows (he and the fog came and went), and an un-terrific commute to a job I had at the main p.o. as assistant to the assistant chief stamp seller and parcel post person. What's known as a job with no responsibility, no seniority, no salary but "a chance to meet the public." (A lot of winos peel pennies out of their pockets slowly for one stamp, old ladies tend to think they're getting cheated on their change, and the people you end up liking best are the ones you have no occasion to notice.) However. It was good for my circulation to have to get up, vertical, every day and go out.

At my age Keats was down to a skeleton, no doubt about it, and Schubert too, I think. My mother defended Emma Goldman and one of the Scottsboro boys before she was thirty. And the room in Sausalito was all I had managed to become, the essence or the dregs. It was all bed, with a bit of a mess of a kitchen that looked well equipped but never had what I needed when I needed it. There were some plants that my absent friend Anita had equipped with wicks one time when she couldn't be home to water them, and I kept the wicks in but I was so busy doing nothing I could barely remember to fill the containers for the remote control. All my clothes were in a muddle on the closet floor, a sailor's knot. Stan's never even came out of his duffel. The place had the regulation cat smell and piles of socks mounted against the baseboards like dust mice for the cats to knock around. Now that I think of it I can't imagine why Stan had so many pairs of socks when he had only one pair of pants, painter's overalls, with old hankies glued inside the pockets.

Behind the bed was a shelf where he kept all his Trotskyite books and they'd fall down on us, very unfunny, at all the wrong times when one of us thrust a hand up without thinking. (An undiscovered form of contraception, but as you'll see, far from reliable.) I thought he must need them there somehow, to remind him who he was, how different from what he must once have been. One of the books should have come down with a bang the night he gave me Tippy—I mean I thought that for a very long time, maybe something about the labor of women—but he was so intent he barely moved, so I was on my own, careening along blind. I was mixed in my feelings about it—a couple of Mexican abortions down, and one bad infection that scared hell out of me in two languages, and I didn't want to go through that again. But then when she came back to claim her room, Anita told me Stan was famous around San Jose, a regular Johnny Appleseed. He had half a dozen bastard kids around and they all had the same blacker than black crimpy hair and bandy legs and three-piece nose, angled like the presidential range. How old-fashioned. I had seen men who loved fatherhood exorbitantly, but when I thought about it it was only Sophia Loren who had to wear her apron high over their macho dreams. That made me sick. I felt like a laughingstock. We should have formed a union, all the girls talked into motherhood by Stan Belsky, dupes of the dupe of PLM.

You see, he had made this pitch to me, quoting Norman Mailer, about how masturbation was worse than murder—or was it suicide?—and contraception made fucking masturbation. Something like that. I'm not good at remembering jokes. He had a debater's style that just overthrew me. I kept remembering how I had always fallen first in spelling bees, and had flunked my essay questions, all tangled up in reasons, causes, why.

So he'd argued me into bed with his small vocabulary of elite specialized words, all dialectics and oppression and, can you imagine, exploitation. Then he talked with his hot breath in my ear, talked me out to sea, and convinced me it would kill me if I stayed on the pill. He could see it in my eyes, un-health, cancerous denial of life, see all the white, he'd say, pulling down my bottom lid till it jumped under his fingers and I was a little kid with a cinder in my eye. When I told him, in our first month together, that it was a bad time, dangerous time, he very nearly raped me then and there, I watched him turn silver, turn purple, turn jeweled with the sweat of some lust I'd never seen before, and I swear he broke records, he had me ten, twelve times on that weekend, we never even went out to get the mail off the porch. If he could work as hard at any job he wouldn't have to live off women. We talked very little after that. I was angry, I felt like the victim of a gang bang but I'd been there too, nobody'd locked the doors on me or held a knife to my throat. I think I had been waiting for something to happen, something definitive to shake me up.

When I told him I was pregnant he closed his eyes. Satisfaction, or terror maybe. Whatever it was it wasn't mine, I didn't know how to feel so I felt nothing but nausea. To celebrate he took me right off to bed and of course could do nothing, I remember he could barely get together the energy to touch me with his grimy fingertips that smelled of cat food. And within a week he had gathered his analyses of mass movements and PLM work sheets and was gone, back to San Jose, mission accomplished. I think he expected me to understand, to *know*, and to remember him as some kind of god, what's his name, Zeus was it, who made Leda in mid-air and then dropped her flat as though she had some safe way down? Well I'll tell you: I felt more like a garden that's been thoroughly fertilized—all that bullshit—and then planted. And I was left to ward off the blights and pests, and then in the end to harvest myself, somehow. Tippy's birth was no fun, I went through it nearly catatonic, and every time the doctor complimented me for keeping quiet (a true psychologist) I swallowed a little more shit, a little more pain and thought, when I can let all this out and not kill somebody or break into little slivers, then I'll be fit to be a mother for this child. Meanwhile I was keeping my mouth shut. You know, there's a time during labor when you feel like your whole stomach is going to crack open and you'll end up all over the walls. It isn't even pain I'm talking about, it's this feeling that something else is controlling your body and it's going to smash you up from inside. I kept lying back in between those contractions thinking, I'm being punished, I'm getting exactly what I deserve, I'm going to shatter like a bottle and then I won't feel anything, that's all I want, and they'll ship the pieces to Mother in a dustpan, and I'd sleep a little and then it would pick me up again and stretch my skin to bursting and then loosen and let go. Tippy, whose legs are not bandy and whose nose is beautiful and straight, is what you call a hybrid—to get back to gardens —and when they showed her to me I was about ready to try to convince them they'd made a mistake: there shouldn't be such a reward for surviving righteous punishment. I thought the pain was what I should have and nothing more, and all that blood between my legs from a wound that would never close.

❀ ❀ ❀

I wanted to do what immigrants used to in the old days— shoulder, fist, elbow my luggage, hoist my baby, and walk from

my port of entry to the first tenement that said ROOM TO
LET/INQUIRE WITHIN.

But you know where the planes set you down now. There I was
in the dead center of Queens, in a treeless parching sun with a six-
lane highway all around like a fast-moving moat. The baby kept
on crying. In the distance no skyline, no city, only this primitive
geometry, a tall white rectangular motel doodled in the margin of
my vision. Standing in front of the Arrivals building covered with
desert dust. No shelter and a hawk is going to swoop down and
take me away if I don't move fast. If I'd had a destination I'd
have been able to escape that hard light. But look—this is exactly
the point, I know it finally, exactly the point where I fall apart
each time: I don't appear to have as many destinations as other
people. Choose. Choose something. Forever unprepared, an F for
readiness. Alternatives all fogged up, lessons half-learned. I had
$54 in my bag, left over from three bonds my mother bought for
me when I was seven. I had lugged them everywhere my life long.
They had been lost once and stolen too; retrieved with tears beyond their cash value. But they stayed with me as though they
were lucky and I respected that. Gray-green curlicues I never
stopped to look at, I don't know what they said or even what they
were ever used for. The margins were full of elaborate pin curls.
Did they buy tanks once, my money? Boots for a dozen boy sol-
diers to go marching in? All I needed to know was that I could buy
a ticket *out* sometime without having to hock my shoes or beg any
man. Joe had said one word too many in the voice he would use on
a dog famous for its poor breeding. I had packed every shred of
mine and then some. I had gone to the bank with my bonds
which had swollen marvelously in value—was it unfair for me to
reap the rewards of my mother's perverted ability to think ahead
twenty years to this moment? I had found a standby seat to New
York without a thought for where or what, and only half for why.
I didn't leave a note or say goodbye, it was (thank God) my last
self-conscious gesture of invisibility. *He won't even notice I'm
gone, oh he won't even notice that I'm gone, he go lookin' for his
laundry ticket and he see what he gone and done.* Twelve to the
bar. I'm here to be free but I move slowly, loaded down, to a
phone booth, and find a nickel and a slug—Stan used slugs to

deny the system its undeserved spoils—and call my mother. Her money bought my ticket home. All I have to pay her back with is myself.

She's in a meeting. When she's done with this one, the secretary assures me in one of those unindented voices you can't get a handhold on, she has another one. "A busy day," I suggest, embarrassed for her, because she doesn't know she's failing me in my three minutes of need.

"No, just the usual," she says, sighing, accepting no help from me. "Whom shall I say has called?" She has the grammar and the elocution of a Radcliffe graduate. What in the hell awaits me, vocationally speaking, with my two years of failed college and my thousand unfinished credits, half in frivolity, the other half in depression?

"Nobody," I assure her and my eyes fill one more time with self-pity. The baby's on the floor of the phone booth, her corduroy carrier laid down tenderly in candy wrappers and the silver linings of cigarette packs. She yawns at me.

It is a dangerous instant. There are alcoholics and junkies, and there are said to be nymphomaniacs, though I have my doubts about the predominance in them of matter over mind. Then there are just women with the wearies, vague all over. There are a lot of us. I have gone home with so many men for comfort, I have crawled into the crooks of their arms and the hammer locks of their legs, and told myself I loved discovery. I have even told myself I loved men, but I haven't had any evidence of it, really. Not really. In that I am my mother's daughter, though she'd be the last to admit it. But you see, I kept making myself a waif, an orphan, which means making myself perpetually grateful, glad to be suffered, making no demands.

So there is the energy of men moving all around me now, and I know I can just step into it anywhere. They hurry and they loiter, they're almost all in summer shirt sleeves, rumpled with the heat that's banished inside the terminal. Most men are easily distractible, all but the ones who have plane tickets in their pockets anyhow; and therefore, I suppose, I'm contemptuous of them. Most could be inveigled right into my life for a night or even a year. How else did the last ten years get by me? In an hour I could be safe. The arrangements are social, you know, not financial. You are the kind of person things happen to, accidents, madcap coincidences, you sit down next to someone or you pick up someone's lost briefcase, you find yourself alone in an elevator or at a corner table in a cafeteria with someone; the point is, you are never really going anywhere, not in a hurry, and so there's time. There's the semblance of real intrigue, too, where there is none. We would meet and meet again. The baby would sleep or she'd watch me quietly, see where the sticky web comes out, how they fly in. Watch me pay my dues and get my supper. I have—I am trying to say—the instincts of a whore and the looks of a high school senior. It is a combination that makes most, if not all, things possible. With the sole exception of satisfaction, peace, permanence.

But remember, I had prayed my instant of fear away. I had sworn off anything that could make me be a burden to the good Lord in whom I didn't believe but who had saved me nevertheless. So there is only one other kind of burden I can be.

I found my mother's building by one of those instincts that's awesome. My suitcases were carried, dragged, kneed, toed, and the baby just went right on squalling against my chest, captive. Every now and then I'd listen to her howl right under my chin—this really strange and fitful full-tilt shrieking—and wonder what she was trying to tell me. "It's all right," I'd mutter, "all right, all right, all right," but it seemed a nasty omen and I couldn't seem to break through with a single word she needed.

The old building is surrounded at its base by a whole new bed of shops as colorful as a flower garden. Its lobby has gone fluorescent, a leap into the twentieth century for all that aged marble, and walking into it is like entering a transparent plastic bag: the sound of my heels disappears, the baby's howl echoes stunningly, it's enough to make me look for stalactites over my shoulder. I take the 11–20 elevator without a hesitation. For all I know she isn't even in this building any more, maybe they dumped out the offices to paint them and nobody ever came back. Eight years of silence wells between us, three thousand miles deep.

But of course she's there. Not that children's dreams deserve to come true, but that Gerda Stein is not a woman to move until the wrecker's ball taps a third time at her window. She probably has a ninety-nine-year lease with an option to renew.

They've gussied up her office too. A rust-colored rug comes all the way out to lap against the elevator, and they have a rubber plant they must have ripped off from a bank. I don't know why they bother, really, the offices probably still look like stables in the back. They were always furnished in a period I called Early Martyrdom, with accessories in Late Social Action (Non-profit). It was kind of touching and undoubtedly it convinced you, if you came to hire them, that they would be dead serious about your case and take too small a cut of the winnings (but you'd be a headline in the ACLU bulletin). I remember the odd hours of my childhood, Saturdays sometimes, when I'd get to come and see what it was that kept her so damn busy all the time. Try to see, I mean, what other child it was she came to every day that wore her out and sent her home exhausted and abstracted and ready for the phone after supper. There were permanent blue shadows in her office that won out over the motes of sunlight at any hour. It was a place where you might expect bolts of striped ticking or ladies' girdle elastic to be brought in for approval: that unadorned this-is-business-gentlemen-how-about-a-cigar look to the place. It wasn't even beautiful there and she still preferred it to me. I hated it but pretended not to so I could come. The long mournful windows with their chipped brown radiators underneath. The old scuffed wooden desk from which she had taken the name sign, confiscated to the bottom drawer under mimeograph sheets (I had plans to steal it and put it up in my room, that's how I know, but I never got up courage). In its place she'd hand-lettered a small sign, black on gray, which declared in the words of some hero or other what I only now can begin to appreciate for its arrogance, its self-exemption, if there's such a word: ONLY FOR THE SAKE OF THE HOPELESS ONES HAVE WE BEEN GIVEN HOPE. How comforting to know without question which side you belong on.

It's my friend at the front desk. She's Black. I should have known nobody else would say "Whom?" to a stranger on the phone.

"Is Mrs. Stein still"—I figure I'll try a big word, I need them as much as she does—"incommunicado?"

She gives me a funny look and consults a wristwatch the size of a halved apple. It makes her wrist about the width of a used matchstick. "She is, she is," she says. (*Chides* would be the word.) I won't forget this little interview because in it I am somewhere on the greased and narrow edge between hysterical laughter and calming tears, and I have to put the baby down, she is breaking my neck. I drop her carrier, sort of just jerk my arms out and let go of her, onto the desk, sending the in/out box over the edge on one side and stapler and stamp licker and a few other instruments of clerical torture over the other. The baby is yowling again, oh shit, she opens up so wide I can see the tiny icicle of her uvula quiver. It looks like it might break off. The girl has stood up. She is wearing a two-piece print dress, about as short as any juvenile delinquent and truant from Central Commercial High School's, and there are eight or ten bare inches to account for between knee and hem alone. How can Mother put up with such a thing, I wonder, and then I ask her where is the john. I want to kneel down beside the toilet bowl and evacuate the contents of my entire life. There are these half-dozen large pictures cut out of newspapers on the wall behind this girl's huge glory-haired head, but the only one I see is the biggest, of my mother, also in a two-piece dress but one containing a minimum of a dozen yards of damask drapery goods, accepting an award at which she is glaring suspiciously. The sight of her face—emphatic and intolerant even in murky newspaper gray—is still and forever a finger down my throat.

"The washroom is reserved for employees and invited guests," she tells me in that same ledgeless voice. "Exclusively."

I'm not going to make it. "If I could only get through to her, I'd be an exclusive invited guest, goddamn it," I shout, very far away, like someone abusive coming toward me across the room. "Please watch this baby," I plead and run off down the hall lurching this way and that as though the deck is rocking.

I hear her voice raised after me—maybe she's only politely inquiring after the baby's name. Crouching in the gray stone fire stairwell I have another talk with myself, this time on my own, without the impetus of an imminent crash landing. My throat is unsteady, the way it used to be when I was a kid just finished with the hysterics—you know that nervous click, that lunge of your caught breath against your tonsils and your lungs all out of phase? I sound like somebody else still, subsiding from a year-long cry, I echo off the dungeony walls of the fire stairs. I do not want another great discovery about myself, one is enough for the day, and a lot of good it did me: I had promised to keep smiling and within an hour I'm a shambles. Peace, goddamn it, peace, I coax myself, hissing inside my head. My mantra. You will make peace between who you are and who you are not, and when you see your mother, when, if ever, her meetings let out and she comes toward you shocked but ungracious, never caught out by surprise or delight, you will cry if you want to, and begin over with her, and then if you have to, begin over and over again.

In the movies I would cut there, and wake up in my mother's bed, refreshed among clean sheets, a ribbon in my hair. She would be sitting beside me in her chair, bent forward, anxious, troubled; she'd have worked out in her head a whole new schedule for herself, allowing many afternoons just to be home with me making the hundred pounds of chocolate pudding we'd missed when I was little, and the patchwork quilts she was always out of town for. She would hum in the voice of my grandmother, whose hands she would suddenly have, veiny with arthritis and perpetual dishwater. It's enough to make you swear off movies.

I say to the girl when I come back (and find her coo-cooing at the baby—oh mortified, I'll tell you, I'm tickled but she hardened her heart even further after that), I say, "I'll just wait right here for Mrs. Stein to finish, but will you please tell her, when you can interrupt, that there's someone to see her?"

"*Whom* shall I say?" she persists, bending straight-backed to pick up my rumpus off the rug, flattening her lips in censure.

"Don't say anyone, OK?" Maybe I can make a conspirator out of her.

She opens her mouth to announce office policy on acts of conspiracy but I wave her away and sit down in an orange plastic airport-lounge chair to check the baby's diaper. Maybe the tears are for wetness. "She has to come out sometime, right?"

Stones from the receptionist. A stone for compassion. "She sleeps here once in a while," she offers me generously. "Once she stayed the weekend on the couch in her office." She makes a shitty conspirator. I'll remember that.

I change the baby with her feet in my lap. As usual she howls when the cool air hits her bottom. (If only I did that, she wouldn't be here.) I let her howl. Maybe she can wake the dead in there.

After half an hour a young man thrusts his head around a blind wall toward us, then retracts it. A scout, come to see if the place has turned into a welfare office. Now my mother may surface. But the damn baby has exhausted herself on tears and falls asleep gulping and that bait's gone. I empty my head of expectation and drowse.

Then when I'm thoroughly numb, back on the plane again in my droning head, I hear voices coming down the hall. Three people are talking at once and my mother continually, her strange staccato like a fender bass. She and the young man are seeing a nun to the elevator. Mother towers over the pale woman, who is wearing one of those voluminous old-fashioned habits. She isn't the kind of nun you'd expect to see in the offices of a coven of civil liberties lawyers. My mother is more than corporeal, though, she is flushed with energy and alarmingly young to me. Not young, I mean lusty, almost, sensual in the excitement of her talk. A ballsy lady, one of my friends once called her and that's about right. She leans slightly forward when she gestures, she comes so close to the old nun's restrained transparent face, and speaks so loud, the nun takes a small step back for air.

Maybe she sees me out of the corner of her eye, maybe she doesn't. But something changes a little on her face, her concentration breaks whatever the reason, and she leans her hand, palm-first with impatience, against the elevator button, once, twice, three times. The nun is dismissed, no appeal. As my mother turns back with the young man—the elevator hasn't come yet but when she's done, she's done—she glances at me and passes and keeps on walking. The receptionist, standing, holding papers against her chest protectively, is beginning, "Mrs. Stein, there's—" but my mother has turned back to look at me. I swear she doesn't know me, she is turning without thought, toward some familiarity she couldn't have defined. A tropism for certain kinds of faces. I am hunched in my chair, legs apart, eyes dazed with monotony, a baby she knows nothing about—you realize she knows nothing about her—stretched open-legged in my lap in shirt and damp diaper. It's one of the times I've wondered if my only problem might not be an essential lack of dignity; a recessive gene.

At the time I remember thinking, it's fear I'm seeing, and I relished it. She has the puzzled tentative frown of someone who thinks for just a split second, maybe I can get away, maybe she hasn't seen me, and then gives it up. I know the look, I live my life behind it. But I am sitting frozen, watching her; and I have been watching her, I have that advantage. Her hand is out to the young man beside her, blindly grabbing at his sleeve. Even so, in a voice calm and unhurried, all its questions held at perfect bay— oh, years of practice in the courtroom—she defers to him and says, "Sam," and clears her throat. "Allow me to introduce to you my daughter, Renata." She has the sound of a shaky pride down, for sure. "Renata"—and she turns to me where I sit rumpled and afraid to jar the baby awake to tears—"Samuel Eisenstadt, my newest partner. Our *junior* partner."

The young man smiles at me, his mouth perfect with the teeth of a born politician. He won't sit in this Late Non-profit firm one day longer than he has to. "A pleasure, Renata. Have you been waiting long?" He's already half-turned to go.

It is cheap but I have so little resistance left—what the fuck could I do to surprise this woman, short of dying? Bring her Siamese twins? I nod casually, tossing my head. "About eight years," I say, and the tears begin.

❀ ❀ ❀

Now I have to tell you that it was my mother who hadn't seen me all these years or heard a word from me either (a sign of excessive caring or a sign of none). I certainly had seen her.

The first time it may only have been the illusion of my mother that I saw, or my own thin guilty ghost. I had just given up on college for the third or fourth time, work kept getting in the way of my other plans and I was no damn good at any of it. I had moved into a commune up near Woodstock. This was such a long time ago, it didn't even know enough about public relations to call itself a commune, it was just a load of friends in a big half-painted wooden house, and I was concentrating chiefly on getting sunburned in unprecedented places (great pain for the very blond), hoping the atrophied parts of my brain would rejuvenate like some begonia bulb in case I ever needed them. I was in a bar with a TV on up in a corner, and I saw a woman on it who looked like my mother nearly forty years older than I—sitting there, picture it, having the gooseflesh under my arm petted by my current semi-literate lover—only she was in Alabama, Selma, and I saw a highwayman, whatever they're called, patrolman, taking careful aim. His boot was laid so studiously against the place he wanted to rip open, like some golfer gently teasing the ball a couple of times. And then I saw him pull it back and swing, but I never saw the face of the woman, only the way she hunched such familiar shoulders over her breasts and stomach and rolled back and forth like a Shmoo finding its balance after it's been pummeled. I never saw whether it was my mother or not. But something about the contours, the weight of the figure, a little top-heavy, plus my being where I was salting my beer, they all made me want her to turn her head to me, whoever the hell she was, and forgive me. And I knew she wasn't about to. When kicked she lay still for a minute but she wasn't dead, only in pain. Then the camera panned over the crowd and it was a mass of these curled-up bodies, like slugs, protecting their soft parts, all of which in me were peeling from too much sun too fast.

More recently she had been verifiably there, listed in the evening newspaper between stand-up comedians and rock singers plugging their albums. The book she went on to hawk the first time—*Conspiracy of Silence: Government Constraint and the Chilling Effect*—was hardly bound for the best-seller list. But she seized on the offers of TV talk shows, she protested, very publicly and complacently like a religious fanatic, because she truly loved, as truly as ever the Pope could have, endless audience. She wanted, she once told this to Irv Kupcinet who only smiled uncertainly, to issue herself in paperback. Ah yes, he had nodded, of course. He was thinking of movie stars, Debbie Reynolds, maybe. But no, he did not understand—she held up a hand and chopped his suppositions in half, in quarters. She said that the shows were fantastic opportunities for instruction. It was worth putting up with the appalling discomfort and the general level of the discourse. (He kept on smiling.) I've never been convinced that she sits there in that wash of hot light feeling self-sacrificing all for the sake of her "democratic" period, for the money that helps her firm take on charity cases. I think she glows back at the lights and the applause and that faceless camera; to an audience so distant and vague she can even afford to be kind. ("Those little drawings have always come for me in the courtroom, you know? No cameras allowed where I go to do my work, only the caricatures, cartoons. Do I really look so much like Golda Meir, Irving?") Now the real Gerda Stein can stand up, repeated and repeated on the monitors around the studio.

So she was constructed for me more often than not, for the last four or five years, entirely out of the dots and spaces of the TV screen. Her face surfaces out of it bearing, endlessly, an expression of what you could only call tolerant indignation. Like Queen Victoria she is not easily amused. And—you know the way everyone has two unmatching eyes? Usually you can see it in a photograph. I saw a picture of R. D. Laing once, and you could isolate the stringent element from the harsh and the yielding. And Nixon . . . eyes at two degrees of meanness, one the rabbit's, the other the hunter's. Painters usually get that wrong, they do eyes like mirror images. Well, Mother distilled on TV shows her one cunning and her one ever so slightly more vulnerable eye. The brow is down on the hard side, thick and almost straight. Unwillingness to compromise, saith the fortuneteller, and incapacity for beauty unless it takes her by surprise and asks nothing in return. Eyebrow a slash mark of heavy pencil, like the fat No. 1 Eberhard Faber she uses, unheard of, impossible to get, she shops for it the way some women go looking for rare night creams or gorgeous wines. And the other eye—whatever is soft and forgiving in her is in that one, unguarded once in a while, eyebrow raised: there's a way in if you can only find it.

So this is the expression she keeps in front of the camera, out of all the things she could show: disdain trying for mildness and failing endlessly. And who can say this isn't what she's become. It does no good to curse about it: like the time I ended up in bed with Stan taking insult on insult, being plowed and planted. . . . She too is reduced to her leitmotif and it can be translated into a theme song to accompany her on the long walk across the stage to the bank of couches where she and the M.C. exchange personalities in these great clumsy blocks of cliché. What would you think if you woke up one morning to realize that you come before millions of your countrymen introduced by the theme of the last movement of Beethoven's Ninth? "Ode to Joy," Mother, the trumpets slightly flat, a jazz beat abetted by snare drum and fender bass. The first time I heard it I wanted to cry. Now Tippy will learn to giggle and clap her hands to see that someone in her family actually comes to her announced by a theme song just like the animals in *Peter and the Wolf*. Then, "Ladies and gentlemen, a truly gallant heart—Miz Gerda Stein!" says the talk-show barker, eliding the facts of her marital situation irretrievably and just as well. He had spoken of her as "the great émigrée lawyer, herself the victim of Nazi brutality." Not true but always an available epithet which I'm sure she encourages. Considering her accent, which she works to maintain ("Ziss is not troooo, Renata"), and her general air of grimness, which you can only assume she's earned, it's not surprising that people are disappointed to find out how long ago she came here, how she went to Harvard Law, how she had her choice, come in or stay out, and picked her bits of American-ness with finicky exacting fingers. She never was any good at languages.

And here she is, by now professionally unattractive. I'm sure viewers turn to each other with affectionate little grunts of condescension and familiarity when she walks on with her crammed leather bag like some crazy aunt ("Oh, there she is, look, Harry, you've got to see this Gerda Stein!") prepared for whatever bargains the cameraman or the ushers might be offering, first come first served. Her skirt is slightly long, old-world not old-lady long.

Just to appear life-size she has to become larger than life. So she indulges her natural idiosyncrasies. What a way to lose your discipline and become a freak, a victim of your virtues. I'd better stay away from live cameras, god knows what I'd do. . . . She's grave as a doctor diagnosing a terminal condition, off and running, deep into a case that's been in the headlines. She's defending, for example, a man, an oil-truck driver, who had tried to burn down City Hall. (Half the city would have helped set the wicks if only he'd asked.) Lots of laughs and nasty cracks by the M.C. during which Mother looks uncertain, forever ill at ease with laughter at her work. She spends most of her time on these shows justifying the defense of indefensible and unpopular people. She's found the perfect profession to contain her perversity. No, it's not money (feigning outrage) and it's not notoriety, but democratic principle. "You have not heard of this, *principle*, ever?" she goads the M.C., who mugs at the question like a first-grader who's forgotten how to spell cat. I have examined it, turned it over, and I think it's her attraction: her work is chic, right? With the sensationalism of loving the unlovable, of forgiving the sinner, for the sake of democracy, that abstraction we learned in elementary school that smacks vaguely of Christianity. And here's somebody who'll fight grimly for it like a convert, her life is a rebuke: didn't St. Julian lie down with the leper? That much even I know. All with a little fillip of instruction tacked on and how the California audience loves to think it's learning while it laughs. "Did you know the fourteenth amendment also—al-zo!—protects people who choose to fall out of airplanes naked onto lawns marked Reserved for Greeks? One time I had a case, let me tell you about it, I must say I took it against counsel—" A joke without a punch line. One has to love this woman, there is nothing else to do with her.

The night before I decided to leave Joe to his self-satisfaction and come home, I saw her on Dick Cavett, I remember watching her heavy lips in their rapid easy movement. Beautifully formed lips, actually, with a great many surfaces. Faceted, refracting. I rarely noticed. What was it she had? The tension of charisma, the deeply charged confidence of a public person. Personage. I suppose I knew, but I came home anyway, how this woman, if she came to sit in my kitchen and drink from one of my mugs, would make me think she was going to burn right through her chair. Or crush a cup. Make all the tender bones of it just crumple, and catch a handful of coffee, and blame the cook. But still—but therefore?—I came.

At dinner.

R: Do you always take taxis like that?

G: No, don't be foolish. I should run through my entire salary in a week. But the baby—

R: What, "the baby"? Would she be contaminated down there?

G: Well, look, my dear, she is a California baby, correct? So you must try to protect her, ease her in slowly to our noise and dirt here. Do not shock such a system.

(This is the kind of care, the random scattershot kind I recognize in my cells—the kind you give when you're not sure where to begin or what might really matter. It's sort of like providing, I don't know, knee-protectors to a barefoot child or underarm dress shields to a nearsighted cowboy. How did she ever get me through infancy and childhood alive?)

G: You have a ticket to return?

R: To San Francisco? No.

G: And there is someone you have come to see here?

R: (Puts fork down in peas and looks at her mother, a long time. G. is incapable of showing anxiety: all those years in court have finally given her the face of her father, my grandfather, who was a so-so poker player.) I came to see you.

G: (Narrows her eyes, looking for the cheap shine of a lie.) You did not feel I should be forewarned?

R: Why? Am I the plague or something, would you have gotten a shot?

G: Foretold then. Please, no quibbling. (Still assessing. In someone younger, or someone who didn't happen to be my mother, you'd have called it brazen study. If I thought I could buy off her anger at eight years' abandonment with my presence alone I was too arrogant. She wasn't sentimental. She persisted.) I could so easily have been out.

R: But you weren't, right? Things work out. (R. shrugs. There's got to be a lot of room in your life for shrugging.) I've been away so long and so thoroughly—

G: Yes. (Nods.) It has been extremely—complete. To your satisfaction I trust, out in the big world.

R: I only thought (and R. was never going to have an easy time with sentiment, unless it was with certain men) I just wanted to see you, do I have to have reasons?

(It was a time for *her* to shrug but she was too constrained. Took my statement under advisement. Took it to have it tested for forgery or counterfeit printing. Consulted with some judge who did her favors. Returned it to me shredded. No go.)

G: You must have had some better reason to be here suddenly across my kitchen table.

R: (Shrugs again. This could get to be a nervous tic.) The alternatives, Mother. (Close to tears, turning herself in.) I'm not good at protecting myself against certain kinds of dangers.

G: So I can imagine. (Said with some satisfaction; sniffs once, like a dowager in a play. What might it take to bring her to her own unimaginable brink of tears, which is rumored to exist somewhere but which I have never seen? I have seen her disappointments turn only to righteous anger, but never to despair.)

R: You cannot imagine. You cannot even begin to guess.

(R.'s daughter Tippy is crying in the bedroom in need of three or four things at once. R. cannot even bring herself to the side of her bed to let herself be seen.)

GERDA

How can this be? That I was yesterday here in my most comfortable isolation and today there is my daughter, alleged daughter, sitting in my armchair while I walk about distracted, thinking, should I, after eight years of abandonment, bring fruit or wine, a hostess, welcoming? Should I concern myself about her past or let it alone and think with her about her future? How does one commit small talk with a daughter? I cannot, even, with sheer strangers.

Out of the past, of course, with neither explanation nor apology, has issued this tiny pale child named, rather foolishly, "Tippy." (But that, at least, is preferable to the genuine full-dress Theresa, the name of a saint when last I looked, may my mother forgive her. I wonder if she has chosen this in defiance of us all or merely in her supreme ignorance and unconcern.) She laughs and tells me of a friend, in that disorderly life she has come from, who has a baby without any name at all, a baby who must be named anew by everyone who "relates" to her. So she exists in the eye of the beholder, very apt indeed for the depthless subjectivity in which these children are condemned—self-condemned—to live. And if no one "relates," does she then cease to exist?

Renata says nothing at all about the birth of the baby except that it was "terrible and wonderful, you know?" Well, perhaps I do know. Can it be we have accidentally shared a thing or two?

44

So we may as well let the bygones be. I ask her what she shall do now and she shrugs. She claims to have come to "visit" me, but you may understand that I have my doubts about this, though motives I have none.

"The two of us," she says, smiling, but I cannot read her expression, the girl is a stranger to me either because she has changed or because she has spent her lifetime being opaque; both. "The two of us here without men, just like the old days. The virgin mothers." Her laugh is not in the least bitter, it is casual.

"Well, men are something I have never missed, Renata, to be quite honest. You may find it more difficult to live a life of—" I look around at whatever is my life, my good life, but most of it is not visible here.

"Of chastity."

"I should never even have called it chastity that I have lived, that implies so strongly the—scent of men which you are at pains to ignore. I have, as it were, had my nose elsewhere."

At which she laughs outright. "Well, now watch me do that too." She yawns and stretches. She is still so ethereally blond, her father's pale hair as unfamiliar in my eyes as the saint's name in my ears. Even her eyelashes are negative, wholly unrelated to anything of mine. How is one to believe flesh is of one's flesh? My motherhood is like an old rumor I can barely, faintly remember, like a book I read so many years ago I have forgotten whether it may have happened to me or has been invented by another. Who is she to me that she can arrive out of the blue sky of summer here, and assume that I shall succor her and this frail baby she calls my grandchild, and be *right*?

What am I to think, her sharp little nipples, perfectly defined, point within circle, peek out at me through a gaudy orange polo shirt grown fast to her skin. "Oh, Indian," she replies when I inquire what it is supposed to be, thinking I have intended a compliment. Is this meant to be a wanton provocation of the population-at-large or, conversely, so cozy, so familiar and defusing that, nothing withheld, no man shall feel the need to seduce her for mere curiosity's sake? I suggest to her some clothes appropriate to New York City: California, I believe, has its own more forthright code. For this I receive a look I well remember from her sullen adolescence. "I shall lend you money if you wish," I tell her, rather shyly, looking again at the wide eye of her right breast which is lower than that of her left. If I were a man and not her mother what ever would I make of that, winking at me?

❀ ❀ ❀

It was, believe me, an exceedingly minor riot. Things deserve to be a lot more uproarious for the wardens at the Women's House of Detention than this, ill-planned, which commenced with the throwing, as though it were a grenade, of a soggy canned dinner peach. One of the women, however, had a gun of a sort (which, on examination, proved to have three smashed chambers, a bargain, and so the inmate who used it was more brave, even, than mere triggerwoman for a riot; she played a game of Russian roulette with a great many lives). But she was lucky—or unlucky, as you will—and the contraption worked and she shot off, or at least into, the rear left buttock of a matron fondly called Keyhole Katie because it is she who is despised in this vile place for performing the vile entrance examination, vaginal, for drugs and weapons. And another woman had somehow managed to keep her cell unlocked; how has yet to be determined. Note that the escape attempt, for it was nothing less, could have been commenced without that kind of violence, would in fact have thrived in silence and calm, but that the occasion for revenge was clearly irresistible. And so the "sister" brought down her enemy with a single shot and the others gave orders, opened cells, swarmed and hustled and were, with little exertion, instantly overwhelmed. Things are not so simple as they were in old Western films where one stole a big gold key from off the warden's belt and set loose the entire jail, out into the arms of its waiting womenfolk, all without having to answer to the intrusive efficiency of the closed-circuit TV.

This history was reported to me without comment, nearly without *tone*, by Sam, who, when I arrived in the morning, suggested I call someone named Nedda Purchase immediately; she had been trying to phone me at home and had talked only with Renata. "I offered myself," he told me very innocently, "I could use a little diversion, but I think that's a little too ecumenical for the current faith. They want a lady."

"Oh, the boredom of that," I began, "the supposed compliment of being chosen because the x chromosome of my father—"

"I gave them that whole number, Gerda, trust me, I told them you don't enjoy command performances based on anything but recognition of your extraordinary merit"—he bowed and tipped his imaginary hat—"but they weren't buying. You appear to have a mandate."

"Well, if I go it will be to correct their misapprehensions then. They will be expecting a soft sell."

"Go get 'em, Gerda."

This is not the time for it but I shall one of these days, a slow day, have a talk with Sam for his insolence. Every time I attempt a scruple, an impartial judgment that diverges from the main chance, I see him smirking. His favorite descriptions are of clients or opposing attorneys or judges who have been "suckered into" one or another uncomfortable position. He is vain, ill-mannered, elegant, and small, and he shall be smaller by a bit when I have done with him.

Nedda Purchase. Yes, I tell her—she of ACTION, the Ad Hoc Committee To Insure Only Niceness or To Invite Occasional Notoriety, or some such nonsensical acronymic assertion. I shall come to speak with them. Not to negotiate, they have already been whipped back into worse than compliance. Of course things go worse after a rebellion, she need not tell me that: common sense dictates that the dog who snarls, let alone bites, will be beaten into vicious collapse and either become a cowering cur or a kamikaze savior with a holy plan (and I should imagine that with nine hundred separate souls, or whatever the number, crammed in here, there will be an even sprinkling at both extremes).

My taxi careens uptown as though to the raging riot itself. "Is there some emergency?" I ask the driver.

He turns a broad densely wrinkled face to me. "Listen, in this town it's an emergency when a lady's late for her beauty parlor appointment. Aren't you in a hurry?"

I was, of course, but I said, "No, I am not, particularly. Please do me the favor of not murdering a pedestrian on my behalf."

He shrugs. "Suits me. But I'm used to getting hassled from the back seat there, you know?" In falsetto: " 'Buddy, can't you move this thing, my kid's got a piano lesson.' 'Why don't you learn to drive, fella, I got something I gotta get out of the freezer.' "

I sit back as we lurch up to the light before the bridge. "You have truly an exalted sense of the occupations of women."

He laughs abruptly and turns, expecting to see me smiling approval, since I am clearly exempt from his caricature.

"And please to keep your eyes on the road. With your defective vision I would rather you paid closer attention."

"Ah shit, you're one of them too."

"One of whom?" Could he have failed to notice I was female?

"Boy, talk about surrounded," he mutters. "Closet butch. I want to tell you, my good lady, nothing's gonna be the same when you guys get the gun, I really mean it. The whole city's gonna look like the inside of your purse there, all jumbled up, we won't be able to find where you put the goddamn George Washington Bridge."

He is not interested in the niceties of my indignation. "This corner will be fine," I tell him and give him precisely what the meter reads and not a penny more. I lean in his window as he counts out the bills and coins and, finally, the fifteen last pennies, and say into a corner of his tufted ear, "But we shall handle the budget beautifully, don't you think so?"

The building is ringed with police and it is necessary to talk my way past them. "Invited, attorney for the inmates," I mumble endlessly if prematurely, and hurry past sufficient musketry to put down an insurrection of a hundred thousand. But they are relaxed and sloppy, their guns well housed, and on behalf of the women caged inside I find myself wishing they felt more threatened. Another frivolous defeat.

Nedda Purchase meets me and pumps my hand most vigorously. She is a small and earnest black woman, young, in a very military blazer which I imagine gives her some amusement, and a defensively cheerful red scarf around a large burst of that "natural" hair they all affect now, even down on the farm I dare say. She is, she tells me, "a free lance" in women's affairs. A lance indeed: St. George in navy blue, 5 foot 2. Who, I want to know as we walk noisily down the hall—my shoes squeak on this floor as though there were an inch of water in them—has invited me here to speak with these inmates?

"They'll tell you that."

"But who," I persist, "is responsible for my invitation here?" I should have been certain before I came, and had I not been too eager to administer my corrective lecture to them about knee-jerk feminism, I should have been more alert.

"Well, you," she says, wide-eyed, "no one coerced you into coming, did they?"

Exasperating. I do not trust her innocence. "Miss Purchase. I am asking on whose behalf I have been asked to speak with these women. Theirs or the authorities'?"

"Well, my goodness, you're a very well-known woman, aren't you? We thought you—"

"But who is 'we'? For whom do you work?"

She covers her mouth with her hand like a child caught out. "I only made the phone call."

The assistant warden—warden away like the king of a small country overthrown in his absence—is a large ax-faced woman, surprisingly young. She is built more or less like a cliff, I think, many feet of flat surface up and down, the last of the pioneers, still in need of a sturdy bone structure to get her through hard winters and handwork. (There is a Walker Evans woman in a faded housedress, Alabama dirt farmer's wife, whom I have seen a thousand times in memory; perhaps with a college education and a tan cord suit and nurse's shoes, she would look like the assistant warden's sister.) But she has gentled herself somehow, this woman who is referred to as Thomas (Miss?)—neutered is what I am forced to think; she is like a great sexless St. Bernard going a trifle soft not in domesticity but in fear that she could otherwise do damage with her size alone.

"They've asked for you in there," she tells me wearily, gesturing over her massive shoulder, "and we're trying to listen, believe me, we want to hear anything reasonable. Even though we've got them calmed down and we've got the upper hand, I really want to hear them. We're encouraging a dialogue these days, you know what I mean." Good Lord, have they been holding encounter groups, touching, feeling, weeping together?

"And this episode is a result of the enlightenment, do you think?"

"I don't think I know, Mrs. Stein." She is breathtakingly honest for a city official. No bureaucratic ambidextrous hedging? "It's like dealing with little children here. No matter how much respect I may have for some of them as human beings, they're going to be testing your limits all the time, and you've got to expect it."

"To say the least."

"It's not easy to re-tool."

What a stunning up-to-date display of modern terminology, it puts one in mind of the newest executive furniture. In a soft and reasonable voice this unholy mixture of metaphors: psychology, technology. What will the streetwalkers and addicts and shop-lifters upstairs be like in their "re-tooled" condition, I wonder. New mufflers at the very least: docile or merely "in touch with their true feelings" through poetry therapy and t.l.c.? And have they yet installed an orgone box or a sauna for every cellblock? I smell some college of criminal justice in the background: the Enlightened Jailer and Executioner, Contemporary Wardenry, I-II. "How long have you been here?" I ask Thomas. "I have never heard your name."

"A month," she says and laughs softly, bitterly. "No, two, actu-ally. My first and my last, Mrs. Stein."

"Yes."

"Please try to make them understand if you can that it's easier for us to be tough in the old way, everything militates against humaneness in this place. Even after Attica."

"Especially after Attica, I should imagine."

"Maybe. Maybe. It's a struggle just to hear people when they talk to you, there's so much static. But—nobody's going to care much about this, really, but, see, I actually feel this kind of thing is a sign of health, improving health. It's like unblocking the sinuses or something like that, you know, every spring you get a cold because your body has to adjust to a change in climate. So in there, they can feel things beginning to move a little and—"

Good grief. "Enlightenment and tenderness are not quite enough for them, I should imagine, or stroking by the hand of the warden's assistant. If it does not extend so far as the abolition of this place."

She stiffens as if I have accused her of something other than simplicity. "Well, that's not about to happen. What's about to happen is that we bring back the cudgel and the rack. Why can't they tell the difference between their enemies and their friends?"

I nod. "Because their friends wear the same uniform they do. Have you never noticed the similarities?"

It is a small room I am taken into, cinder block, an oatmeal pallor and texture. In the frigid fluorescence there are half a dozen women, a few leaning against the wall, two seated, one cheek each atop a bare metal desk. And on the wall, oh my oh my, a technicolor picture of the mayor. Possibly it is for darts.

"No cops!" one of them shouts when the warden puts her head in. "Lock the fucking door, huh?" She is a smart-looking chippy type who still manages an elaborate hairdo somehow. What will that takes. One could achieve conventional wonders with the sheer pushing power it must demand to straighten and curl again that iron hair with the amenities they provide here.

"Well, we'll be right outside," my pioneer friend sighs, abnegating her height and breadth, gentle as a concerned mother. "If you need us." Hot chocolate and oatmeal cookies—one expects her to bring such goodies.

"Come on, we get to talk to our lawyer in con-fidence," the young woman says in a nasty schoolgirl's voice. She should be slapped for freshness.

"Hey, you know me," she tells me when we have secured our privacy. "Don't you recognize me?"

I look at her quite blankly. She has the brass of a singer in feathers and sequins, a little fist of a voice.

"Last year, two years ago, whenever it was, you went to court for my friends and me, you don't remember. They took us in on Forty-seventh Street and you said we had a couple things coming to us they wouldn't give us."

"Like our rights," a woman behind me said.

"Yeah, even we got rights, man, we went around feeling real cool when you got done with those bastards. And I was one of your, you know, what's it, defendants."

"No, you were not a defendant." I had to smile. "That time you were on the giving end, not the receiving."

"Well, anyway, you were cool. We wanted to give you a party or something, you know? But we didn't think you'd want to come, like *really*."

"Your name is—"

"Sherry."

"Yeah, they named her after Harvey's Bristol Cream."

"My mama never got next to no Harvey's, man. She tried, though."

"Just didn't have your talent."

"Ladies. May we talk about what we are here for?"

"Do what the lady tells you," Sherry instructs them most primly. "She got her head on right."

And so I listen to their grievances, which, Lord, short of the one true grievance—shall I call it the one true grief—are not very daunting. Always this happens: the true rage is not to be approached, and so the symptoms dribble forth, pathetic in their insignificance: kitchen and bathroom reforms, meat five times a week, more rolls of toilet paper, and the right to wear something other than these worn gray neutralizing sacks. The chance to re-establish a pecking order, one might say, based on the old terms, not on strength or personality merely, "the thing itself, the bare forked animal," but on beautiful clothes, the true tokens of exchange of respect, awe, intimidation. (And when the prison authorities refuse, they too seem stupid and petty, but then that is their only point. They can give nothing, can only take away, and the more they forbid, the closer they think they come to holding these poor souls in the palms of their hands.)

"Well, the administration at this very moment, at least, seems very enlightened. On the scale of things. I should be surprised if we have any problems here. How do you feel about this new warden of yours, this Thomas?"

The automatic groans. The shrugs. Someone offers, "I'm scared to be alone with her." Snickers.

"She's a eunuch," says this Nedda Purchase. "She fronts for the massa."

Sherry volunteers an ounce or two more. "She's OK, I mean she don't seem to think we got the leaping plague in here, but Nedda knows, she's a fucking warden, so it's all, like, another con, you know?"

"Yeah," says another, "I used to have this cat, I'd try to get her in her cage, you know? So I'd get down on my knees and I'd tickle her right on her little titties, like, all up and down, and I'd blow on her head right between her ears, she was a sucker for that, 'here sweet little kitty,' and then whammo, she'd go in the box and the door would come down before she knew what hit her and there she was, man. Same old shit no matter how you slice it."

Things, I must say, are peculiarly unfrenetic in this discussion, there is a quality of sweet reason that I do not trust. I have been told from time to time that I am "insensitive," whatever that may mean. I believe it is an epithet that is used only in cases of gross disagreement: I see but you are blind. But the fact is that anyone who has gone to trial frequently develops a truly tactile sense, an appendage, let us say, to the back of the head with which one reads the ambience of the courtroom, assesses the tactics of the opposition. Possibly this is not a sensitivity that carries over into one's relations with, say, one's daughter, but that is a different story. Now I have spent many hours among these people, and whatever wrongs may have been done them, grinding incapacitating wrongs, I cannot deny there is often a stridency, an immaturity and noisy bickering audacity in them (the "hookers" are the noisiest, like chickens) and that is troublingly lacking here. There are, further, certain exchanges—eye contacts, I should say—that cause me to feel like a substitute teacher in a children's classroom waiting for the pail of water to fall on her head or the tack to appear on her chair.

I am not, after all, among friends, in spite of Sherry's warm memories of the party they almost gave me. They are examining my willingness to interpret to them certain possibilities of legal relief. I have surely not begun by chastising them for their damned attempt at wreaking havoc. But I am well aware that, whatever my reputation for impartiality may be, I do not look like their kith and kin. Do I not have—my age, my style—the look of nemesis, of an authority? No, I do not "swing," nor do I approve of those who do. Must I love them to serve them, or they love me to be served? To me the answer is obvious and not troubling; to them it must be more difficult.

Nedda Purchase, with the exception of her initiating comment about Miss Thomas, has been entirely quiet throughout. I turn to her in the silence, a chill bleached-white silence through which has run only the buzz of the fluorescent lights like a fine line, and say, a trifle impatiently, "And what more? What further demands shall we consider—not demands, pardon me, requests. I forget we are not in a demanding posture right now—while we have their ear? Surely—"

And at that, good Lord, it is unbelievable even in the remembering, in that blank instant in which one is erased—not even surprised, you see, one's consciousness merely eradicated—at a look from this Purchase, a nod, less than a nod, all of these women rise and descend upon me, what are they doing? It is half terrifying and half, I must insist, amusing, a giant mugging, all hands on, and rough. But what they are doing is toppling me backward on the desk and muzzling my mouth with the red kerchief from Purchase's hair. My nose fills with the cloying smell of some pomade; someone makes a tight knot under my ear. I cannot call or warn, only flail foolishly like a great beached whale. Am I to be raped or murdered, have they all gone insane? My legs are pinioned and it is quiet. Intense concentration, this is an operating theater, no laughter. Outside sits the warden and an army of guards! And they are stripping all they find beneath my tweed skirt which is to my hips, they are tugging at my girdle with the most inventive curses, and then, stunning the pain—trust me, humiliation is a passing inconvenience, a social response—this is the sheer high-colored pain of flesh tearing, collapsing inward. And then one of them thrusts so much of her hand inside me I see from above only her dark wrist like a tree limb protruding.

"What you got in there, sister, any TNT? Any Hershey bars? You got a razor, maybe, a pound of hash?" She flicks her fingers ungently and looks into my face. I cannot think how my eyes may look from where she gazes serenely down on them. *Witches*, I think, *witches were said to pass hair balls, jewels, dead mice.* Always this deepest most secret cache was suspect, open to speculation by strangers. . . .

"You see what that feels like now? You get it?" She tosses hair out of her eyes. "You like it when I comb all around in there like this? I got to make sure you *al*-together clean in there." To the others, rolling her eyes: "You never *can* tell what these damn crazy folks might try to bring in here." Under the kerchief I bite my lips numb.

"Let me tell you something, lady," another woman says, and I see her for the first time. She is not young or spicy, she is the kind of wife and mother who stands, worn and rarely smiling, lifting and putting down, lifting and putting down a shopping bag as the long line slowly moves, to visit her husband in *his* detention. Her crime, whatever it was, was workaday and unglamorous: no turner of tricks or robber of banks. "I want to tell you this, see, doing this, that's more human, it got more Christian love in it, than what that matron do to us when we come in here. You understand what I'm saying?" She waits courteously, as though I could give her an answer. "You, at least you got a chance to have some feelings, right now, right? You angry, or you want to put out my eyes, or you scream bloody murder if we took that thing off of your mouth, but see—" She flattens her dark lips as though at a terrible taste. "But see, she stand us up here with a law in her hand, she got this statute that give her the right to take our clothes away, our wedding rings, everything, and we supposed to stand there, nothing but the wind on us—"

"The air conditioning," somebody says, "'cause it's not where *we* stay," and nervous giggles, relieved, I think, ripple all around.

"And then we got to squat down and she squiggle her fingers around in there and, see, we can't say nothing. Like some machine. They call it a procedure on us. Not one word, or we start out on the wrong foot in here and that mean we eat shit from the very first meal."

The woman who was playing matron more gently removes herself from me than she had entered. She holds her hand up and looks at it comically as though it were perhaps now mine, not hers. Then she wipes it on her dress. "All in a day's work," she says, in a voice just like the warden's, deep and subdued and unnaturally checked: out of a box with the lid clamped down.

I rise, dizzy and still in the most searing pain, and sit on the desk with my face in my hands. Desperation is, yes, one of the world's most common weeds; and they think my garden has none. They are "humanizing" me. I am to be grateful. Perhaps I am now expected to advertise this trauma on their behalf.

But what do they want of me, I think, shared anger? I cannot afford to be angry the way they are. If I were as wild with rage as they, I should be in here myself and then what good? *There will always be someone outside; there must be.* I raise my face, which is all asweat, and with a control more hard-won than they can ever appreciate, say to them quietly, even consolingly, "Look, my friends, you cannot make me angry." No, they are not my sisters, my sisterhood is non-negotiable, non-transferable, and non-democratic. "You cannot make me angry because I understand what that was all about—I do, I assure you. You assume that I come to you complacent, protected, I go home to my filet mignon, my cocktail—well, all right, I do. I admit that I do. Not without certain regrets but I do. You think, she is therefore more of *them* out there than of *us* in here, she is only on the border line of sympathy, she is *for hire*. Am I correct thus far?" Wide eyes on me. "Well, please be good enough to give me a sign."

"Right," says the older woman, conciliatory. The young ones hang back. "Agree. You come and go and you *theirs*, that's the God's honest truth, that gate swing closed, everybody out there got something we want."

"Right on!" Echoes of assent. They are attentive as schoolgirls to see if the operation has been a success.

"But you shall not find a lawyer amid your own numbers, you know that you have to turn to someone like me, correct, and you say to yourselves, 'Well, we shall at least compel her attention, we shall buy from her a passionate performance,' is that not what you decided, that made you perform this—rather theatrical gesture here? She shall share this humiliation with us and know, experience our disgust and fury, perhaps go storming out and then think better and return and be wedded to our cause with the heat of her anger—and as a woman go forth and battle for us."

No SS knock at the door with fists, but the considerate tap of the poor warden, driven to consistency in her means. "How are you coming in there?"

"Fine," I say, steadying my voice. "I hope you have not been waiting there. Another few minutes, if you will be so good." Her footsteps retreat on that peculiar floor. How may anyone steal up on anyone in this place? One would have to be a barefoot Indian guide.

The women are waiting, moving around a bit. I have not betrayed them. "But you see, you forget that there must remain a difference. I am hired to be not a woman in particular but a kind of—a craftsman of your pain. In your service, or, say, a surgeon who cannot become too involved or his hand will shake. I need to have my mind clear and my—"

"Bullshit," says Sherry. "I'm sorry, but it don't hurt nobody to know what it feels like to get trashed inside, that's all. Trashed. I'd like to do it to the judge, man, but he don't have no hole except between his ears. I bled a whole week when that bitch got done with me."

I feel a grinding in my stomach, these are baby teeth but they work away at me these days interminably.

"But you see, I object to that argument. There are those who must keep their heads clear, what have I except my head—" But it is not sensible to argue, and when I talk I feel the nipping at my stomach wall. I do not want to convince them. They are serious, and I suppose that is all I dare ask. Street theater has come to the House of D.

Nedda Purchase, who is either a conspirator or a more passionate woman than her navy blazer will ever disclose, picks up from the floor her blood-red kerchief, her flag of war. Nine tenths of it disappears into the thick hedge of her hair. She probably brought the gun in there. "Nobody has a written guarantee to have their clear head protected. If I get fucked over, you get fucked over. That's all. It's simple."

"Yes, is this a constitutional principle? Or one of the Ten Commandments I may have missed? Suffering shall be spread equally among all parties, to the relief of none? Well, leave ideology for a moment. I may find it within me to forgive your—violation, shall I call it, even to go so far as to respect it. But please do not expect my congratulations on your strategy. Please, this is asking too much."

"Goddamn it, don't forgive it, nobody wants your forgiveness." She puts her large head right against mine, her shaggy hair makes a shadow around my vision. "OK? You remember it, don't you ever begin to forget it. And tell the people about it."

The people. I am, in disgust, the one to move my head away. The edges of my sight clear. "I shall be glad to negotiate your grievances with the assistant warden, who I think is a fairly reasonable woman."

"Wait till the warden come back, we'll have to start all over again."

But no, I was certain we could make some progress. I try to convince them that they have to decide whether they can support this warden or take a hard line and ignore her relative permissiveness. "No one out there is ignoring it, they see this little business today, you may be sure, as a mandate to tighten up, to clamp down on you with unparalleled force. So you must decide if some minor reforms will do or if this is to be outright war."

"Here kitty, kitty," says Nedda Purchase, shaking her head vigorously. I send a sharp look her way but she does not receive it. She meets, instead, Sherry's eyes.

"Well, if it is war I suggest some decent arms and a respectable battle plan, ladies."

They look in their many different directions, for a moment most alone and unsisterly. Trapped, all of them, and the short hours of their lives stealing past outside the windowless room.

"And if you choose war, I would also suggest that you choose at the same time another attorney. You may inflict whatever indignities you wish upon me but you shall not teach me to spite your best interests."

"As you see them," says Miss Purchase with some heat.

"Of course as I see them. Who else is to do my work for me?"

"Us!" she shouts, and we all turn to study her. She tempers her voice which has gotten away. "But if we hire you don't you do what we want you to do? If we want revolution and not reform, if we want war, don't you have to help us make it?"

"First of all, I didn't realize you were incarcerated here, my friend. Are you absolutely certain you mean to say 'us'? That is a confusion I despise." She is looking at me peculiarly. "There is advocacy, and then there is overidentification. And it behooves us to keep them clear." I pause, still studying her. "That is unsentimental and unfashionable, but it is a necessary distinction. Now, if you organize a feasible plan that is within the law—" You have, I wish I could say, broken enough laws already, that is why you are here and I am not, and democracy has nowhere a thing to do with it.

Nedda Purchase shrugs, making light of it. "Oh shit, what fun is that?" And she sits down on the edge of the desk and studies her nails.

And there I leave them. I try to get the authorities to approve a group of convict representatives, I want to take along at least two of these women to show my *bona fides*, though I trust I can protect them adequately alone. I lose on that. So there is much shuffling back and forth between negotiating rooms. The mayor's representative comes and lectures them for a while; they yawn throughout; I cannot blame them. The pain I am in makes me alternately sharp and dull. The juices of my stomach quibble and quarrel with the walls, they tease and bite. And the pain to my most intimate parts—well, let that be.

At three in the morning a day and a half later I bring them their winnings on a small tin plate. Everyone by now is numb, they have quite accurately read the situation and ceased to care, the good news has no taste. The older woman, Jo, slumps in a corner, her face blank. "That's what it come down to, don't it, a mess of slops. Two more rolls of toilet paper a month." She turns her worn hands over and over, dark, light, dark, light, studying, perhaps their habit of emptiness. "Next time somebody in here get a gun, come and let me use it on myself first."

"They are calling this a victory in the New York *Times*, my friends," I tell them. "Inmates Win Concessions, something like that." Nedda nods vigorously. Yes, she ought to know.

"Mazel tov to the New York *Times*," says Sherry. "I never

could stand them anyway because they never had no funnies. Snobs."

"Mazel tov?"

"Yeah, I learned that off this Jewish pimp one time, it means you can shove it."

"We win," says Jo. "You mean, what's her name out there got no more job is what you mean."

"Correct. And goes to her next job somewhat less sweetly inclined, I should imagine. You see what kind of power you have."

Even the fluorescence in this room seems to have taken on the qualities of stage lighting, rising and banking with our own moods. Right now it has a sullen greenish cast.

"I think you are going back to your places in a few minutes," I say to them. This freedom in a locked room has only been a gift of the confusion of these days. A parting gift from Thomas. "There are a lot of men with flashbulbs out there."

"The finger," says Sherry amiably. They fluff their hair and pull their dresses smooth. They are disappearing into their cheerful perpetually raucous voices: these are the women who shout out the windows four floors down to their pimps and boyfriends in the street. Many, most of them, belong here. Whatever I may want to amend in the bail or plea-bargaining or arrest structures that caught and surround them with their sticky threads, they are taking more than they are giving to the social good. But neither do they, any more than I, deserve that witch's search, and it is the point I could not win. (Amnesty for the inmate with the gun I dared not even broach; I had too little to bargain with to risk such a weak thrust.) I shall file a suit and win for them perhaps some kind of relief from the search. But delay, delay: find a plaintiff, enter a plea, an appeal, wait it out whatever it entails. These women are not made for gratification postponed, that is a refinement of the middle classes. This time there shall be no party for the attorney to decline.

Nedda is the first to leave and for someone who so identified herself with the bereft she does make a quick and tidy exit. I catch her at the front door. "Miss Purchase," I say, not quite ready to accuse, but only because I lack hard evidence. "I shall not forget you. I forgot that Sherry among her many milling friends in that case, but I am not about to forget your efforts here."

"Thank you," she says guardedly, looking at the door as if she were an inmate about to regain the fresh air at last.

"I have no doubt you shall be thanked sufficiently by your friends."

"Well, they didn't have much to thank me for."

"Those poor women we have just left are not the friends to whom I am referring." I hold the door for her. "Do you know, I had thought at the beginning that these women may have found in you a facilitator of their contact with the outside world. But I think there must be a better word for what you are, no?" She eyes me warily as though I might spring on her. "And what will you do the day you get someone killed? Will you receive a bonus, possibly?"

She looks hard at me. "That will depend on who it is. If it's a lawyer for the inmates, I get a trip to Bermuda." And she is gone briskly down the street while I hold the heavy door for myself alone.

Why did I not walk out after that desecration? The subway shakes its spastic way downtown and I think and think. Shame for their desperation or shame that I too am vulnerable like all of them? Offensive act, and yet they know precisely how offensive, know better than I. Now I must again heal closed like a pruned tree, *dorten*, as my mother called it blankly: "there." I have done so once, I shall do so again.

RENATA

Nothing has changed since I was sixteen in my mother's sanctum. On the way uptown in the cab that first day Mother was uncertain whether to warn me or to reassure me that things were pretty much the same as usual on West Eighty-third Street. She had her friends among the derelicts and the bench warmers along Broadway and I could see it as we sped by, the combination of doormen and hustlers, bodegas and bagel shops. All of it was gray stone, too, and shades of tan and brick; fresh from the coast my eyes were used to white wood and cupolas, frivolous shapes and peaky porches full of flowers. Her building was the same sagging old thing too, ageless, or maybe aged at the start, only its layers of grit deepening hopelessly. All the landlord did for the years I lived here was fight rent control; I don't know what he does now but none of it gets done with a paintbrush. Its dark corners are unsafe caves, the wrought-iron outer door has, I swear, been raped by someone so overtaken by passion he's bent the bars outward to open a vast hole dead center, and then shattered the inner glass and got down to business. (A TV set from Mother, small and not particularly valuable. The tape recorder he left sitting in the middle of the hall with a note that troubled to inform her: STINKS with an arrow. Surely, Mother said forgivingly—admiringly, I swear—since she'd lost so little, surely the craft of burglary becomes its own reward.)

It's still the apartment I grew up in too: dining room table sunk under papers, never used to eat on. Window sill in the bathroom is piled high with books no one else would dream of bringing to the bathroom (where the people I know, who have subscriptions to *Mother Earth News*, secretly go to read *Cosmopolitan*). Mother reads at the breakfast table, reads at the dinner table, or she talks on the phone between mouthfuls. The only difference my absence has ever made is that she took my old pink room for storage and it is a forest now that can't be entered without a machete. There is a 1959 calendar on one wall, the Scotch tape turned brown and brittle; inside the door is a small picture of a boy whose name I can't remember, with very short hair and a smile of deadly emptiness. Over the bed, ghostly, is a vague crayon outline of a heart and a welter of initials inside; the boys' faces are exactly as indistinct in my memory. The first night back I stood in the doorway holding Tippy on my shoulder, trying to reminisce, to be warm and sentimental. The child who lived in that room was so secure she dreamed of violation, of girls followed and forced on the roof, caught in alleys, asleep in bus stations. For a long time I was preoccupied with atrocities—crimes, assignations, accidents. They didn't seem to happen on the eleventh floor. Once before it became a natural occurrence a man stole a TV down the hall by impersonating a repairman and carrying it calmly into the elevator in broad daylight. Old Mrs. Scurf fell on the fire stairs and broke her hip and finally died of it, but not excitingly. Newlyweds across the way (who seized Mrs. Scurf's apartment before the funeral was over) screeched like animals who had fought themselves extinct, but they emerged every morning beaming at each other. Maybe she made good coffee. Once the super told me he had found blood behind the apartment house near the airshaft but he didn't have a clue. Dogs, probably; somebody's undercooked calf's liver. I went to check on the stain every day as though it might whisper a clue to me, until the rain took it. Even when a girl from a Catholic school, no friend of mine, was raped on the roof of a house on Seventy-third Street—they had heard her calling long after dark, I remember, and found her stuffed into a big metal box that held tools and ashy incinerator grates, and it was days before she could stop her teeth from chattering and utter a word—even then I felt more envy than horror. Experience! Drama! Irreversible events! If they felt pain that was what I wanted too: my mother had forbidden the world to cause me pain, that was to be a thing of the past. Very un-American. History was to stop at my door; the lions of the past, and the boys uptown, they were all slain by the doorman, that's what we were paying him for. If Mother'd been hired by Hamlet or Macbeth, there'd have been no tragedy, you know. Once she got her foot in the door of any madness she could argue you out of it. She took me on trips to the slums, I suppose to cultivate compassion, but all she did was make me feel smug and lucky. I walked over orange rinds and coffee grounds and urine running down to the gutter through the cracks in the sidewalk, and I tried to keep my nice shoes clean. . . . I suppose I'd prepared for my profession of petty dissipation the way other girls dreamed of Hollywood, of ministering in white to sick children, or raising perfectly matched families if they'd had none. The endless hot summer of my virginity in that apartment that had never contained any man overnight, god. It made me smile. Nobody I knew had gotten what she dreamed of more easily or thoroughly than I did.

Night after night now Mother comes home and I serve us supper out of an amber bowl that had been her mother's, a one-dish casserole I had learned to make in order to survive when I was cooking for fifteen at that Woodstock place. I know she hates them, she thinks they run gloppy gravies willfully from one food to another, confusing its tastes and textures and softening all the firm parts as though she had no teeth. She's right but they seem so perfectly to declare our differences that I can't resist. Joe said I live my whole life like a potluck supper heavy on dessert. I love to watch her sop it up with pumpernickel: what can she do but pretend it's an old-world soup? Then in despair she turns and offers Tippy the last half of her bowl, like a kid feeding her spinach to the dog under the table. Tippy loves it. It's the only time her grandmother speaks to her.

Oh a month of it, two months. I went shopping with money she left for me in the welter of papers on the dining room table, I bought some neat tailored blouses and skirts. I felt like a female impersonator. You have to understand that all my clothes for the last couple of years—in California you only need to keep your middle covered out of season—have come from thrift shops or from friends swapping. The idea of walking into Ohrbach's, where nobody talks to anybody else and the salesgirls eye you—eye me— suspiciously, I must wear my shoplifting potential like a sandwich board, and then of holding something up to a very clean bevel-edged mirror and catching the gaze of this half-familiar thin blond girl with one frightened eye, and then of paying 7 per cent, 8 per cent tax to take it all away . . . I'd get the hoard home— Tippy would be getting heavy on my back—and pull it out of its crackling high-style bags and lay it out on Mother's bed, and then let Tippy sit in the middle and see what she'd crawl toward. Then I'd assume that was a good color and maybe I'd keep it and take the rest back. Or I'd put it all in the closet and make excuses not to wear it. When I put on the clothes and buckled on a belt with a stone in the middle, I looked altogether frail and bodiless, cer- tainly sexless. I guess that's the point: ready for a no-fold no-spin- dle no-mutilate job and a half-carat diamond on my left hand.

When I suggested that I might try work (vaguely, out of terror, but in a voice that probably could be heard) my mother glared at me with less than total sympathy. I was surprised. I had made the gesture I thought she wanted.

"Have you ever worked?" List any major illness. Previous billing address.

"Sure. But kind of—casual jobs. Post office, waitressing, keeping somebody's health food store open one summer. That wasn't bad. I once worked for a week at a place called Nature Girl Undies. I had to answer the phone and say 'Good morning, this is Nature Girl.' "

She's got a glare like a corkscrew. In another inch. "You would most likely not like it, Renata. Work, I mean." As if it were caviar or retsina, something for rarefied palates. And back to her *Wall Street Journal*.

"I might not like work? What's that supposed to mean? Who in the hell looks at it that way?"

She looked up at me impatiently while her reading glasses kept their aim. "You are a mother now," she said in the most distinct let-there-be-no-misunderstanding voice. "Why do you not do one thing at a time and try at least to do that well? I have not known you to have such a record of hot passions about work . . ." and she let the accusation dwindle off into innuendo.

I wanted to say, "But you, but I," only I'd have sputtered like a little kid caught in a lie.

"You see—when you are ready for a true career, not a job but a profession, you see—then you come and we shall talk seriously."

Timidly I made a final offer. "Maybe I could do a little filing for you or something till I figure out what I want to do. Help that girl out front. . . ."

"Cornelia needs no help, believe me. She is a girl to whom we gave that job straight from the bottom. If you ever were to meet her family you would be so astonished, the worst of Bedford-Stuyvesant, not even the best, but the girl has a will—" She clenched her fist nearly out of sight, fervid always about other people's fervor. "Imagine, she does not even have a spelling problem, I don't begin to understand it after a life with rats and welfare and men in and out the revolving door to her mother. . . ."

The necessary connection between a promiscuous mother and a spelling problem was not made for me. It was evident and I felt sure it expected both too little and too much of this Cornelia. It also left me out, I who had a brilliant mother who kept all her doors locked and who could spell in a quarter of a dozen languages. I who let it all slip by.

"Did you go looking for her? For the job?"

"We did. Especially we looked in the most unhospitable soil. We dug down very deep to find her."

"And you are satisfied with your little potato."

"Do not be rude. But yes, she is another daughter to me. In addition she is hugely efficient for the firm, you would be quite amazed. I wish her to go to law school someday."

"Ah, she will, for you. Probably. To make it up to you."

"No, she is not so grateful because, you see, she knows, there are people who know what it is to deserve what they deserve, and life will in the end humble itself to them and not the reverse." She looked contemplative. "I was so much like that."

"Me too," I said, gathering up the breakfast dishes, on which I had served apples in an unrecognizable invertebrate state. "Everybody gets what's coming to them. I thought that was a legal truism."

"What's coming to him. Or her. In the singular. I should not have to tell you that."

With her paper napkin she patted all around her mouth like a lady with a lace handkerchief, and folded it back over its stains to be used again.

I poured her a cup of coffee and put it down with an angry clunk in front of her; it splashed over the edge. She gave me a rebuking look and shook her newspaper once to undo a crimp in the fold. I stared as though she'd cracked a whip. Waitresses who do that get no tip. Wives who do that get no allowance. And broken-spined daughters? What do they get in the first place that they might lose for such an infraction at breakfast?

I had a strange dream. I was very late, I pushed open a heavy door and ran up stairs two and three at a time. I knocked at an apartment door, unfamiliar, and finally resorted to my shoulder to open it, and when I had burst in what I saw was a huge carcass on a bloody plate in the middle of a table. There was parsley all around the picked-clean bones and little potatoes sitting like fisheyes in coagulated gravy. All around the table the chairs were pushed back as though the diners had left in a hurry. I sat down on one of them, a big medieval-looking chair with a high dark back, and began to cry. And that was all. It was very dark in the room when the dream ended but I had no idea what it was about. Only that I woke up incredibly depressed on the verge of a headache with the feeling I'd been interrupted in the middle of something.

The other dreams from this period were not strange, though. I had begun to find men in them, coming upon them the way people must discover blood in their stool: with a lurch of fear and a strange relieved certainty. At last. So that's how it will be. Expecting pain, tears, eventual extinction, but thinking, at least I know. Back to work. They waited for me like a certain kind of death, like drugs wait for someone to go back on the needle everytime the going gets rough. They waited for a point of low resistance when they would come for me, in one form or another. Delivery boys and architects, blond acoustic guitar freaks and air conditioner salesmen with swarthy necks: no preference. A career, not a job, as my own mother said.

So I lay around in bed forever in the mornings like the depressed housewife I never wanted to be. A bottle for Tip and then back under the covers for a warm hour or two of hazy floating, putting off the day. A lot of memories of my earliest desperate breaks for freedom: a boy named Roger something who wrestled with me under the battered Steinway in the auditorium when I was a freshman at Music and Art. We did everything we had planned to do, only with all our clothes on, locked up tight because people kept opening the door and calling out names. There had been a student performance of *Carmina Burana*, on bleachers up on the stage—god, I had slept through it (I was an art student, exempt from loving Orff), I felt battered by those punchy chords, those Latin curse words, whatever they were—and almost everybody had finally cleared out and Roger had managed to keep me there with the most outrageous eye maneuvers, he used his eyes like some whole tribal language, if I'd seen anybody else do it I'd have laughed myself weak. But he had me, all right: for one thing he was the lead baritone so there was prestige radiating from his shoulders like divine light. For another I was fourteen and had just discovered French kissing, which my friends and I discussed endlessly, making faces, in search of some explanation for its popularity. All I remember, besides this sort of foiled grappling under the piano, done behind the asbestos curtains of our winter clothes, was that I had to go home on the subway alone and it was very late. (Well, Mother, *Carmina Burana* is a *very* long piece.) It never occurred to him to take home a girl he'd kept out for purposes of mutual benefit, I guess: sex was supposed to be like a Dutch treat, you each gave and got and provided your own transportation.

And I thought a lot about my first try at a decent college. I commuted uptown from this same apartment, this same bed was the one I couldn't get out of mornings when I had nine o'clocks. For a while I was doing well in math, in English, so well in French that my teacher, who was a very old gentleman reputed to have been a lover of Marie Laurençin, engaged me in these long arduous conversations *en français* outside the door of our classroom. Either he enjoyed my accent, which he kept trying to convince me was Parisian (naturally), or he needed a few minutes, MWF 11, in which to lean gently against the blondest girl in the class, whose breasts (she had just been told by some infinitely younger man) could be (should be?) outlined with a compass, under blue lamb's wool or ticklish yellow mohair. At first I would step back carefully to conduct these conversations with some propriety. But one day the poor old man had asked, grinning as wickedly as his dry cheeks would let him, if *peut-être* he should use Sen-Sen to keep me from moving away from him. His vest gave out a sad rubbery smell and the nerves in his cheeks twitched regularly, in class and out, they were so regular they could beat the seconds. So I moved forward, even to the point of unfairness to M. Vaucheron. I think I considered it final proof of the disastrous unreality of this whole college scene that I couldn't for the life of me picture M. Vaucheron making love to Marie Laurençin, as though course credits and reserve readings had done it, and not sixty years and the death of everyone's dreams, everywhere, given time and space enough. Duffy, my poor friend Duffy, urged me to drive him insane. This because she was big-busted in a sort of useless unprovocative way, flat-hipped and freckled, with hair the color of a dusty Irish setter, and so she lived mainly in such hostile daydreams, in which the charms she didn't have, had she had them, would move men to the edge of suicide with the name Francene Duffy on their lips.

I got through the days on coffee out of paper cups, and more cigarettes than I could handle, but they gave me a sense of sin without immediate danger, and of course an endless amount of conversation, none of which could be recalled the same night. Probably a quarter of it consisted of cattiness about teachers, mockery of the most serious ones; a matching quarter of cattiness about other girls—this was a girl's school, my first and last—and it was sort of studded with male teachers. Cloves in a doughy apple, the only spice. That left the other half clear to talk about men.

When we finally met them, glimpsed outside the subway kiosk or up on the steps of their library across the street, they were consistently disappointing. But they were all we had so we concentrated as hard as we would have if they'd been deserving. Men? Boys. Some wore their pants high, with two inches of white athletic sock showing but rarely with the bodies of athletes to justify the socks. No waists. Men need waists, subtle though they may be. Duffy and I discussed it. Elegant all over, you shall know their naked bodies by the bones of their wrists. Duffy, who had none now that I think of it, believed in ankles; she had a dozen subterfuges to get a glimpse of calf and ankle, which she tried to convince me betrayed style and breeding as surely as a long second toe. Half of them still looked like they carried the flag at assembly and wore those earnest pen and pencil holders like little leather penises that bobbed on their belts while we fifth-graders giggled.

Our friends gave themselves away being seen in broad daylight with such callow men. Duffy and I went perfumed from gym to lunch to bookstore, prepared for some accident more pleasant than the kind our mothers had always made us wear clean underwear for.

In some winter month of my freshman year I was walking along Broadway very slowly, not thinking about accidents. I had stopped in front of the shoe repair shop on Broadway and 109th to look at the Italian shoemaker's windowful of coleus, his tangled wintergarden. I saw a murky dark man behind me, much taller than I was. His reflection surrounded mine, that's what I remember; not what we pretended to talk about or how he dared me up to his apartment after half an hour and a cup of coffee at Chock Full O' Nuts. He enclosed me entirely, with inches to spare on all sides.

As he did all of me, which is what I had in mind for myself: that and not essays on Milton or the *Song of Roland*. Italian, ugly in the striking way of Continental faces whose parts assert themselves as though each were all there was: a face of nothing but eyes, of mouth, of nose. Like a kitchen full of his shouting gesturing aunts. But (I told Duffy the next day, too excited to eat, waving my egg salad sandwich whole) he is large enough for all the parts to squabble amicably. He transcends his parts. Multo, mucho, whatever the hell it is. Macho, said Duffy morosely. He kisses his fingers when he talks. So does a Sicilian hood, she said. So did Mussolini, I'll bet.

Well, he kissed my fingers too, and more. He was given to peeling my clothes off very very slowly, it was his way of paying homage. He said. To Woman? I asked. To you, he answered, making his eyes, his forest of eyebrow, one huge eye against mine. He had a good many tricks but I had never seen them before, so they were not tricks. All the grubby men I'd known had been boys, I decided that in the first five minutes, they were all so hungry, so needy, they were like locomotives out of control, crashing, splintering, undone. Giuseppe's principle appeared to be undivided, selfless, nearly unfulfilled attention. When I talked (which I did with uncustomary eagerness, a tactical error I regretted later when I discovered tactics) his eyes would widen and he'd nod slowly, gravely, like a kind father to his frantic child. When I allowed myself to be undressed, it would take half an hour and he'd barely be to my knees. Even my imperfections he admired, my moles, the single outrageous hair below my left nipple. (Queen Esther was perfect, I used to think, they examined her from head to foot and she was flawless.) But he seemed to approve. However little he said, he was still there, he kept wanting me back again.

I tried to admire him similarly as he lay beneath my awed hands but he was so still, so attentive, following my eyes around, never relaxing under them, that I'd see him suddenly as a patient stretched beneath a doctor's lamp waiting for my arrival at some conclusion. Once he got up to move I'd arrive at the conclusion all too quickly and he'd be offended and shake his head. What control you have, Giuseppe, I marveled. All those helpless boys who'd ruined their slacks and my best dresses trying to get to me too fast. Puppies not quite housebroken. Control is all there is, Renata, he'd explain very coolly, disapproving. You should have been a surgeon—an attempt to make him smile. I noticed that he did not sweat. Maybe he wouldn't allow himself to, it would be a sign of effort. He told me he was a devotee of karezza, the Indian art of intolerable postponement: you lie side by side forever and ever and consummate your love, your whatever, without touching. But that was for later, after I'd mastered the first semester's work of holding still. He pointed to the pink prickling flush across the top of my chest one time, like whisker burn. You see, he said in his voice so deep I heard it gray, that's the way I remember it, he probably forced it down there; it sounded the way print looks on paper.

See what?

See where Giuseppe has taken you to.

Ah, I murmured. So. I didn't know that happened.

It could be—he picked his way across the English language as though it were rubble and he had to walk barefoot through it— that this has never happened with another?

He was not quite right but his pride insisted on it. Ardor alone, no particular skill, had raised such a rash, whether I'd seen it or not. The lights were not always on. He is vain, I decided. And you? I asked, looking down at the dewy sweat between my breasts, chilled. What proof do you give of where you've been?

Ah—he laughed his dismissive laugh. I was much younger than he was and he liked that and had contempt for it. I bit my knuckles, afraid to think. Ah, you can tell where I am, no? Men are given no places to hide, it was not given to us to be—what do you call it—fakers at this business. What shall we feign, we per- form under the whip! He laughed at me again. But I meant more. Where he really was, not where his assorted parts might be, mo- mentarily, performing. Giuseppe, I began, and stopped.

Control, he was saying quietly, slipping into his long socks, his terrific shoes. It was two o'clock. He had an Italian class to teach. An Italian romantic poetry class, he made the girls wriggle in their seats when he read to them. I thought of Roger the baritone who had no control under the piano. I collect stars. God knows who I'll marry. Control, it is a wonder, he persisted. Salvation. It makes an art—one of the finger-kissed words—out of a dirty job. I was astounded that he intended this as a compliment. How he rolled my black tights so slowly down from the top, half inch by half inch, like pastry dough perfectly rolled over, his long fingers strumming my clenched stomach gently as they passed over it. I lay without breathing: he had all the breath. So that when he got all the layers of cotton and nylon off and had come to me—he had accomplished me? subdued me? ah, made me. I came to the word and stumbled over it for the first time. Made me. I buttoned my blouse with my back to him. Was it possible that somewhere, somewhere hidden even from himself, this Giuseppe hated women? I had not yet read about Don Juan, the theories of his latent this and suppressed that. It was an extraordinary moment, in which the possibilities in the world, for complexity and perversity and deviousness, opened up at my feet like a well, a cistern hidden under piles of leaves. I had thought all this was so simple: you get over your terror and lie down, you worry about having babies and your mother finding out and even about motives on the crudest level—he is, of course, the best baritone in the school—but not whether the man in bed with you has to overcome his disgust to touch you, but needs to touch you anyway.

Control, I said, not looking up from my small troublesome pearl buttons. Control and *tristesse*, right? I felt like a pretender with such words in my mouth, words for M. Vaucheron and his Marie. Giuseppe was smiling. At my pretensions or at the speed with which I had learned the language, the ceremony of insincerity?

But I didn't let him go. I decided instead—taking the steps down from his apartment quickly, flying along in the peppery winter air, thinking god, I look like a girl who's just been properly fucked!—that I would try to learn some things from him but not others. (I hadn't read *Faust* yet, either.) Technique, not attitude. Skill, not that cruel withholding. I'd show him up at his own game, I'd use his use of me: a quick course in the Italian tradition.

Giuseppe was so eminently presentable that not only did my grades begin to show the strain but I lost two friends simply for being seen with him. A *tall* Italian, can you imagine, Duffy had warned them. She had become my advance man, tagging along to get some vicarious pleasure at the very least.

So I spent the late afternoon in the stacks with him learning control. We'd sit where we couldn't quite be seen, though we could always be come upon—where geology and topography met, something like that—and our fingers would work with great concentration, our faces unmoving as though we were in the middle of a crowd. (There was a story afoot, dragged around and embellished by Duffy, that a couple—no names were ever used but it was clear *she* knew who they were—spent last Saturday night in the "beau parlor" of the dormitory, where girls chastely received their dates or kept them waiting interminably, and the girl who sat on her boyfriend's lap surrounded by navy blue accordion pleated skirt, was indeed receiving him, in full view of the classes of '58–'62, without so much as a reflex twitch. They both wore *blazers*, for Christsake, Duffy would howl with such depthless disgust I knew she'd give a full year of her life, now or later, for an hour of such corny perversion.)

And here I was with fingers positively tenderized by a pink hand lotion I thought smelled like an aphrodisiac, sitting beside an unflaggingly ready Italian instructor—a professional, I knew, and my heart would rise and sink at the same time—groaning with agonized delight, all of it turned back into my chest. Giuseppe, I'll die, I'd whisper. You'll kill me. Please.

To which he'd answer, with his instructor's aggravated patience, sounding just like my botany teacher when I confused her damned pomes and simple fruits: *Renata.* Please to what? That is what I am existing for. To do you this service. Let me. As though he were refilling my glass with his very dry vermouth. My dear girl —turning the pages of his everlasting Leopardi—ah, let me.

❀   ❀   ❀

I said that nothing had changed down through the years except my own room, reclaimed for chaos like an abandoned meadow. One more thing, though: the cleaning woman had changed. "Colored girls" were out, Puerto Ricans were in. And though I had nothing better to do than keep the kitchen counters polished, even at the risk of insulting me Mother kept her "girl" on— daughters you can always get, I suppose, but a good maid's hard to find. Her name was Mrs. Huerta and she came as a surprise.

I was in bed, half asleep but conscious of the guilty knot that wound and unwound every morning in my chest. Came a click at the door and footsteps in the living room, rustle of papers, the closet door opening, closing crisply. The postman always rings twice. Do muggers come in the morning? I was torn between leaping naked out of bed and pulling the covers up to my neck. I thought of hiding Tippy under the sheets but if I grabbed her she'd make more noise than she did sleeping.

But the steps were a woman's—my mother, back for something? —and then a song began in the kitchen, and the song was in Spanish. Pots banged, the dishwasher slid closed with its dull clank, china on plastic. I put my clothes on and went out to see who had appropriated the house.

She was a woman to quash all my (shameful) categories. A large woman—my mother's size, maybe, but her flesh deployed differently on the bone. She was small-busted and wide-hipped, with a bit of stomach buckling her aquamarine skirt—but all of her spread in such a way—how do I say this and make her sound both pleasant and familiar? She is loosely hinged. Comfortable. With a little turn she could be sluttish, but she doesn't make that turn. Say she's the kind of mother whose children know she still goes to bed with their father: no apologies. More blond than not, with emphatic eyebrows. She doesn't own an apron.

"Well," she says, and "Well," I say, and we laugh. She reaches a hand to me but pulls it back and shakes it. "Bubbles." It's been in a bucket of Mr. Clean. I like the idea of shaking hands with a cleaning lady, though.

"Visiting Mrs. Stein?"

"Her daughter. I just moved in this week."

"Her daughter! She never told me she had no daughter." She's a little angry, at both of us, I think. "I had her down for a lady nobody ever got theirself next to." And she did hoot, with a dripping sponge in her hand.

"Well, it's Mrs., you know. Only one, I guess, and not for long."

"Oh well," she said, "the world just likes to surprise you. Where you been all this time? I been here more than two years, down on my knees cleaning behind her books, keep the bedbugs out of the sheets, she never mention nothing."

"Around." I got myself a piece of bread for the toaster. "She never mentioned me."

She shook her head. "Or a husband either. You got quite a mama there."

"What do you mean?"

"Oh, she's a one in a million. Ten million. She could knock off Muhammad Ali if she wanted. Just talk him back in his corner."

"Just what everybody wants in a mother. Have you seen the milk?"

"No milk I don't think. She's no kind of shopper you can depend on, you got to run up behind her about some things. But I bet she keeps her office up."

So Catalina and I got in the habit of talking. She sings half in Spanish and swears in the other half. She's so professional she carries all her detergents and rubber gloves around in a bag like a doctor, and she's very exacting. To buy some pride, I guess. She likes to tell me how she ordered my mother to buy the proper mops and sweepers and plastic bags. "And did she listen, I scared her half to death."

"Hey look," I said one time and trying not to apologize I gave her all my unworn New York clothes, my Ohrbach's specials bought with such pain. Catalina's not my size, she's much bigger and thicker but she pulls them all up differently and manages not to look sexless in all those silky blouses. She loves the shoes for church and the skirts and the impenetrable belts. Maybe she does all her bending during the week, at work, and they must be uncomfortable enough to feel right for a good godly Sunday. When she smiles her one gold tooth winks at me. And Tippy saves her biggest grins for Catalina.

Once in a while she brings one of her two sons and her daughter to wait for her. Mother had a party on a Saturday night and she dragged them all along to escort her home when she was done straightening the chairs and dumping the ashes. She wouldn't travel at night and her husband wasn't having any.

The party reminded me so much of my submerged childhood I just stood in all the doorways and gaped. Voices were kept to a very low hum; occasionally a burst of laughter was sucked back in quick as if someone might regret it. It's no wonder I spent a lot of nights as a teen-ager dancing and howling to records, just to wash the sound of all that good taste out of my ears. Mozart at a party

. . . for years I heard Mozart as a kind of orange-brown color, the exact color of the lampshade that threw a genteel den-warm glow into the room. The sherry they drank was the same color. The only people who didn't drink Mother's sherry, I can see them, were a couple named McCall, Stewart who was a reporter, I think, and somebody-Ann, who brought their own Bourbon in a messy A&P paper bag, always made a gesture of gift-giving with it at the door—"How nice, dear, we can surely use this," Mother would be forced to say and take it from them—and then Stewart would reclaim it off whatever table she'd put it down on and cling to it like a raft, the two of them would, all evening. They'd leave behind the creased bag and the nine-tenths-empty bottle which Mother would throw away with pursed lips, along with the cigarette butts and Loren Weisbacher's wet cigar.

No one ever said a word to me at these parties, after the hellos. (There was no reason for me to know until Tippy how blessed are the nights without children, when you don't want to have to explain a single thing, or slow down, or watch your language.) There was endless discussion, passionate but even, of tax law and estates, of conspiracy charges and government evasion, of chicanery in high places. Sympathies were assumed to be with the dregs, the losers; they were also, I realized later, anti-Stalinist, all the old pilgrims had long since trooped back from their disastrous romance with the left—only their reputations would never catch up with some of them. I don't think they minded having me, wide-eyed, in the room; maybe they even thought the discussions would have a civilizing influence on me. But certainly no one ever addressed me by name. My mother would hand me trays out of the kitchen and I would pass them silently. Once she handed me a glass of sherry, absently (she was not one of those European mothers who encouraged drinking among schoolchildren. "Who was it," I once heard her ask, "who taught my poor father to shuffle a deck of cards?") so I drank it and fell asleep in a corner with my head against a bookcase. I would go around feeling like one of those Velázquez princesses, a compressed grownup, only in plaid wool slacks, with a slightly belligerent lower lip and Aryan hair, and I was privy to the confidences of the royal chamber; also, of course, I was unable to make head or tail of what I heard. Judges were rated for fairness and reliability and uncompromising stances against communism: kindness to the A.D.A. One man's winning points were subtracted for drinking which incapacitated him at inconvenient times—that kind of thing, human, I could grasp out of all the abstract lawyerly gossip, only the abandoned husbands, the woman lawyer, no friend of Mother's, about whom Mother said the only kind words I'd ever heard when someone reported that she'd been seen in tears after a losing verdict. (Were they kind words, actually? Now that I remember it, somebody said, "Gerda, it could happen to you sometime," and I wondered if he meant losing or crying.) My mother would herd her friends back and forth from living room to dining room with the rough efficiency of a cocktail waitress, scolding and crooking her finger. As the evenings wore on everything would loosen a little; women would begin to sit with their legs slightly apart, men to belch quietly, hand pressed to chest in apology, chairs were moved at strange angles as though to let them breathe.

I found it insulting and deliberate that I was so invisible to them, only another plot of my mother's to deny my existence. Mother was at the center, a large woman in her own house, husband and wife. Her friends knew her far better than I did. Her hands moved with more grace than you can imagine, considering their size. They drew stories in the air as she told them.

Which left me nothing to do but embarrass her. One night while preparations were being made by Carlotta, who was arranging little shrimp on crackers with a twist of her whole body every time she laid one down, taking her hand away quickly as if it were burnt but humming with great satisfaction (and eating every other shrimp)—I didn't say to myself in so many words, How can I wreck this? It was so perfect, the caramel-colored light pouring down in a corner of the living room, all of it held under a glass, like the cake Carlotta had baked that was magnified and protected and impenetrable to my fingers.

So I ran away. I suppose it was a sign of my terrible consent, my contempt for myself, that all I could do to get myself noticed was to eradicate myself entirely. I knew a boy who set a fire under his parents' bed; what a heroic act compared to mine. I am telling this story because I wasn't missed till after eleven o'clock. Mother said later she thought I was taking a bath. I'd have disintegrated by then. Carlotta was in hysterics, being supported by Mother's hard clasp around the shoulders at the police station. No one was relieved to see me, only furious. I had walked down Riverside Drive along the outer edge of the park, carrying all my warmth, what felt like my only possession, inside my winter coat. I felt like a small tight ship moving secretly without lights. I'll never forget the happiness I had brought myself, discovering I had legs and guts and perfect understanding, having utterly destroyed my mother's party. I thought, I can do this any time, it's like getting kidnapped, only I kidnap myself, and all I want for a ransom is my mother worrying, my mother in tears, desperate, rending her clothes.

When the police cruiser found me and took me back, after we got through with the precinct interview (they were trying to make sure I hadn't been abducted or molested or other such unsubtle business) I saw they had gotten to the perfect little shrimps, the ones Carlotta left them, before they'd missed me. A few tiny rejects lay in a briny puddle, capsized beside chips of sesame cracker. The chocolate cake in its glass coffin was untouched though. The kitchen light, when I was marched through on my way to bed, shone off it in brittle squares, undisturbed. Oh the self-pity I took to bed with me! I lay there clenched in a knot hating her and hating myself, even a failure at *not* being.

Now it was Catalina's children who slouched around the outskirts of the living room looking for something to do. Her daughter was beginning to have little breasts that pointed straight out like dares she couldn't follow up on. Even I wanted to touch them through her fuzzy pink sweater, because they'd be soft as rabbits' tails (and I know she hated them, she wished they were full and hard, her weapons). Catalina is already worried about Tina, who'll be giving it away in stairwells soon, behind shoestores and supermarkets, anywhere anybody wants it. But each time we talk about it, all we can do is look at each other helplessly and smile—why should our daughters be any purer than we were? The world will always be a place where warmth is exchanged, all the small flames joining, for us to warm our hands by. Well, why should we ask our daughters to stay cold just because they were our babies once?

Her twin sons, from what I know about them, are very different, pure lead and pure gold. One of them, Tico, came over to me at this party as I was coming out of the bedroom. I'd gone in to check on Tippy, afraid she might have trouble sleeping through the noise; but when I got inside I realized that my mother's parties weren't going to loosen any plaster. From her crib it sounded like an ordinary evening with the radio humming. Tico was standing in the doorway. He looked hungry.

"Hey, what's that supposed to be?" It was a gambit as good as any other; he led with his chin to a square hanging on the wall behind me, a huge batik called "Castle" that some artist had bartered for my mother's services one time—kept him out of the army, I think, to go on saving the world for its cottage industries. The castle had turrets and banners hanging from its great stony-gray squares.

I laughed and said, "What does it look like?"

He shrugged. Tico was one of those kids, sixteen, seventeen maybe, who spend passionate amounts of energy looking cool and careless. Somehow he had made his face, not a bad face, come to a voracious point, an anteater's forward thrust. Still he looked so far from depraved he must have mourned himself in the mirror: too many open places still. Too many points of entry to shame him. Small eyes and a wide mouth—he might even be secretly generous in his own way. His mother would be the last to know. "Look like a jungle, maybe," he offered, bored, but hovering around on one boot and then the other.

"I was thinking it looked sort of like a castle, you know? The kind kids dream about, didn't you ever dream about knights and kings and stuff like that?"

He picked a few nuts out of a paper cup and threw them into his mouth from a spectacular distance, and shook his head. "You gotta live on Park Avenue to be dreaming about kings, man. I used to dream I was Roberto Clemente." Another nut flew in. I thought he'd choke. "Hey listen," he whispered as though he had something to confide, and he came very close to me. "How about a little, unh . . ."

He was trying to bite my ear, absolutely earnest.

"Come on, hey, I didn't know you were a fuckin' school-teacher," he whispered, sounding abused, the very worst insult he could muster, and pressed up against me so hard I could feel the steel rivets on his leather jacket. Well, I didn't know either. If I looked alarmed he probably took heart at his menace. But—I *have* changed, I thought from a great distance where some part of my brain wasn't frozen with gin. In spite of my horny dreams. Maybe I'm aging. This felt like incest, this could practically be a son of mine breathing beer into my neck. Fleetingly I saw a boy I'd once spent a weekend with in Taos, so young his chest was hairless and looked like some marble David's. All I remembered about him—nothing like his name or how I came to be there—was one long brave erection he wore around the room like a flag and saved for-ever, he wouldn't let me come near him for fear he'd use it up, to say You see? You see? But I kissed Tico right straight into the salt from the mixed nuts, and felt against me the hard and imperious—is that the word? imperialist?—center of the boy, like a tree branch I might put all my weight on and never bend. I kissed him for as long as he wanted, for an old times' sake he wouldn't have understood, till his twin brother came over, wearing the same face only not nearly so aggressively cool, and said, "Hey man, leave the lady alone, you gonna land up in jail that way."

So Tico put his heels back down and retreated to nurse his hard-on in the general crush of warm bodies. It was nice of him not to object that the lady had liked that, salt and beer and all. I wiped my mouth with the back of my hand, feeling positively in-dented in three or four places. "My brother don't mean no harm," said Alejandro, "he just some kind of sex maniac, that's all." He raised his bottle of beer to me in a small salute and smiled with one broken tooth, one perfect one and a gap in between. He reminded me of Ollie the Dragon, my oldest friend.

GERDA

I have held a small party, and at the party a discussion developed which has haunted me. My friend Theodore Rasp was arguing a kind of determinism in families—all this the result of a fiery fight with half a dozen of us regarding preventive detention of children. "But look, haven't you seen it—madness in one generation, madness in the next, the statistics are extraordinary. I wouldn't call it a death warrant exactly, but there's a better than even chance one of those children will end up in trouble. Suicides the same. And alcoholics, god, I've got a friend whose parents were so caught up all their lives in AA and all the rest of it that their daughter—this girl who had positively *reviled* their drinking all her life" (Theo is knocking on the table point by point, keeping time) "that, wouldn't you know it, she took a quick trip through it all herself. Like she'd been waiting all her life to put herself through the same doom, it was just crouching there waiting for her."

Fine, I agreed to all that. Still I argued, with much assistance, that a 99 per cent accurate predictive statistic did not give us the right to curtail anyone's freedom prior to the commission of a criminal act duly prosecuted.

But later that evening, watching my daughter sleep fully dressed across the bed which had held my guests' overcoats—she had perhaps come to see Tippy sleep and lay down herself, she is so far from energetic—alone there with her noiseless breathing on my pillow, I had an intriguing understanding for the first time.

This child, you see, in so many ways has not been mine: accidentally conceived, genetically and spiritually she has been her father's only, and he a phantom who passed meaninglessly into and out of my life with the speed of sound? Light? Perhaps not that quickly; in the time it took me to understand I had no need of him, and so to let him go. But she, from the first instant, had his physique, the fair skin and filmy hair, anomalous, alien— *goyische*—the uncertain eyes and blood-ready high pink lips, a certain sexuality in them from the first. Beside her father, Henry May, I would wake sometimes to see his profile, pale even in the dark, like a face in a negative, and feel in the very floor of my stomach the question forming in acid: what am I doing here? With Renata the question was in fact the same, except for its changed particulars: who is she? What incidental part could I have had in the making and carrying of this stranger, this stranger's child? And since, you see, in my carefully planned and exactingly executed life there had never been the dream of home and children (I had neither accepted nor rejected them, only had never sat down and thought the requisite thoughts) it was so easy to see her as an aberration, a kind of growth on the perfectly shaped body of my life. . . . Well, where does this fault lie that she bore me not sufficient resemblance to involve my flesh in hers? Somewhere between mother and child? Between father and mother? (But we were never that unit. Consecutively we were, first he the father, then forevermore I the mother.) Certain poisonings take place, *in utero*. Done. Accomplished without consent. One fights them at best. No blame attaches.

(I recall, good Lord, watching the child in her bath one evening —Carlotta's day off, I should guess—seeing her shatter the water over her little thighs like glass into a thousand fragments, and discovering how early a small girl's bones imply the roundness they will grow to. Yet, holding her out of the tub in a huge yellow towel that drank up moisture like a sun, with the small blunt downy lamb's nose of her sex beside my face as I dried her, I thought, no, no, she shall never have a woman's sex, it is not possible to move from such soft innocence, pastoral, to such wrenching hungers, such abandonment. But it was true she had her father's nature, lustful, never cerebral, and when she early became embroiled in her first little affairs, as a teen-ager, I knew she was caught in a track and would follow it straight wherever it led her.)

But this is not what I had wanted to speak of. I have suddenly had the understanding that Renata—my prodigal daughter—has indeed returned to me after her peculiar exercise of a family tradition, my family's. I had simply never seen it, never stopped being on the defense to think, you see, that her disappearance was not truly a function of her endless personal argument with me.

My memory of Renata's disappearance from my life—she thinks she was never a part of it to begin with, of course; she knows only the tradition of American mothers tethered to the kitchen door within hearing of their beloved children's every cry, not of any European convention of nannies, nursemaids, governesses, women free to have households, continue their work lives, keep lovers and husbands as well. (Interesting: we smile, patronizing, at Freud's circle of Viennese hysterics and yet we make our own, if not repressed, then bored and narrow hysterics. What have we learned of the physics of the mind, which like the physics of matter declares that anything compressed sufficiently will surface elsewhere or explode?)

However. One May, late May, Renata waited, suddenly patient, to receive in the mail the last of a series of postal cards from her college professors condemning her final examination grades to F's and D's exclusively, her courses flunked or miserably botched. She wrapped them in a red ribbon, tied a bow, and placed them upon the folders on the dining room table where habitually I worked. A pretty present for me, but she wanted no sympathy, in fact, which she would somehow have to have used to take a step up, or back, or forward, but a step. What she wanted (say I) was a scapegoat for her anger at herself, which was final: sufficient anger is resignation, after all. Ah, so they were to be *my* failing grades, you see, as a mother I had done execrably, hence her indifference, hence her incompetence. However much I had cared for her, she did not approve of the conditions of my caring. I had, I shall tell you, a desire to put her possessions on the street where they belonged—

all clothes and magazines, no books, no hobbies. Rainbow shades of eye shadow and detachable, inflatable, most detectable breasts to pop in and out of brassieres and bathing suits. Rather, I waited for her to return home from her evening—she had already been out when I came exhausted from work. I waited, drumming fingers on her packet of postal cards, but she never came. The postal cards were apparently an "explanation," an indictment without particulars; half the clothes were gone. But a goodbye? I was not deserving.

Yet, you see. This evening a decade later with my daughter asleep on the bed, her face which I have just come from studying so clear as to be terrifying, a child's face inept still at expressing complexities, I have found a new perspective. This is the way I work, perhaps it is the only way to live my life: I see a precedent for her disappearance. And I respect repetition as the true and only movement of history, both public and private. . . .

I who began life as the eldest daughter of a pathetic and lonely Talmudist-manqué—if there is no such designation, let me create one—then lawyer-manqué born on la rue des Juifs in the provincial town of Colmar in France? in Germany? (I cannot be very authoritative about that, someone surely owned and was responsible for that city but like the child of the case judged by Solomon, it was nearly torn asunder in the course of that determination.)

My father, born in Frankfurt, wanted to become a lawyer so that he could fight some of the chafing restrictions on the Jews. It would have been a pathetic battle, fought on the terms already established by the victors, he would have been decapitated before he drew his sword. However, fortunately or otherwise, he was so prevented because he was not permitted to become a lawyer in the first place. He was not so much as admitted to the university. He had a round head, tufted at the edges with hair to which all the energy of a full head had retreated and massed, and eventually it had to be sufficient that, with narrow glasses on his thin features, he looked like a university graduate of fine, even finicky, tastes. It is comic, his life was comic, though not to him and certainly not to his family.

My first whole memory is of my father in his characteristic vigor. He is taking me in a coat that was cut down from someone's

—a cousin, perhaps—to the market in the square in Colmar, beside *le marché aux fruits*. We are in search of some fabric for my mother, who wants to make a pillow. "Why couldn't she have come?" my father keeps demanding of the air. "How do I know what she wants?" He fingers some very pretty bright colors but finally in his mournful way, without conviction, settles on a bleak stripe, gray or brown. It will be like everything else in that flat: barely adequate, and dull. My taste, you understand, is formed early—happy colors do not coincide with my parents' view of themselves, they appear to feel they don't deserve them, that or they think that the burghers of Colmar (who could hardly have cared how we amused ourselves at our own expense) might judge such frivolity unseemly on the part of Jews. All I can remember is that we came home from the market in a heavy rain and my father handed the goods, already spattered with raindrops, to my mother without a word, and she took them with a grunt that was perhaps intended to signify satisfaction. Or even thanks.

So it went for him in the world at large. Kafka, having taken a position in Prague in some office—workmen's compensation, I believe, or perhaps *le douanier*, however one puts it in that divided language—said about the job that it is "a running start for suicides." He said he was obeying an order that commands "You have to earn your grave."

So my father earned his grave a hundred times over. He had wanted to become a lawyer. He had not become one. Why? Let us be charitable and assume one is not born with a predisposition to become a cottontail rabbit. Then let us reverse the question. What would it have taken for him to succeed? Not only himself with a difference but things, events with a difference. It took no special sensitivity to see how things were with the Jews of Frankfurt where he was born. All the restrictions, the prohibitions with their long history dating to medieval animosities. Poor Papa for thinking he could go with sword and buckler and undo history. St. George, St. Joan, St. Morris Stein. And yet, the implications of *not* so thinking, do they make more of a man of one? Or, in fact, in touch with reality, fully adjusted to the bad luck of his birth, make no man at all? Having spent his boyhood, before the age of responsibility, dreaming, he spent his manhood grieving over his early death.

I myself began as I have reported. My reputation as an émigrée from Hitler's Germany is altogether fabricated within the deficient imaginations of sentimentalists with no knowledge of history. I speak with an incurable accent, in which I have announced myself to be in lifelong exile. Whatever the complexities of feelings toward exile—Dante put forth so very gently the idea that "the exile that has been given me I cherish as an honor"—for me this expatriation has been a life spent in badly fitting shoes. Humble as these corns and bunions may appear among the noble head- and heart-aches of history, like the introduction of garlic to a subtle ambrosia it can mean a niggling pain immensely distracting. Furthermore, I favor a certain irony of speech which at times can appear to border on bitterness, and, do you know, this is a terror to Americans of plain speech. They think I must know a great deal more than they do, and it must be of the unknowable: hence I watch their eyes go in hopeful search for the number embossed upon my arm. Pfui. There is only one holocaust that they have heard about, thus they shall assign me to it. They have no experience or appreciation of the multiplicity of situations in this world which, like winding and digressing roads, may lead down to the present. And though in the end, paradoxically, they are correct, that situations in fact replicate each other the world over, and from them people come forth bearing similarly shaped scars and singing songs that celebrate similar moments, nonetheless they are sadly lacking in respect for the multiplicity of real people who inhabit real countries of which they have never heard. Like children, Americans are: once you have dipped over the horizon and out of sight, you cease utterly to exist for them.

Now the older I become the easier it is to think far back, the harder to gather up yesterday's jagged pieces. I have heard that happens, a cliché, and have been waiting so consciously for that slippage to tell me I am old that undoubtedly I have made it happen. . . .

It is easy, in New York City, to think of the dust of my childhood. The color gray, something like a subway color, the cold mouse-skin color of a prison wall. It must not have registered on a child except as an accumulation behind the eyes; an expectation. After all, the city of Colmar and its neighbors, Mulhouse, Schlett-stadt—*en France? en Allemagne?* Schlettstadt became Sélestat from time to time—were built in the fourteenth century. Time for the sludge to have built up so that one could feel that age, as with the skin of very old ladies, first with the fingertips. Everything here, in comparison, seems young, half-fledged.

And with the fingertips my softer memories: say, the grapes. I do not know where the grapes came from into our kitchen. Alsace is solidly paved with vineyards, of course, and one could see them easily from the ramparts of the city, lying like soft green lakes on all sides. I mean rather that my mother ran, I should say con-ducted, like a maestro of small compassion, a kitchen more stern than spontaneous, and we were not much given to munching, *noshing* on handfuls of anything in the course of the day. Still I do see my long dark skirt gathered up into the shape of a sack and stems of greenish-yellowish grapes piled up, myself running some-where incessantly and the grapes most probably my lunch. They were cool and soft but fenced with skin: like a hundred separate organs of the body they fascinated me. I spent hours peeling them laboriously so that I could see the little capillaries beneath their pale green flesh, the inner world of bloodless tracings, or in fights with my brother Addie I would squeeze them from their tight skins and watch them burst like worms, oozing down his shirt front.

Mine was a childhood of moats and ramparts. If I had not lived there I would have dreamed them, as all American children ap-pear to. At best, ducks and chestnut trees. Laurel in season, or-ange trees that gave miniature pale fruit hard as pits. Sharp roofs, angles and gables exaggerated as wooden toys, against a gray and steely sky. The canal, that section of the city called La Petite Venise was very romantic at a distance—trees and flowers closely overhanging the slightly curving water, gray-green weathered wooden docks and little boats tied bobbing to the houses. *Très très belle.* Only up close did it stink. (But then, so stinks Venice, does it not? And Xochimilco is a slum. I myself have neglected to go there.) Only up close were they splintery, the docks, and only half the little gondolas water-worthy. If it were

America, the houses overlooking the water, mosquitoes and all, would minimally be worth a million dollars a month in rent to a good speculator. Colmar in the first decade of the century, however—well, I should not make a vice out of the virtue of un-self-consciousness.

In any event, we did not, in fact, live on la rue des Juifs—you must keep an eye on me, I can exaggerate shamelessly for effect. A ghetto with so public and disingenuous a title was not at this time strictly necessary to make its effects felt even in dispersal. It was on rue Nefftzer where my first twelve years were spent. The relationship I had with the canal was more accurately, too, between my skirts and the silty water. Three times at most did I manage to secure a decently lengthy ride on someone's little boat (three times disappointed, might I add, because no one dared go as fast, or if slowly then as swayingly, as I dared dream, and there were low bridges, incommodious if the water level was swollen in the slightest by the rains for which the vintners prayed every spring). Instead I found a place for myself, down in a rougher part of town, where there were no houses beetling over the canal, where it began to look more like a drainage ditch, and there I arranged my armies of sticks and wet the hem of my dress, inevitably; where, even if I managed to stay away from home long enough to let it dry out, I would still bring with me evidence of what my mother saw as some dereliction of my femininity—a line indelible as the high-water mark on a wall that has held back a flood.

I was a precocious child, of course. Anyone who volunteers to tell the story of his or her life with little urging intends to begin by telling you of his precocity—and the single son among us was a lout: large, beefy, with the square blond face, unprecedented among Steins or Lifschutzes, of an Eastern European *goy*: a Czech or a Rumanian. He was always in trouble. He pushed our neighbor's boy, Fritz Pforz, from his balcony and broke his collarbone; he was singled out by his schoolmaster for special punishment so frequently that it ceased to be special. And, although there was perhaps nothing mortal in his sins, my father rightly or wrongly found himself incapable of bending his authority, nor even his attention, upon a son who so dramatically failed him. In retrospect it appears to me that Addie was attempting a different, easier kind of masculinity than my father's *yeshiva bucher* challenge to authority, which came to nought, his voiceless rabbit-before-hounds crouch. I am certain. . . .

There was one incident, one day on which my mother—who was carrying before her the only evidence of my father's manhood, a mound which became my sister Minke soon enough—her face drawn down in folds of wretchedness, spoke to us of how Papa's job was beneath him, how he should have fought his parents with teeth and nails to become a lawyer, how they should have been forced to send him into a different state where he could have entered university and studied his beloved law. A clerk is spit on and a Jewish clerk, God forgive, she said, not saying God but dropping her voice, is used as a dog sees fit to use a post. My brother Addie with me at table was watching her hands clench and unclench—my poor mother, large-breasted but high-waisted as a child, her face half the time flushed with effort, eyebrows arched as if frozen in expectation—and within a moment of Addie's dismissal from whatever small meal we had, he had trampled on one of my father's hats and broken its crown to shreds. An accident, he howled as my mother raised her hand to him. I didn't see it, he cried, but she hit him once for his action and again for his insolence, for she knew he had spat upon his father. As she dared not do. Yet had she not dared to incite him and confuse him utterly?

And the rest of us were girls, who were valued at half price. But being the eldest I managed to insinuate myself into certain masculine circles when it came to intellectual expectations. My father must have felt a terrible need to avenge himself on the community that ignored his good mind, and even a daughter, frail rod that she is, might serve if she is sharpened to a point. My mother too, I should guess, sensed that I was a chance worth taking.

My parents glared at each other most of the time like mastiffs restrained. They spoke little. To be fair, if my father failed my mother, she at least shared his expectations and his want. And so she shared his guilt, his falling from satisfaction. I always wondered how it was my mother had met my father; she never thought it worthy of explanation. Probably she had expunged the memory, or simply lacked time to speak of it. They are in the end curiously similar careworn reasons for silence. All she ever told to me, since the statement could better contain her bitterness, was that she had been given to unwarranted hopes by the luck, the *nachas*, of meeting and marrying a German. Like a Puerto Rican lady of my acquaintance who calculatingly wed herself to a gentle Mohawk Indian to escape the *macho* temper, and found herself married instead to a man with his lips welded to a bottle. And when it little availed and my father's fortunes collapsed—what could they have promised to be, he a city boy barely educated, but a clerk?—they came somehow to Colmar because of a distant relative's recommendation of the "gentility" of the city—who ever heard of a French pogrom, or a German one for that matter?—and a promise of employment. When they arrived the cousin, second cousin, was gone, who knows where, and my parents were well launched on their career of petty bitterness and failure. Is this a history of poverty? Of love, a month or two of passion? My mother chose to leave her comfortable home with a young man of no prospects. I should guess that she hated herself for her bad judgment, and ever after charged his soul for tempting her.

It brought me grief, from the earliest day on which I understood the process, to imagine how it was that we children were conceived. Surely abjectness is not sufficient incentive for the surrender of a lovely woman. I thought of my mother as the victim of a victim, and each time a baby appeared, loosening her waist, distending her features with a dangerous puffiness, I thought (imagining, like my Catholic friends, that one coupled only to make babies) that, hating his face, she had had to look upon it once again. Eye to eye as well as body to body are children made and in the end was I not correct? For her body perhaps did not despise him half so much as her eye, which saw him, calmly, as he was.

How did I ever learn to love words in that household, though? There was only the speech of toleration, bare co-existence between my parents. Fifty words a day at most, commands predominating, or rather irritation at wishes unanticipated, unfulfilled. Did you buy the butter? Why have you not prepared my shabbos suit?

My father read the Talmud to me, then with me, and I did learn Hebrew—perhaps in part those cadences impressed themselves upon my inner ear. I thought, eventually, that I did not become a writer only because I sensed I was too serious—not that writers are not serious, mind you, but that mine was altogether the wrong kind of gravity to give my imagination a long tether. From inside, from the pit of my stomach I knew I was too tense, too straightforward, I was made of stern durable serge when the entertainers of the world came spun of pastel silks and taffetas full of lights and shadows. I have not been entertaining for a moment in my life. And so, I think, at an early age, desperate with a kind of ingrained sorrow—my parents strangers in their animosity, my brother cruel, a rabbit too in his way but fierce and clawed, who terrified me, playing crude tricks on the girls because we screamed for him like squeezed dolls—I think I opted for reality rightly understood. It would have to serve, if not save, me. In my mind I flirted with words on paper, with the idea of Art (always capitalized), made pools of words to see if they could catch and hold my meanings. They did and didn't. I would brook no uncertainties and I had to find a way to circumvent the need for charm. As if it had been my father's actual calling I took to announcing that I, too, was going to be an attorney. There seemed little chance of such a thing happening, therefore no one bothered to dissuade me.

But this, to which I have been leading, is the story of the way I left my first home, from which I have been going forth ever since, and from which, tonight, I can begin to recognize my own daughter has gone forth and to which she has returned, because it still is possible: her first home. Unhappy as the tale may be, at the end of it we are here. I did become all that my father did not. I have left skin behind in one or two rough places but I am here.

No child thinks in such terms as "home," agreed, yes? What is, is. The world surrounds, but how narrowly one has no reason to suspect. Because to think simultaneously of two places where one might live, here and here, is the beginning of higher thought. An infant does not even recognize a world other than himself, let alone a world out of sight. So. I was, despite what I immodestly call my precocity, truly a most ordinary child and my powers of distinction were already taxed to their limit by the class and religious differences in Colmar. I saw them the way, perhaps, severely myopic eyes take in an abyss: hazy, indistinct, but undeniably there. Looming. Friends were made of a clay of a slightly different cast, we could not play with them on *les samedis,* they were compelled to dress up and be sober *les dimanches.*

It was a Saturday evening, after dark. I have reason to recall because at the gnarled heart of the problem was the fact that my father could not dispose of certain work on Saturday, on the sabbath. Herr Adelbert Brug, the *avocat* for whom he worked, had parted from my father the previous day in a fit of pique at the thought of the copying that was to remain undone at a time of what I take to have been some urgency. He had muttered (or my father had imagined) unpleasant names and accusations under his breath. He had cast one long hard evaluating look at my father, perhaps, from all the way down at the far end of the room, over the pompadours of the women who sat between. It was at best an inscrutable look.

My father, my rabbit, had wavered. You must understand: Adelbert, his only son, was named for this man. What had gone between them in the fifteen or so years of their association that he should name his first male child, in memoriam for his devout father Avraham, Adelbert: the name of an overseer? (A gift for my forbearing employer, he had pleaded with my mother—she reported this to me so many years later. A gift for what? For him to spit at, to disdain? No, only a gift as gifts ought to be given, he had insisted. For no reason, Eva. A *mitzvah.* So. Here he was all these years later, the dust of Brug's legal codes ingrained as fingerprints by now, and still Herr Avocat Brug had not suffered himself to understand the sanctity of the sabbath. Nor had he any reason to, my father in his employ, for he could still arrogantly challenge my father to refuse to come to work on Saturday and my father, not comprehending the first thing about self-respect or even self-protection, could reliably be expected to waver and look ashamed. A suicide. A stick with which to beat himself. Had he ever had the opportunity he wished for himself, to become an educated man, a professor, let us say, he would have been the first to submit to baptism in return for the chance to be a *Privat-docent,* I am convinced, for except in the rarest cases it was only by so doing that one could advance. The keepers need only wait with open hands while some men crawl into their cages.)

Addie and I had gone along to the legal offices with my father this Saturday evening. He was, in his attempt at conciliation, planning to do some of the undone work. I enjoyed the smell of the place, the feel of the yellowed paper, like dry grass, under my fingers; those old ledgers—containing laws against the Jews, against the French?—with their singed look, as though it had been a mild fire that had browned them and not merely the airs of time. My mother, in spite of her vague ambitions for me, was faintly hostile at my eagerness to go with them, but I prevailed. Why Addie came I cannot even guess. To find paper clips or rubber bands for his rock sling. Not out of love for the company of Father and me, who tried to speak about the meaning of certain laws, certain prohibitions, but failed always, helpless on alien ground. This was no Sanhedrin.

We went up the narrow staircase with a good deal of noise, Addie swimming in my father's too large winter boots, banging and stamping like a Cossack, and me, confident beside my papa, drowning Addie out with unaffectionate sisterly curses. The steps were steep and dark and the musty smell started partway up, acrid as the apothecary shop. At the top when we turned, what should we see but half the lamps of the office lit, making islands of yellow concentration, and marooned in these islands, in a manner of speaking, Herr Brug, his daughter Herta, who was his assistant, and one other clerk, Werner something, who was exceedingly small and who put me in mind of an ant, with an ant's narrow dark face and pointed ears for feelers.

My father bowed, astonished at finding anyone else at work, and true to form acted not as if it were natural for him to have come to help, or better, grounds for thanks, but rather as though he had come to steal something. He begged their pardon for intruding.

Need I tell you how mortifying it is for a young girl to see her father in the toils of such self-denigration? And so, loosening my scarf but keeping my coat tight around my shoulders, I sat beside him in utter shamed silence. His pen scratched like an insect rasping against a screen, endlessly, endlessly, and I sat praying that I could disappear. One of the marvelous daydreams of my childhood was that if I truly tried, in every pore, I could become anything. And this terrible evening I saw myself clap hands once and become a gander, clean and white in a kind of apron of fluffy feathers. I remember almost better than the true surroundings—the stiff wooden chair, my woolen coat becoming steamy inside, but I would not dare to move to take it off—the white waddle of that gander in whose skin I escaped from Herr Adelbert Brug's legal offices, placing one scaly orange foot before the other on the cracked floor boards. Fortunately the door was ajar. I heaved myself out to where it was cool, every tail feather.

But, that done, I was miraculously still seated on that chair before my father's narrow desk. He kept his head bent to his task. I studied his beard, which was much the most vigorous part of him, how you could see the little pocks where the hairs began, like pinfeathers. His lips moved slightly as he worked so that, humiliating at this moment, he appeared continuously to be praying. The room was so quiet one could imagine it full of snow; I thought of that awhile, soft cool snow settling gently between all the breathing people, their distances made palpable. Between my father and me there grew a drift, higher and higher, glinting cold like true snow until I could not see him any more. Fantastic obliteration! Would that the world contained such wonders, I should plan more assaults on reality.

And then a sound of curses, in German, in Yiddish, of chairs toppling—all this in the other, the second of two offices to which Addie had gone when we came in. Everyone rising, running, Addie toppling out, bent down as if flung, and a boy about his age —Herr Brug's grandson, I believe, or youngest son, it was never clear—chasing him with a raised stick, broom, andiron, I do not know. Details are never equally clear: my gander, being my own and no intrusion, remains with me in greater clarity. Of course he was called filthy Jew right off, of course being Addie he attempted to grapple with his attacker (or for all I know, his victim—Addie was none too gentle, none too sweet). The only thing I sensed was that there were hidden principles behind this fight. They had begun it as boys but certain boys should not be permitted ever to touch one another, because their skins are raw with ready hostilities; they come well armed by their differences, and are ready to burst and bleed at a touch.

Herr Brug said "Now there—" once as the two rolled past like a single crazed clawing animal and the next I heard was a ghastly bumping down the stairs and the Brug boy, with a hideous grimace, stood, his cheek torn and his Adam's apple leaping up and down as if on a string. His father touched his arm lightly.

My broken brother lay at the bottom of the stairs. Even from the top, I could see he was like a puppet unstrung. There was no way to lie in that position intact, and Addie was no gymnast. Somehow we got him home, half conscious. I cannot imagine how. Because terror is the finest fuel, for my father especially, the highest octane. And that same night—can you believe such a story as this?—we were packing our belongings in every receptacle we could lay hands on and running—escaping into the night, the nowhere of the roads around Colmar that go in deep secrecy through vineyards and flat farmyards. We were running because Herr Adelbert Brug's last words to my father's retreating back were "I shall sue you, Jewish butcher, I shall have you thrown in jail and your pig of a son put away." Many years later Addie testified, in his remaining shattered speech, that the boy had begun the argument by approaching him in friendly fashion, with a collection of something small in his hands—stamps, butterflies, whatever—and then when he had come up close had informed him that Yid mothers circumcise their babies with their teeth. I have never believed a word of my brother's, I do not know whether to believe this or to call it outrageous. But it probably happened since, quite uncharacteristically, he admitted to having taken the first swing. Addie had till then lived (by his testimony) more sinned against than sinning, and so I am inclined to think he took the insult for what it was and brought our lives down on us for it.

If it seems excessive to flee with a family of six into the grim countryside in winter on such provocation, let me tell you that an old French peasant who lived at the first rise in the road up toward Haut Koenigsburg had been shot, a few weeks before this, for having refused a German soldier four eggs he was discovered carrying from his hen house. "*Ja oder nein?*" the soldier had asked. "*Non,*" the man had answered, and falling had crushed all the eggs under his chest.

I have a vision of my mother in a field like a gypsy with her head hidden inside a shawl. *"Baruch atoh adonai"*—the candles guttered in the wind and went out and it was dark. I see no one besides the two of us side by side, feeling the heavy flap of our kerchiefs, like flags, against our cheeks. She lit the candles seven times—lucky number—and no matter how we sheltered them with our bodies they went out. Truly, they went out. The curse of darkness while we fled. My mother stood beside me, a large woman, toothy and dignified, clean for the sabbath, and I could see her tears begin and then stop as if by command. (Her milk for the baby had dried up. Her hair had turned white in a small arrow-shaped patch over one eye. She stayed very far from my father. I rarely saw them touch again.) We passed a fire the next day, some men were roasting something in a yard, we were on the outskirts of Nancy. She marched to the fire and without a word drew the candles out of her skirt, threw them in, and murmured *Amen*.

And so it happens, you see, beginning with this sojourn from what is only accidentally my home—but only one moment in the life of my family (father from Frankfurt, mother from the little Russian shtetl of Birosk)—that I assume their true life's work as mine: exile. How can one be exiled from a temporary rest-stop? Quite plausible. In any event, I can better comprehend the life of a hoarse-throated, one-legged, blind, garlic-scented, God-fearing Malaysian who has lived in any twelve cities of the world than, say, that of my partner Jack Tenney, who was born in Washington Heights and has merely rolled downhill a few miles to the nearest viable neighborhood, barring Harlem, to live in a building which must be nearly identical to the first; and so, except for a short lifeless sojourn to the barracks of Fort Dix twenty years ago, he has moved gently through his life yet to be truly surprised, I would wager, or truly inconvenienced. Imagine. Snug Jack.

We lived in Luxembourg, that incommodious gray castle. We spent one uncomfortable spring in Paris, amid perpetual rain which was meanly timed because it meant that we six—Addie bent in a chair, his face more blank than ever, slack with a cripple's abandonment to helplessness, and Esther, the baby Minke, myself, my mother and father locked in their distances—all of us imposed ourselves with no relief upon a distant cousin André (born Aaron), whose small apartment barely accommodated his own family, plus what seemed to be excessive laundry for ten. Paris had nothing to recommend itself to me—I remember drying sheets, and cobblestones slick with rain and occasional detritus of some shop whose fish or fruit rind washed down into the gutter— except perhaps the river which made me think of home, and all the worse. It was a bad time for nostalgia.

How we lived I shall never know: my mother did it. For a while I remember, but vaguely, she obtained somewhere a collection of bone buttons and laces, and she sold them to ladies and gentlemen who were, I realize now, not truly ladies and gentlemen, since the transactions so often took place on street corners.

We children were out at elbows and perpetually cold. It was too late for us to enjoy gypsy freedom. I felt we had been robbed. The deepest feeling I took from our sad spring in Paris was astonishment and gratitude that the French-German episode in Alsace was, in fact, only that: an episode, not a universal fact of life. Somewhere in the world there were people who could speak French without whispering, without criminal or insurrectionary intent, subject to prison, ostracism, even death. I was so happy for them, these cheerful noisy gesticulating French, as though all of them had just arrived northwest from Colmar and had burst like escapees into their sunny (at the moment rainy) freedom. Most of them undoubtedly knew nothing at all of their brothers' plight under German domination (in which once l'Abbé Wetterle said to the Germans something like "*Vous avez sans cesse le mot 'allemand' à la bouche: la cuisine allemande, la femme allemande, le vin allemand, la chanson allemande! Et qu'est-ce que votre Kultur allemande? Vous finirez par nos dégouter du ciel à force de nous dire que les anges y sont rouges, blancs, noirs!*").

But if you are attentive you will understand how it is that I was happy for them. Never for an instant, though I was glad to be free to speak French (and be ridiculed for my accent), did I relate this freedom or this bondage to myself.

Perhaps we should have chosen Palestine rather than the States for yet another exile; perhaps it would have been the first home.

But Mother was afraid that her work, in the absence of useful men, would not have been sufficient there. She would have been less self-conscious as a widow. As it was she was like one of those ants you have seen who must drag from place to place a huge fly or a crumb far more massive than she. That was what our family had become.

So. Even here we *shlepped*. New York to Boston, where my mother ostensibly had relatives, whom we never found; perhaps they had never arrived. Accidents befell anyone, they appeared to be the only things one could have gratis. To Littleton, Massachusetts, for no reason at all, as far as I could fathom. All I can recall of the unlikely Littleton is, one day, standing at the top of a sort of hill—a gentle rise, merely, which by now must certainly accommodate two gas stations and a take-out supermarket but then was sparsely mottled with New England fir trees—and looking down toward a place called New Hampshire which I had heard was perpetually drowned in snow, just as I imagined the Russia of my mother's girlhood. I looked vaguely in that direction. There was no snow, but no rain either—it was June or July for all I knew —feeling we were dangerously near Alaska and the North Pole. Perhaps I could have found this an exciting adventure, but my spirit was from the start a lugubrious one, burdened by obscure weights of self-pity and worse: pity for Mama, whose stoicism, I suspect, was far worse than would her tears have been. They at least would have freed me, told me it was all right, that she could at least mourn for herself, I should not have to do it for her.

In any event this melting pot was continually subject to stirring: back to Boston on our own. My mother mute among Irish ladies working at a handbag-strap machine. My father useless, weeping in Yiddish, waiting for death. Addie like a toadstool, huge and puffy, sitting at the window, still quite alive, waiting in fact for the girls to go past on their way home from parochial school. In my memory of Boston it is perennially autumn. They kick in their plaid uniforms and knee socks through huge piles of leather-colored leaves and Addie, in his desperation, indifferent to the fact that they are perhaps, on the average, ten or eleven years old, plunges his hand inside his fly and hums his love song, *hors de combat* for life. For life. I have rarely felt compassion for my brother. Rather I blamed him for the entire monstrous waste of our lives, neither understanding enough of how events work their slow or sudden magic on all that is latent, nor granting to wanton chance and bad luck full responsibility for striking us down. Only when I watched him there, caught in his chair as if by chains, coaxing feeling from the most useless part of himself, did I allow myself the most meager twinge. He would turn and see me watching and smile gently, not embarrassed, but as though he expected me to understand how under the circumstances this little life was to be expected, even hoped for. A life sign. Had Addie been whole he should have been no friend of woman; he should have been a mean and riotous plower and sower of seed. Maimed, self-maimed, whatever, I could almost pity him. Even he did not deserve to be so brutally humbled.

A postscript to this. Do you know what my father became on America's green and golden shore? Would you, ah would you believe what he saved himself for? He may indeed have had a whole life to hide, and had he not been a Jew it would have been in a bottle, undoubtedly—the tradition exists—but what he chose to become finally in the land of choice was an extraordinary, helpless, untalented gambler. A gambler. À la Dostoyevsky, for even Dostoyevsky would insist that up close his suicide scheme was a two-bit operation as well. There is no glamour mucking in your powerlessness, even if you are a Russian aristocrat. So you see—his wife in a sweatshop, none of his children old enough for work, and he in a state of perpetual bemused unemployment, he would steal away with what money we had and squander it at pinochle and gin rummy—so it was not roulette at Monte Carlo, one can, with sufficient application, get drunk on cough syrup as well. As far as I can reconstruct, he never won; he only managed to prolong his losing for as many hours as some men put into escalating triumphs. One year, my mother told me this very much later, he managed to spend close to $5,000 by his own estimate. And since we never earned anywhere near that sum, perhaps there were some temporary winnings. But back they went into the fire where they could not so much as be touched for their momentary warmth. Why, my mother pleaded, could he not have chosen a cheaper humiliation—infidelity, say, that would have taken from her nothing that she really wanted anyway. He spent a good deal of his time in tears, repenting as regularly as any alcoholic. He did not appear to be, nor want to be, happy gambling. He never sneaked in at dawn exhilarated, shoes in hand. Perhaps he was just unhappy enough, so exquisitely did he dance on the knife point of utter annihilation. One time the police actually came looking for him, for debts past due, I presume—whom did he play with that they could enlist the *Polizei* in settling their affairs?! He hid, like a righteous Jew in the path of the SS. My mother in all her dignity lied for him and then took to her bed for a full day. Whenever, in those years, I saw him he was meek as a lemur, already sliding down into one of those daytime depressions that finally enveloped him in a permanent stupor. My mother had told us, in not so many words—or rather in more words, for she had begun to chatter nervously to fill the long silences in which he sat —that in America one did not need father or husband, nor even luck. Only determination. Gambling, in addition to all else, was to her profoundly un-American, archaic: it depended upon the power of prayer and not of will. And the prayers were directed downward to a subsoil I believe she thought this America too shallow to possess.

My father finished his life in an armchair beside his son's, while his women were at school and work. Mother made a point of leaving them there alone; it was the only cruel thing I had ever seen her do. They would sit unfed, incapable of moving to the bathroom or the front door, until we came home to move them, averting our eyes. Eventually, after his death, my mother had to give his old green chair to the junkman because Addie continued to look for him in it. He would whimper and whine like a chained dog when Mother set him to stare alone out the window. She stood in the doorway as the junkman trundled it down the stairs out onto Blue Hill Avenue, nodding violently, an unstoppable twitch. Do not scratch the walls! she called out—if she fancied one could see the walls in that hall she was still an optimist. It should have been firewood, she told me, turning back and closing the door, her eyes smoldering with something I should call neither sorrow nor repentance. We would have gotten some warmth out of firewood but what does the old man give me? He never said so much as thank you, lady.

✿ ✿ ✿

I feel I should wake my Renata, whose white shoulders glow fiercely under the intrusion of the street lamp, and say, "Not a word. I do understand the force that moved you in this strange trajectory away; and children, apparently, do not ever explain. We, none of us, Steins, Lifschutzes, have *Sitzfleisch:* we do not stick it out, not at the start. We exile ourselves, we turn and turn again like you asleep, disturbed by this light. But eventually we rest. At least you have come back. At least I see you are of the family Stein." She has heard all these stories, they possibly have been her only inheritance. As a child, after all, she found them infinitely more engaging than word from me about the NLRB or Whittaker Chambers. So I told and retold—I, too, engaged, the words repeating like a—what is that kind of troubadour poem, a sestina? wherein the end of the line tolls like a bell, around and around? *"And so she left. And then we ran. And of course they never saw him, never again. Because she ran. And nothing left. Never again."*

✿ ✿ ✿

It is after nine and I am still at the office. The silence is thick, heavy, the secretaries long gone; not my favorite way to work, actually. Imagine the catching-up those women in the jail will have to face when they come home—the ones with real lives like Jo, that older one, facing the chaos of her lost time.

And my daughter is calling me. I am so eager to come home from work tonight, remove my shoes, rest. But she is in tears.

Renata, I should tell you, since I have come again to know her has made it her business to be a spectacular weeper; incontinent of sorrow, one could say. I believe she thinks that to be so proves her sincerity, her involvement with life. After an adolescence of sullen silences, now she flows and flows, like some flower child's coat-of-many-colors. Endlessly her baby reduces her to frustration. She matches Tippy tear for tear, shakes her in her colic, feels picked on and rejected when the child cries. I do not remember so often personalizing my daughter's discomforts, I did not take them like arrows to my breast. As you may imagine, I find her strategy unconvincing, wholly suspect. It has, shall I say, been to her advantage to attract my attention so; also to make her cunning little comment on our differences, for I—no weeper, surely, only an arguer, a table-banger, a fetcher of large books from which to cite chapter, verse and footnote—I am colder than a terrapin in my daughter's eyes, she accuses me of sins of the heart, and so she seals the accusation visibly with tears.

This is, however, no contest of vindictiveness. I thought in the first moment that she had called because something terrible had befallen her or her child. There was not a single word in her wrought-up speech to so indicate but I would be hard put to guess what other event could so agitate her very private, should I go so far as to say narcissistic, person. But no, she is speaking incoherently of my cleaning lady of all things, of hospitals and dying, of bringing suit.

"Do you ever talk to Catalina?" Am I being challenged?

"Talk to her? No. Not particularly. Our schedules barely overlap, if you will think about it, Renata. Why?"

"Well, do you know her son? Alejandro—"

"Of course I do. She brings him to do her heavy work. He moves the couch and so on. At my last dinner party I believe he became a trifle tipsy. Or that was his brother, possibly. Do wait now, Renata. Permit me to be seated, to get my—rather, in fact, let me call you back please. I have just come in from a long exhausting day to clear up some work— Let me arrange myself here, I am distracted, and phone you up in another few minutes. You are at home, yes?" Because I cannot deal with her in this wrought-up state, the interval will be to calm her or at least put her on warning. One can make the telephone a useful, subtle instrument of will.

She fumes and sputters and pronounces "Mo-ther" exactly as she did at the age of ten when asked to tidy her room, but I hang up and go back to reading my correspondence heaped and falling from my In box. I have tomorrow an evidentiary hearing and am ill-prepared. I go to my little office refrigerator to get myself a V-8 with an egg in it, do not sneer I beg of you, you know nothing of it; unroll my girdle which is, I am happy to see, being rendered unnecessary because futile, finally: my waist is become a confabulation of gray herrings, skinned and mournful. *Feh.* After today I shall not wear one again.

Then I re-call Renata. She is no more in tears. She is bringing me work. From home to the office. Apparently I am to be grateful.

"Renata," I say to her wearily, having quite enough work for myself and a twin. "It appears from your recital of these facts that you want a doctor, not an attorney—to bring him back alive, so to say." The case is that of the cleaning lady who works weekly for me, one Mrs. Catalina Huerta, to whom I am devoted for her efficiency, economy and occasional wit, a spry woman in a sweater and skirt like a girl, who does not disdain, like some I have known, to bend over or reach far or wash windows. She has a son —well, not a son exactly, I should say not hers exactly, there are many complications to which she has occasionally alluded but this is something else again. In any event, like a son; certainly she works him like a son. Apparently last week, on the day after her regular duty at my apartment, he had suffered a routine appendectomy, performed after the similarly routine barring of the door, yet another hospital extracting its pound and a half of Hispanic flesh, may they incinerate in the hellfire of their own hearts. But having been admitted, however reluctantly, and operated upon, having begun his healing, somehow nonetheless he had died. Of neglect, they are alleging, Renata and this Mrs. Huerta. My daughter again begins to weep.

This is an interesting development, I must admit, and the anguish with which she goes on is not a familiar sound in her uninflected voice, for I must admit that Renata has been the most wholly apolitical young woman it has ever been my frustrating duty to deal with. Her impulses are still, if I were to characterize them generously, altogether subjective; self-absorbed; reflexive. There have been many times when I have been inclined to believe she could barely muster concern for her child, who appears to break the closed circuit of her own sweet self. However. Be that as it may, wherever she is I can be assured that only Mrs. Huerta herself could weep more copiously for her son.

"I have no right, excuse me, I have no right to cry," my Renata breathes through the phone, thus assimilating in one day, perhaps one hour, a complex lifetime of unsuccessful instruction from her mother. It has been a watchword of mine, of which I suspect she wearied early, that one must never confuse one's own outsider's sorrow with that of the protagonist—unless of course, as at the House of Detention, one is making hay of the confusion. One mourns but does not shriek, one attempts redress but never vengeance. And, though the Law is a dream of perfection and balance, it is most often only a partial restoration that can be effected: not the flesh made quick but "damages" for punishment and the guarantee of future care: to make peace with the living.

She tells me he was a beautiful boy which, alas, arouses old suspicions: too often has Renata been an appreciator of beauty in young men. (She who thinks a free woman should be empowered to love beauty in all men, while I think she should be empowered to ignore it if she so chooses.) But again, beside the point. "I have met him, I told you. Whether he was beautiful I never noticed, but a fine young man. Devoted to his mother." There is only a boy entirely dead, unnecessarily dead at seventeen. Renata inhales, exhales stickily through her tears. She is sitting with her blond hair fallen intimately over the telephone, I know the pose, the phone entirely invisible, her hand supporting her forehead which, being fair, is blotched as a gingham cloth.

Why do I resist her so, she demands. "You never believe me. What do you think I'm doing, making this up? Am I looking for sympathy?"

"Is Mrs. Huerta looking for sympathy?" That seems to me more germane. Is there not something unseemly about the relations between mothers and daughters? Her tone, which has only recently allowed itself intimacy enough to be capable of taking offense, reminds me of my whole haggling family in Colmar and ever after: a chainsaw whirring, endlessly, endlessly. That kyrie, that om, tuneless, wordless, signifying something other than its particulars. It must be a most comforting sound, this ground bass, to some. Certain children are perhaps imprinted, like ducks who learn to follow close behind their mothers, to the incessant sound of voices nattering; concern, disapproval, interrogation; the sound weaves a nest, makes a moving shadow, whatever is the thing needful for warmth and security.

For of course she feels my reluctance, my resistance to her perpetual projectile tears; it is a very complicated business.

"This is not a question of belief," I tell her emphatically and finish the dregs of my tomato cocktail, where like pepper in the face I have come too late to all the Worcestershire sauce collected in the bottom. "I simply take certain stories slowly and carefully. A professional reticence, my friend, nothing personal about it." I shall not accuse her of possessing no sole professional standard, rigor, what have you; her entropic life is not here in question.

But I can add, and do, "Do not let your animosities run off with your pretty head, my dear." Too bad that she shall hear the word "pretty" as a rebuke. "But if you wish to engage me on a professional basis then you must suffer my style of operation. Otherwise you must retain a different attorney."

She snorts at me, does my daughter. "You have only one style, Mamà, you are always professional." And that, needless to say, is a matching rebuke. "It seems very fitting that I have to tell you about this on the phone, you know? You're never where you ought to be."

But no, I shall not trek out to see Mrs. Huerta in Brooklyn tonight, I am not a doctor making house calls. She swears never to forgive me but I make an appointment for her, with her weeping Mrs. Huerta, tomorrow at ten in my office. I shall soon be home but I would be grateful, I tell her firmly, if we do not discuss this further in the absence of Catalina Huerta, the sole possessor of the necessary facts. We shall approach this mess—for so I fear it shall be, I like doing this service as little as a surgeon likes to raise the knife above the sheeted bodies of his own children—with utmost care and dispassion. At least I shall, for my part.

And so, I think in my seat on the subway, so she believes I am always professional. She lives with her necessary illusion, though whom it punishes, herself or me, I cannot guess. For a girl as intentionally simple-minded as Renata, who early pulled up her intellect like a rooted plant out of a garden and let it wither in air, there are only dichotomies; one is this or that, I am so or such. I contemplate her possibilities with trepidation because there appears to be so little logic to mediate between extremes. Look at her current life: she has gone from her game of revolving beds to this solitary puss in the corner in which the only people she speaks to are shopkeepers and cleaning women: truly this is schizophrenic, and I believe she does it to spite me and my hopes for her.

As for her vision of me, how wrong it is, still a child's kept at bay on the outside of the bedroom door, the office door, knocking for admission. The images I see on the inside! Retching into the toilet bowl the stink of my husband's endless sweating need. Trussed like a gray chicken on that desk of the House of Detention, with a strange black woman's hand investigating beneath me. My blood runs cold.

Would my daughter, who thinks I love only abstractions, believe the sight of her mother only ten years ago, or thereabouts, so assaulting a doctor in the state of Mississippi, town of Gillespie, county of Horace, that I spent four days, I believe it was, in the county jail while extraordinary bond was raised? Yes, I do mean this. One of the high moments for me, of a lifetime! Am I not to be allowed my paradoxes? How deliciously her very own mother abused the tenets of professional disinterest to the point where she stood in real danger of disbarment. How has it happened that, with the passage of time, this tragic incident has become an occasion for such delight? Perhaps it is that I have used only my head and not a single extraneous muscle in all the preceding and intervening years, and that it is a corroboration of some other kind of power (now surely lost to me forever) that I could actually have flown through the air one instant in my life, like Superman, like

Wonder Woman, in the execution of my duties! My daughter should have seen me in that moment of abandon. And must I wonder that these rapists at the jail enjoyed me on my back? Had I been they, I would have felt a torment of delight. . . .

In my year in Gillespie, Mississippi, when I was adviser to the Horace County school integration suits which Renata saw as dry court business, her mother a clerk with a few good spoken lines—I spent so much time in a fit of internal bleeding, pure frustration with judges, with witnesses, with "citizens," they call themselves, the husbands, wives, lovers, children of that town, it is a wonder I did no worse harm, committed no homicide. They had, I do believe, their dogs well trained to bark when I walked by. The suppositions as I walked down the street were flattering to an old lady indeed. I spent months at a time working in the little storefront on the main street, whose window had a brutal crack in it, made by a stone. I lived the while in a motel, anonymous as a fish (attempting anonymity, should I say; no one in that situation is not intimately studied on all sides). I worked in the storefront and argued at the courthouse, had dinner with friends black and white, though if together then in relative secrecy, the shades drawn as if we awaited an air raid. Indeed I began work on an ulcer there. When I was assaulted by long-distance visions of the absurdity of my presence in Horace County I would shake myself and reason that, by that point, once having been flushed loose from my first latitude, longitude, any resting place was illogical or logical: both or neither.

It was midwinter in Mississippi; there was none of the crepe myrtle that I so loved. The ground in its tentative hard frost, undecided. Did you know the South had that kind of season? What did I know—I expected, I think, the Everglades jungle in full red flower all year round. Instead I found a climate in some respects reminiscent of my own Alsace, that indefinite discomfort of cold for which no one is entirely prepared or defended, not after a hundred years of predictable chill. The people lie low in winter there, passions gutter and go out. I sat in my office and the other attorneys and I, we burned with a higher flame than our gas heaters with their little reflectors, their Austrian mountain-peak villages painted hopefully above the rusty coils. The whole state of Mississippi, of the South, resting on its back, feet up, eyes closed, no work, no food. The heat may melt desire and slow work in summer, but in winter there is a mild ice lock, a hibernation of the spirit, pure suspension. The season when cabins spark and burn down. Our rooms smelled perpetually sweet-sour, dangerous with gas fumes.

And comes the day, you see, when one little girl flung back the door to our office, where I was making I believe a demographic chart of de facto and de jure segregation, perhaps the hundredth so with a small variation—alone I was, they were all out taking dinnertime depositions—and shouted, whites of her lively eyes huge and terrified, so shaken it would seem she had not really expected to find a friend anywhere, "Miz Stein, Rosie Jo hurt, you gotta come." Bent at the waist to insist. Was I resisting? She looked then as if all her short life she had only been preparing to be a messenger of blood. Years of practice swept her to me, like water that will rush to one side of a tipped trough, had her take my hand and pull me out into the street.

Running in her tight dungarees, still leaning. Like a jet-black footman on someone's lawn, holding a lantern over some house number a mile away in East Gillespie where there were two-car garages larger and sounder of structure than the houses of my clients ten at a time. Where was her little peaked cap?

We ran down the quiet main street, it was dinnertime and the stores were beginning to close, then over the frozen ruts, the clean blacktop. (A picture I carry always, a feeling, a small ache, really, of the shopkeepers of my childhood rolling down the long corrugated shopfronts. A desolation, purplish-gray, the air losing its warmth to evening. The New World, here, has always looked raw to me without them, unfinished, nothing can properly close that remains all window.) Seen from the sky we must have blown like leaves. An old woman running, it was a death blow to my dignity. What fate had ever blown me here? My large bones rattling loose, braids toppling from the shelf of my head, ankles turning at this speed even in my solid shoes. I am happy at least to have been spared the sight of Gerda Stein in full girdled flight. I was well beyond sixty then, you see, ample, bolted together tightly. I have not spent a lifetime dancing. Nor, alas, could my Renata see me, however illuminating the vision might be—we need our own private television transmitters, or will enough, to send by aura alone the complicated messages that separated twins are said to share.

He was not at the edge of town. He was miles. Miles. We ran along drainage ditches. We frightened dogs and children. When we found the knotted crowd we were, I swear it, halfway to Memphis. In the deep shade of the culvert, baseball jackets, one pea-green sweater like stagnant bayou water. An old man in a hat too big for him; likewise his jacket, which had been elegant in its, in his youth.

"Thelma get the doctor," they all said, assuring me. My feet ached from slamming the stone ground. I did not know I would remember my poor feet ten years later.

Rosie Jo was a child—sixteen, was he, and already martyred? His mother was at work in a white lady's house, his father did not for all intents and purposes exist. Ah, Mrs. Huerta, if you knew. At least I presume your boy had his own appendicitis, it was not compelled upon him, though of course that hardly means he had to die of it. But Roosevelt Joe Louis Bass had begun his day in perfect health, bony and rich-colored, of enviable muscle and, so I was advised, vast skill on the basketball court, and hopeful. Is there not a statue in Riverside Park—somewhere along the river?— "to an amiable child"? The first one to go, the next day he was to go, to the white high school named for that Bilbo, that early sena- tor of degenerate mind and habits, who wanted niggers flayed, but legally. We had been coaching Rosie Jo, he took our instruction gravely, his large eyes still and impossible to read. All we could guess was that he was willing, and would be dignified. Whether he felt his celebrity a duty, an honor, or a curse we would never know. We had picked him for being amiable; we wondered, many a long night, if that did not simply mean he had bought (and we abetted) the ruin of his good nature. We were coaching him in imperviousness, inoffensiveness, invisibility.

And now his blood had seeped in all directions. It was running down, maroon, into the drainage ditch, down to the sewer and out to the river, out to the Gulf of Mexico, enough to turn the tide red. Enough at least to soften the hard freeze under him.

You see, I could not find his face. He was turned every which way and where his face should be was one chewed ear and the grated back of his brown neck. He was a doll whose head was turned around. Could that be done to a person alive? I remembered Addie at the foot of the stairs of the *avocat*'s office.

"Better don't touch him!" My Negro friends—for they were still "Negro" then—were a chorus, every one unanimous. "Leave him be, doctor be here in a minute, turn him over."

Jephtha Willey cried out from inside the little clutch of men, "Let her touch him, don't make no difference now." She set up a wail fully worthy of church and covered her face in her thin hands. She swayed like a Lombardy poplar in a wind.

The doctor was white. Why, one may wish to ask, did it take him an hour to come, we were right there at the entrance to the high-speed highway. He was waiting with his feet up, no doubt, for the blood to well and thicken and it did; in time it will. Talk of suing the Brooklyn Memorial Hospital!

Thelma had gone to call an ambulance in her one-fender De Soto. For whatever reason the doctor drove his own Porsche back. (A Porsche in Gillespie, imagine. A tatter of lace in the junk heap, *schlag* in the charnel house.) He parked across the road and got out leaving his black bag behind. He made no acknowledgment of us and, using a good deal less care than would any passer-by, bent and pulled Rosie Jo over onto his long twisted back.

Jephtha screamed.

"Been doing some Saturday night cutting," the doctor said, most cheerfully. It was Thursday morning and Rosie Jo had been hit by a car before or after his beating. I believe there may have been tread marks on his bones. Then the doctor asked— laconically, so routinely—"Do you want his face? Anybody?" We fought, I believe, our own battles to keep from putting his eyes out but we must have looked very obedient in our silence, a little church group perhaps out on a nature walk, studying an aberrational growth on the highway margin. A handsome hulking man this doctor, but small, you would say he was sad-looking, with his dark raccoon-shadowed eyes ("Eyes looks like two shit holes," Thelma muttered into the cold air) and carefully combed-down hair the way they wore it once upon a time in offices along

Madison Avenue. Knowing a good deal of what there is to know about the city of Gillespie, Mississippi, necessary for work, one might say—one keeps one's hands near the scales to apply weight where safe, where necessary—I will add that this particular doctor's life was haunted by rumor enough to have made one feel no sympathy, under ordinary circumstances. Hints of sexual innuendo tend not to elicit my greatest feeling; such complications are to my mind far worse than tears for weakening the constitution which needs all the strength it can muster from emotional rigor. It is suddenly clear that he is a soulless Hun who deserves his luck. May his wife and his warmhearted secretary conspire to have him slaughtered in his bed.

"I guess I'll take him in," this doctor said finally, looking abstracted, like a sheriff in the presence of a live felon. He blinked a great deal. Guilt, I should say; his soul's reluctance to face bright light. His fingertips were a urinous yellow.

I made a hundred fists. "This is a child you have here. Is he *alive?* What are you saying? Is he dead or alive?"

He looked at me reluctantly. I am a tall woman and I was glad he had to look up, it was the very least he could do. "You needn't shout, lady." He swathed me with his attention then, from head to foot, he reamed me out with his eyes. "You his mother or just what?" And a smile. "His girl?" He gestured to my waist: white blouse pulling out of a tweed skirt, the calm detached forever from my body in a single shirttail. "You one of the missionaries trying to get these boys to stop eating people?"

The small crowd raged forward at him and swept over him. Or, more likely, it raged backward as if it had been hit. I cannot remember what anyone did, to be quite honest. He was leaving the bloody mess of carrying all that gore to Rosie Jo's friends and accomplices. "Let me go spread some newspapers in my car," he said with a look of the most housewifely distaste, as though we had slapped a stale fish on his dining room table.

Rosie Jo's mother was on her way. A car had stopped—good Lord, the white lady's shiny whatever-it-was glistening just beside Thelma's car like a chariot—and Rosie Jo Bass's mother eased out of the back seat at a good hundred-yard distance. Nearly dignified (I would say it ran in the family, that aplomb that had got her son volunteered for death), she pushed out legs first, or perhaps she was arthritic or otherwise slightly hobbled. She left the lady unimplicated, waiting like a chauffeur, came trying to run, but slowly, painfully, her white uniform shoes not quite lifting off the ground.

That was when I leaped upon the doctor: when, seeing her approach and knowing who she was, he turned to go. Is this cause for pride or shame, tell me, or only for six months' suspension from the bar? I opened my mouth wide and—my dentist would not have approved, he will not let me eat so much as an apple—I took a bite out of this doctor's neck and it was real flesh in my mouth, surely for the first and last time in my life: rubbery, salty, it made me retch. Never would I have supposed Gerda Stein to be capable of such a fantastic act as this. Talk of professionalism, my daughter. What a taste.

The doctor fell over in surprise if nothing else, this large old woman on his back like something fallen out of a tree, and not even the boy's mother, you see, and I tore him with my nails and my mouth in as many places as I could break through to. The more tender and private the flesh (under the Adam's apple where it sagged, always hidden like scrotum flesh), the more blood I drew. He may thank God I had no knife, I'd have thrown his sex in the bushes like a peach pit. We might have grown a poison tree.

For this act I was treated, I should add, to a marvelous gamut of responses: to a severe dressing-down by my co-workers, who were not there but who were too embarrassed to allow themselves a speck of satisfaction at the tale; to a three-minute tacitly congratulatory Huntleybrinkley interview at the time of my emergence from jail four days later at no small cost to my friends and office, who raised the bond; to disdain by the non-violents and awe by the community at large. Rosie Jo Bass's mother never did do anything but shake her head, which was almost more than I could bear.

It was no dream, but neither was it Gerda Stein. Clement Slate, an office-mate new-minted from Yale Law School, suggested tenderly (when it seemed permissible to joke, the project in no dire jeopardy for my rashness) that it was only "the change." "If you don't mind my saying so, Gerda, your last taste of a good-looking man."

From me only a look I hoped, for our future work relationship, he could not read.

In any event, I shall admit that—helpful as this incident was in dissolving, on the spot, I would take an oath, my incipient ulcer, I am not about to repeat it. I may do any number of things once, more than my daughter imagines, I cannot even predict myself, but when the occasion again arises I shall, alas, have to be armed. That is the difference between us: that I repeat no mistake while my wits are with me. Accidents of judgment are to be forgiven, if at all, once and once only. And they do befall again, one might as well accept that. My entire career is posited on the assumption that everything recurs, only in slightly altered form, for which is required, as for justice, eternal vigilance. Hence precedents, hence the protections and forewarnings of written history, which we are at pains to consult, understand, and obey. All progress, one's own and civilization's, hinges on this ability to learn restraint.

So this act, whether deranged or noble or both, had its precedents within my lifetime; one might have to call it vengeance. It was the act of an outsider with whom the consequences would never catch up. Having been cut free of my past the one, the first time, I was cast into a lifetime of freedom. One accepts such freedom of movement like a doom, a taste of certain death, do you understand that? I was not easily to be hurt or frightened. Perhaps that is all that is necessary for mere humans, not saints, not martyrs, to act. Most obviously I had done it for Rosie Jo's mother, who had a life to go on living as best she could, bereaved or not, in Gillespie, while I had none. Had come from nowhere, in whose peculiar accents I persistently spoke, and would soon return to nowhere. Mine was a privileged freedom which compensated—at such times—for my rootlessness. So you see, even the Lone Ranger could afford momentary lapses into heroism. They did not truly cost him so much, surely not so much as children believe, for he habitually vanished, did he not, into some canyon, some purple sunrise, leaving only his silver bullet behind. Should he not merely have been called The Exile?

When I arrive at home the lights are off. Renata and Tippy are huddled in a corner of the couch in an exaggerated posture of devotion: two children in a storm. Shame on her.

  ❀   ❀   ❀

Renata and Catalina are, to begin with, considerably late to my office. Do I have appointments? Do I keep to a schedule? No matter, my daughter is a poet of sorts and refuses to trammel herself with the bourgeois services of a wristwatch. Between them there are, I know, many children to be dispatched to school, to baby sitters, subways to be headed off, a trip—how can we aggrandize this into a great pioneering venture?—actually a trip below a *river* from East to West! Why, they deserve to be panting when they arrive twenty-five minutes tardy but rather the two of them, Renata and her Mrs. Huerta (no longer *my* Mrs. Huerta), appear like two young girls who have been window-shopping and have simply forgotten the time. Their cheeks are pink.

Catalina responds to my outstretched hand with admirable strength. I set great store by handshakes, I believe they tell more about vigor and pusillanimity than eyes or even words can ever manage, being under more conscious control. Her handclasp tells me she is direct and unembarrassed by her power; I am more content to deal with a woman of equal weight, in balance, than with the weightlessness of someone like Renata.

Nor does she appear to me precisely my image of a mother mourning. Later I shall make the dreadful mistake of implying such an idea to my daughter and she shall be furious at me, accuse me first of bigotry, then of a want of imagination, allege that I would have to be treated to a special performance of the Pietà to give credit to a woman's sorrow for her dead son.

Renata sits beside her with her breath clenched up, like a child struggling for obedience. Always wan, she is paler than a midwinter sun this moment. My daughter is not only weightless but boneless. I am reminded of a chicken breast—that kind of invertebrate pink. How does she get through the day? Take away her hysterical sexual menace and she appears beside Mrs. Huerta a small anxious girl I can barely remember.

I put aside preliminaries and ask Mrs. Huerta to tell me the entire situation. In detail, if she can; I shall hear necessary facts that she may not appreciate.

She lights a cigarette and pulls in on it slowly, her mouth full of smoke for a long time. Then letting it go in thin streams that come out like tusks, she begins, "Well, a week ago Wednesday—"

"I interrupt for one question. This Alejandro whom I have seen, is not your son?"

"Oh, you want to know all that." This apparently is altogether a different story.

"Yes, all of it, it has bearing. There are those who like their clients to boil down their information as economically as they can do, and those like me who would rather take the task of doing that. So, I shall not mind, tell me all you have to tell."

"She means she doesn't trust you," says Renata, who does violence to irony. I am not sucked into a reply.

But this Mrs. Huerta can take care of herself, I shall not worry myself for her.

"OK," she says, "OK. I got four children. Had. Two of them you could say don't belong to me. I mean, you know, giving birth to them, they were my sister's twins."

"Your sister's."

"Zulma. Only all her life she got a lot of troubles, she goes in Pilgrim State Hospital now and I think she's gonna stay in there forever. She always had things wrong in her head, like. I don't want to say this but she was a very slow child, she always look at you a long time if you tell her something, you think she was, like, maybe reading it off your lips or something. So after she had Tico and Alejandro I think it all got such a big thing she just, I don't know what you call it, she just got tired and, like, she just collapse. Sat down and never got up again."

Catalina Huerta cocks her head to see if I am understanding. She speaks with a certain modesty as if there is still a lot she does not herself claim to understand, but she is giving it serious consideration. Also she laughs a lot between sentences, not in amusement but as a sort of sign of bewilderment, I should say. Each little laugh signifies another queer fact of life.

"See, she was very small and young, she was like this cat I had one time, it had kittens too early or it wasn't big enough inside yet, I don't know, and they all died, and she started bleeding and —anyway, Zulma was just a little teen-ager, you know what I mean, my Tina's age." She shrugs. It is self-evident to a roomful of women, she says by her shrug, that there are children and there are women and a sharp line between. I have a foggy picture in my mind of little Indian princesses wed under grand royal canopies, still like the little sister of the Song of Songs, who had no breasts.

"Well, so, for all anybody knows she finds herself a little boy himself who still practicing, right? Or somebody who likes kids. So Zulma and her little *novio*, they make these babies somewhere, two at a time, very efficient, they don't got to do it twice, I bet! And the time goes by and then a couple months more and one day there is Zulma tied to the bedpost. Mamì is shrieking and tearing her hair. And the babies are starving, who can blame them, their mother's thoughts, I don't know where they are, on the moon, they're on toads, they're walking around on her stomach, she's buried under the sand pile up by the concrete works, up to her neck and it's rising, she needs a knife, Jesus, you know what I'm talking about? She's going to kill herself.

"Like that. And they put her in the hospital and she still there. To make her happy they made her so she couldn't have no more children. She pleaded and she called in Jesus and Mary and all to give their permission, I don't know. That's what they say. I never knew why she was so sad about her twins, they must have been the prettiest babies anybody ever saw, they were like a present somebody gave her, you know? And no one ever was mad at her for having them. You think they were the first babies born without the church, without a father? Huh." She carries on these little arguments with herself, rhetorical. Her head bobs in answer.

"So the twins were with Mamì, they did fine, they drank bottle milk, it cost but, bad luck, there was no one right then to wet-nurse them and anyway two of them! I think they got so big because they say cow's milk makes bones bigger, a little too big even."

Renata is eager to have a part in all this; she is nodding vigorously.

"But Mamì made a deal with Freni, the man at the store, to help him clean it up half the day Saturday and sometimes Sunday, scrub and sweep, and for this he gives her all his dented cans of evaporated milk, enough for almost a week."

"Perhaps, Mrs. Huerta, these are a few more details than we strictly need, we should get on with the story of the twins and you yourself?"

"Well, but. OK. Mamì died. That's how I got the twins for mine, and I had to go and figure out later if I wanted them. She had asthma all her life, still from when she was little, it seems like everywhere there's people who can't get any air to breathe, all the poor people—you know, the ones who don't have the money, and the other ones who don't have peace, take your pick.

"Well, you don't want to hear what I went through when she died, I only tell you I cried so much I got water-wrinkles that wouldn't go away, there's Zulma all empty staring out into space, and all our four brothers gone, and my Mamì in this fresh hole in the ground, and two baby boys clamoring on a messed mattress in the corner. Uncle Pedrito helped keep food in our mouth but then little by little he starts disappearing into another fat woman's house—I say there's somebody for everybody, he's all bony so he just like to have these pillows under him. So I begin to learn how to keep children alive, unh? I sing them asleep, I'm very proud of myself." She pauses and looks all around as though she has just awakened. "And then—I know this don't have to do with the laws and all, but I got to tell you this because it says something about my Mamì, this incredible good woman, and how much it cost us to keep the twins eating. One afternoon I'm in back of Freni's bodega where Mamì did the mopping and I'm doing the job now because we go on needing his cans of milk a long time yet, right? and what do you think? It's about the second time I'm there and he comes and he don't ask me nothing, he just comes over and he gives me a very quick, you know, a very deep lesson in what a man is, you know? I'm seventeen, I'm scared and I don't know nothing like that yet. What he can do. And I find out sometimes it's a good thing to shut up. So then I stand up and go back to work, the mop is standing right there dripping down on the floor, running dirty water everywhere, I go and I'm a little weak you know, God knows what I was thinking and Freni's trying to be nice, get me relaxed, he goes out in front to unlock the door for a customer and he saying over his shoulder, 'Hey, you got a lot of your mother in you, kid. A certain style.' And he wiggles his hips a little, see. 'Be happy,' he says, something like that, 'and save a little for me.' So then I understand and I don't know whether to laugh or cry or what. And when I go home I look at the twins and I think, yeah, you got a little of your mother in you, and somewhere a papa for a minute, sixty seconds maybe, probably less, and you got my Mamì too, and now you're drinking from me. What do you think about that?" A very lusty laugh; she is better at irony than my sheltered daughter, who did not stay a virgin half as long. . . .

"You never went to court for them," I say, trying to keep my eye on the ball, as it were.

She only sighs, a sigh from very far back in her life, of satisfaction or resignation I have not a clue, and shakes her head. "We don't go to court over things like that," and she tells me this gently, it is a lesson in immutable sociological fact that I should know. "We all got each other's kids, you know, it's how poor people live, colored people too. We just trade around a lot to help out, nobody ever got enough to give away to kids to worry about who gets what, is it legal and all. Or wills. I never heard of nobody going to law about kids." Mrs. Huerta certainly does smile at me, saying that: saying, Mrs., you're a lady-in-waiting to queens who never lived on my block. I nod and accept it.

"And now Alejandro when he is grown?"

Now she rearranges herself in the uncomfortable leather chair, wriggles her shoulders as though she has finished the first lap of a long car trip and is buckling in for another hundred miles. She is a very interesting woman for me to observe: there is in her a quality very familiar to me, that resignation, that unsurprised recital of woes for which she asks no pity, and accommodations for which she begs no forgiveness. What, she is asking, poor all her life, was I to have expected? Anything that befalls the ones who climb—their feet slip, they plummet or are pushed?—well, what did they expect? Yet she is so very different from my mother, she is not *sad*. Though the little laugh of punctuation is not joyous it attests to a kind of gentle bemusement and nowhere to anger. It may even be her propitiation to her gods. Simply, she does not appear to me to feel herself wronged. Even my daughter, myself, we are grudge-bearers, we feel ourselves owed happiness, and thus are we up to the brim with self-pity when it does not befall.

"I won't bother with my other two, my girls. I only say about the twins how cruel it is, Alejandro got to be the one to suffer." She pauses to examine her fingernails, her first sign of pain. "I hope God will forgive me, but it's Tico who make trouble all his life and Alejandro goes around with the patience and the light in him. Tico was up to Juvi once already for robbing the meters which he did because his friends were doing that." She looks at me for a judgment but I shall give her none. She is blinking back tears, rapidly.

"But that don't excuse it. He come to me with his head in his hands and say, 'Help me, Ma.' His father, I mean Al who I live with, he won't say very much because he don't think he got the right, so it falls on me. So I go help him plead in court and he gets off on probation and he's all kisses and he helps around the house exactly two days and then he's gone again. Gets picked up for breaking into the Flagg's shoes down Fifth Avenue, Union Street? I don't even know if he got a habit, I don't care really. To me Tico's the one who pinch his brother all his life, he goes roughing up kids in the schoolyard and for no reasons—I think he likes to hear their heads clank together, you know that kind? He always did that, two at a time so they hurt each other, bone right up against bone, and he never got to get his fists bloody. Then he comes crying out like a saint and martyr." She sighs. "When he was fourteen Tico was a father, just like his mother, can't wait, this tall Edith down on Carroll Street, a friend of his sister, she puts her skirts up for him and no judge in the world, man or lady, can say for sure whose fault that is, right? Don't try and tell me." She holds up a hand as though I were about to utter a ruling. And no laughing, this is ground she is sure of. "It take two, right? and one was this son of mine, he don't even shave yet, no hair on his chest, he must have to stand up on a chair to get to the place he need. Tico never admitted nothing, he told me he never said hello to the girl. Well, that could be, plenty of harm a horny boy can do without ever saying hello or goodbye. I'm a grandmother, what do you think? I mean, me for Zulma, it's all the same by now.

"Well, what happened to Alejandro. It's so simple you could break your heart." A long pause in which she gathers breath invisibly. "He come one night, he suppose to be sleeping, this is Christmas vacation, he come in the kitchen holding onto his side and he say, 'Ma, this hurts terrible.'" She is going to act out all the gestures, she bends far over, buckling now, to emphasize the pain, and it twitches briefly on her face. She is a woman who fills my office with a generous light, I would like to touch her electricity. But Renata is pulled tightly into herself, one hand holding the other arm awkwardly as though she aches or has a chill. "So I give him a look, right sides I never liked much, or left chest. 'You been to the bathroom today?' I ask him that, he never remember to wash his ears if you don't tell him.

"So he say, 'Yeah, Ma, but this is a different kind of a pain, it's so deep and—black, like, I never felt nothing like this, it mean some kind of trouble. I'm sorry,' he tells me, imagine, he's apologizing. 'I wouldn't ask you only take me to the doctor please.' His eyes are like little pin points of bright lights, flashbulbs, you know? Very very bright, they scare me most. He got fists in both hands. Well, you got to know he's the kind of boy, he never make no more trouble than he have to, his friends don't know the half of what he help me at home, his room, everything. He got no poisons in him like his brother, they make him hot and evil. He's going to go up to the community college the year after next, he's planning already, trying to put away money for books, he keeps loaning it to his brother to piss away.

"So we put on our coats, it's not too late and we go. Al, Aníbal, he's sleeping in his chair, I just take my chance, he'll be asleep when we come back, his head's way flopped over on one side like a little kid. I don't like that, feeling all choked up seeing Al there, that tell me I'm very scared of something, I mean, like this is the last time something, or I'll remember when it was like this, you know that kind of thing. Like you're already way into next week looking back and you can see yourself. I hate that."

She shivers, the way I recall myself doing at the age of twelve or so.

"My Alejandro's face is all white, he's only a boy but he's twice as tall as me, I swear. I take his hand up and lead him and he come with me like a lamb, he's all soft, you know? And we go around to the Memorial, the hospital.

"Then we get there, in the EMERGENCY. The run-around. Doctor this and doctor that, we sit down, we stand up, go here, go there. Alejandro, he got sweat balls on his face, he's going around holding his side, he keep on leaning like, I don't know, like he took a bullet in there. Not a word from him, though, his lips biting down. So—what? You could say they're not in any hurry with us, huh? What can I prove? They say they're so busy, no one gonna come out and announce over the loudspeaker, you know, 'Oh, a couple spics here, we going to let them sit awhile, cool it, you know.' I mean, I'm only saying it was one long time. They had one of them big clocks like in a school? Every minute it jumps, you know, makes a big click—hiccup—and I'm watching it and watching it, I'm holding Alejandro around his shoulder and he's stiff, he's an iron pole. The pain. The light's so white in there it look like the frost fell on everybody, we all been there all winter. . . .

"So then they come and take him away. 'You wait here.' They send him back in ten minutes with an ice pack. No explanation. I don't see no nurse, no doctor. He gets to tell me, oh the doctor say it ain't nothing, a swelling. 'Irritable appendix, something.' Ice gonna make it go down. Shit. He still white as a bone, though, you know? Shivering? The ice can't get inside his belt anyway, it makes this big pee-stain on his pants is all.

"So we get halfway down the block, he puts his hand on a tree, rest his head down across the elbow, the joint, and he cries. 'Ma, Ma,' he says, 'I'm gonna die.' My grown-up boy in his tan leather coat with the big fur collar like a gang king, only he's true and clean—he cries and cries and holds onto his side, so I stumble right back with him and this time I just roll right past the desk with him—this little redhead tight-ass nurse come running, she's shouting, 'Wait, lady, you can't,' but I can and I yank back one of them curtains on some doctor, he's poking in a white lady's eye, getting out a damn cinder or something, and I roar like a pig, 'Goddamn it, my son say he's dying and you go give him ice cubes!'" She looks at me and then at Renata imploringly. "Ice cubes!"—and puts her hand on the back of her neck, under her bobbing coppery hair as though to cool herself right now.

"Well, so they almost gave me a shot of something like I was some escaped animal or something I was shouting so loud. It sounds funny now but it wasn't funny then. So, you know, I got the doctor scared of me and the lady with the cinder just sort of gets up and edges out the curtain on one eye, fast. So my son lays down then, just sinking down, and the doctor lets me stay this time, he pulls Alejandro's pants down and he's touching him firm in this special way and Alejandro quits trying to get up, just lying with tears all over, getting wet on the paper table. He saying 'I'm gonna die, Ma, don't let me die.' But like regular conversation, you know? real quiet and the doctor gives a nod to the nurse and they put him on a table and wheel him out. His legs keep bending. So I know how much it's hurting him.

"So then I got to sign these papers about how if anything happens and this and that and he's going to get his appendix out. *What if he went home with your ice?* The fuckers! They all just get up and leave me standing in the little room with the curtains on hooks like it was a shower. The nurses all wheeling around quiet, they go around in their rubbery shoes like some kind of carts, and I'm holding the paper towel sopping from the melted ice. 'If he listened and just went on home and died? Then what?' So why they were looking at me like I had to be crazy? Was I crazy? It's my son they got there."

I can only shake my head. I can see, though, how her very size, her high color, something altogether vivid about her might make the nurses wary. They would have to begin, of course, with their habit of uncooperativeness, their prejudices, their rigidities, but still—this Catalina, if all her bolts were, let us say, just loosened a quarter-turn, might put them in mind of some woman they had seen on the wards, ranting. I can imagine it: do not all vivid people seem exaggerated into caricatures at certain moments? I believe I have so appeared. This poor woman's very passion is her undoing.

"So I start to cry and cry and finally somebody comes over and asks me in the first half-nice tone of voice I heard all night would I come and get some coffee. But you know, she gets paid to take care of the crazy ones, the social worker or something. So then all she did while I drank their hot brown shit-water, uch, was sit and stir weak tea and complains about how she got to work nights like this and then go home and get mugged. Kids, she says, yeah, some of the nicest-looking kids these days come up and knock you on the head for your purse. So she's probably thinking, oh that son of yours, good thing he's down in bed or he might come stealing up and let me have it."

Catalina laughs. It is disarming: either a great deal of perspective or none at all.

"Well," I manage to say into the silence as gently as I am able. "And tell me, then, did he die on the operating table or in post-operative or just what?"

Renata looks at me quickly, almost a warning. She does not like the question. Neither do I, nor the fact. She is still clutching one arm with a white-knuckled hand. Mrs. Huerta breathes and laughs in the presence of death, but Renata is too terrified to hear. I dare say she still holds her breath when she passes a cemetery.

"No," Mrs. Huerta says, "he didn't." She looks into her lap a long time. "He did fine. They said it was just in time, them with their ice. I saw him after, he woke up real slow, he kept licking his lips, you know, but I could see he was OK. He had a terrible ache where they cut him but it was different he said, 'I can take this OK, it's just a regular pain.' He was just amazed he didn't die, is all. I mean"—and she shrugged—"when I can see his broken tooth he's smiling. And there it was, first time he was showing it. So it was real good. People came, Al and his friends came, his sisters, except Carmi is too young, they got those dumb hospital rules. I said, can you catch appendicitis, but they said, no, no, you don't ask no more questions. Like they're still tired of me from the night I brung him in, I'm a troublemaker. So his friends anyway, they brung him stuff, candy and joke books, he had one friend who gave away his own copy of *Playboy*. And everybody hung around and laughed a lot, a lot of life came in with them, you know, that dull old green room he was there in. And some girl I didn't even know sends him all these chrysanthemums? Something to think about.

"But see, the only thing was every now and then he'd say 'Oh, this hurts' or something and I'd look at his bandages and they were—aie," she shudders, "foul, horrible. I could smell them, you ever smell a corpse? So I said, what is this, don't they change these things for you? He say, not much, no, Ma, you would do it better. And cheaper, I would remind him that."

My eyes were actually widening at this. Good Lord. At this point I must assess her reliability as a witness, for this is an extraordinary claim she is making. "You do not know any of the particulars. How often, or what was used—"

Mrs. Huerta shrugs. "How do I know? I only see there's this terrible mess on his poor side, the pus comes through the gauze, it even make a stain on the sheet. You got to believe me, Mrs. Stein. It could make a strong man puke, if you saw it. And he's lying there in it.

"But see, they don't like to listen to me. I went one time to the head nurse on that floor, she's sitting in that middle place, you know, the station, whatever they call it, and this Mrs. Lucas, she's the one in charge, she's a lady about as big as two pillows and she smell like a whole rosebush. And she has this big dislike to me. I don't know why. Don't ask me. Maybe because I'm a PR, maybe she just don't like my face. I'm prettier than she is. *You* know. So I was polite, just like a little lady, and calm. But she turn this powdery-pink face at me, this mouth like a fish, it floats open real slow like she lives in the water? I try to tell her what a mess this operating scar is and she just opens that mouth up like a movie star. Greta Garbo. Oh? Oh. Oh dear. Well, we shall see that, hmmm. Daring me. All, like slow motion. I want to rip her into little bits, I don't got to tell you, get her moving. She turns real slow, she don't look like no gray lady, I'll tell you. So she makes me wait outside, she goes in to Alejandro and comes out so late I know she was in there changing the dressing herself but she won't say nothing. She just sort of nods like, well now you can get off my back. 'He's fine, dear.'

"And first thing I know he's got himself a fever. His eyes get that look again, everything's all, like, tight in the middle, you know, the way people got sort of spokes in their eyes? Or like ice with cracks in it—well, his are all—I can't explain—like throbbing. I don't know." She gives up. "And his hands are sweating and dry at the same time.

"They give him drugs, I don't know what, nobody tells you nothing if you're only his mother, and he don't do any good on them, he pop out in these rashes all over, itching and scabs, and before I know it—" She covers her eyes, bent at the neck, and Renata fixes on me as if with some satisfaction. She is tensing her foot, it quivers and kicks. "He goes moaning and flailing around and they just—come put me out of there. They don't let me stay with my baby, this Lucas, she takes me by the wrist and shoulder both, polite but hard, so it hurts, and walk me to the door and tell me visiting hours are over and I should be glad. They are *not*. A doctor is going by, one of these million Chinese doctors, Arab, something, all these strange doctors nobody else will give a job to —and he's going by, whizz, and this Lucas is saying, whispering, something, 'He's souring,' and I'm thinking *souring you! souring you!* Filthy pigs killing my baby and they throwing me out before I can even see him." She pauses a long time.

"He was all better! You understand that. Ready to go home almost. So look what I do, they make me. There's a cart full of stuff, I don't know, medicine, dirty dishes, basins, I don't even see, I just took it and pushed it up against their fucking station and it tips over and it all falls down in chips and hunks. A good noise, it goes on a long time before it all settles, and there's this foam all over, running down the hall in streams, and something's all red. . . . It did me good for a minute but, you know—" She shrugs. Adequate words will not come.

"Then they take me and lift me by the arms, two orderlies they are, and put me on the freight elevator and that's it. They tell me I'll get arrested if I try to sneak up there again. So—" She stops. "That's the end anyway.

"I go sit in the lobby—what can I do, could I call the cops, they'd take me before I even got done talking, who do I have to call, my friends they get spit on their faces like me. Renata—I got to say I just didn't think of." She shakes her head slowly. "What was anybody supposed to do but God then anyway. He was out of his head, Alejandro. I heard him up there, he was calling out names. They must have been kids in first grade with him, I recognize some of them, Juana, Delicato, Jaime. John. He was moaning, once he made this beautiful sweet moan like a man with a woman. He was all getting eaten out, like. . . . And then they come all whispering and say, No more. Nada. Nada. Circumstances this and complications that and his own fault he couldn't take the drugs, and did he ever have a drug problem? They say that to me, this beautiful clean boy lying up there that they killed. There's his arms if they want to go look and they're as clean as yours and theirs. Anyway—that's different drugs, right? I think they were trying to do a number on me." She looks at me perplexed; possibly this has just occurred to her for the first time, and I suspect she is right, too.

"Into the garbage where they wanted him, one less of them in the world to scare the nurses when they go home he might mug them or rape them if he could get their legs pried open with a goddamn bottle opener. So when I got up to see him laid out you never seen nothing so sweet and clean in your life, he could have got married in them pajamas and the hole in his side all draped white like something in some fucking convent."

Her mouth is twisted to one side. Through this entire story this woman has, in a sense, deflated. She is leaning toward me now in her conviction, her feet flat on the floor, I see how her shoes are scuffed to cardboard at the tips, and all the bird-breast puff gone out of her sweater. Humility is in her hands, which are bony, incongruously so, their skin seamed and red, and she picks at a thread on the slick knee of her skirt.

Renata has covered her face with her hands and is absolutely still as though forbidden to show feeling. She shall not dare to weep before the mother herself. The two of them struggle massively for dignity.

And so I rise and walk to the window. The glass again is dirty, it is waxy as a lithography stone—why do we retain that bunch of laggards who are to clean it? At this moment I would give anything I own to be far away, asleep or alone. On a hillside peering up through elephant grass, even if the sky were just this gray.

Then I must begin to explain, as slowly as I would reason with a child, that I cannot be of help.

While I make clear—as clear as I possibly can—my quite convincing reasons for this opinion I can see my own Renata's eyes go distant and hard. (What is it Mrs. Huerta said about wheelspokes in the eye? She put it nicely.) But why have we been wished upon each other? Renata's eyes flicker at me with the cold light of stars and she says not one single word more to me before they pick up their coats—no word to assuage me, my sorrow in the matter, my regret, my stab and turn and stab again of pain, as though I hold perpetually in my hands a most marvelous gun, a gleaming most serviceable rifle, which—in times of crisis and dire jeopardy—will only click and will not fire!

Mrs. Huerta's coat is a large size of some egregiously artificial air-blown squirrel. Renata helps her on with it, most proprietary, and they leave. I try to put a consoling hand on the cleaning lady's tousled-fur arm—it has the dead dull feel of a sick cat's fur, you are familiar with the way the spring and oil seem to drain out of them during fever, then return. Renata glares steadily at me, to the point of self-consciousness, like a child holding her breath to make herself faint. Mrs. Huerta, most interestingly, looks rather more indifferent. Unmoved, undisappointed, except by her own story which made her pale and keeps her so. But during my recitation of the realities of litigation the emotion drained out of her face, her constricted eyes relaxed, and she appeared not massively concerned nor disillusioned. I am led to wonder what she may have expected; why at all she came here. I mean, for whom. I feel cursed all the way to my ankles as they leave, but as you would imagine it, not by my rejected client, who is so complete unto herself and so beyond hope. Only a daughter dares to hate so hard that she can move out the door stony as the statue of a martyr being wheeled toward full visibility, where my colleagues wait.

RENATA

I was trying to get Tippy to bed and she wouldn't go. Jesus, she's gotten into this terrible habit of clinging to me and not letting go. It scares me. I pull one hand off and she catches hold with the other, I pick the fingers of the other hand up one by one and she flings the first one down on my shoulder and pinches. I feel like I've got a leech on me. "Please, honey," is how I start, but by the time I end I'm quivering with anger. Wouldn't you think she'd want to protect herself against that? When I fling her down, her fingers finally extracted from my back, she bounces flat on the mattress, passive, and that scares me even more. She is beautiful, I think, and sometimes I worry that there may be something wrong with her. There's this—disease, condition, I don't know what it is or why but I've read about it and it only seems to strike babies who are strangely lovely. A gruesome mystery *that* is. I bend and look into her eyes, which are bright and moist and seem very normal, and she grabs me again.

I hear my mother outside, banging around to tell me she's home and will I please come in to see her. Better than an inter-office buzzer.

"Poor child," she says when I come in. "Can you not let her stay up on her grandma's knee awhile? I have some penny rhymes for her."

Her grandma's knee all of a sudden. The child has barely seen that her grandma has a knee, let alone penny rhymes. The two of them are alike: hands around the neck when someone's calling you.

"Don't tempt her, Mother. She's finally down and that's an accomplishment. Anyway I think she's getting a cold so she needs some sleep."

By which I meant, don't you invite me to take chances on her and then turn around and blame me when she gets sick. Do you know that I have been held responsible for the child's adverse reaction to her measles shot? My mother deserves to be rich and feared.

"You acquitted yourself nicely this morning." My mouth is already twitching. This is going to be bad.

"Renata, you did not try to understand my position with regard to Mrs. Huerta." She searches behind her for the chair, surrendering, and sinks into it much farther than she seems to have expected.

"Mrs. Huerta," I begin, already weary.

"If you gave one minute of your excitement to a consideration of the merits—"

"Merits." I'm still standing. I come and try to tower over her but that backfires, I feel ridiculous, as though I'm waiting for a seat in the subway. "There are no merits. Your legalisms." She takes in a deep breath of exasperated patience. "They didn't poison the kid in broad daylight in the cafeteria. They didn't run a shiv into him at the main desk." What am I going to do for breath? "So they couldn't have killed him, he probably killed himself, he was probably stealing drugs or, I don't know, what?—fucking the nurses every night, maybe. He probably died of exhaustion, right?"

"Renata." My mother exhales a simple gust of shock. Every "fuck you" on the walls of the world is her very first one.

But I'm eating myself up word by word. I'd never make a long-distance runner; never make a trial lawyer, I should say. "So it's hard. So you can't prove it one-two-three. So the doctors won't tell anything and the nurses'll lie through their teeth. So what? Is he just another fucking little spic to you?"

"Renata," she begins again, hopelessly condescending. "It is to my disadvantage that I have some respect for reason as a means of procedure. Ordinarily it tends to give one a certain confidence, like faith. I recommend it. But being in the presence of someone like you becomes too much like standing before a violent, a proselytizing atheist. Your Mrs. Huerta has had a tragic misfortune—"

"A misfortune." Some words shouldn't exist, they diminish everything in sight: *dismay. regrettable. misfortune.* I recognize the winded feeling from way back in my life: when we argue it's like falling on my stomach from a high place. I'm going to die panting.

"Yes. But what is so offensive about the word 'misfortune'? Would it help matters were I to abandon caution and allow myself absolutely to be convinced that her son died of neglect, when it may very well be that he died of terribly sad, unpredictable, unavoidable, natural causes?"

Mother sits tensed, both feet pushed against the floor as though she expects a car I'm driving to veer off the road; as though she could stop it.

"I believe I have had conversations like these before, but they have always been political, you know. The dichotomy has been between so-called revolutionary and so-called reformer; or between Zionists, let us say, and supporters of Al Fatah—whatever the cause at hand, you dissidents have always been affronted by anything that remotely smacked of logic in the hands of the unvirtuous. It is as though your weapons had fallen behind enemy lines and now all you can think to do is to dare me head on, bare-fisted, with obscenities and this repellent shouting, unprotected by the shield of reason. But you see, you must understand that you shall not touch me here, you are a child fighting with an open hand."

"Shield is right, I'm glad to know you see it for what it is, anyway. But why are the others always the dissidents, tell me that. Because you've got all the power you can define everybody else right up against the wall, right? And anyway, what does this have to do with revolutionaries and dissidents to begin with? Why do you have to drag the whole world in? I'm talking about *one* boy who was neglected to death—wished to death—I'm not trying to

start a war, I'm—you spend too much damn time stuffing everybody into your class actions."

She waves me away. The arguments she dislikes, she ignores.
Only in civilian life can she get away with it.

"Now I listened to Catalina. And I respect the woman, she has
always seemed to me to be remarkably keen and intelligent—"

"Why 'remarkably'?" I want to know. "Is that so damn unusual, don't 'they' come intelligent very often?"

"My dear. I would like to finish without your belligerent assistance if I may, please." She closes her eyes for a long minute. "I
shall eagerly await the day your daughter addresses you with such
respect, my lamb. It is a knife to the gut, in case you do not believe it. Your Tippy will learn just what her voice can do, and is
that to be recompense for me? Am I to feel gratified that you
shall at least share some of my pain?"

"What are you talking about?" I am practically spinning in
place by now.

Mother puts her head down on one hand, very theatrical; then
she appears to recover herself, if she was ever lost. "But all right.
To continue. It is a well-known fact that the mother of a son
newly dead will not make your most reliable witness."

"Ah," I nod, "she will not?"

"No, she will not. Nor will she, and who can blame her, have
all her facts in hand, marshaled in usable form."

Must she make me into a child? "Then you make them usable.
What do you do all day? You go and get them and you organize
them however the hell you want to, whatever compulsive way you
like to have them, and then you sue the bastards and you have
them punished. At least you try. Or do you only do things that
raise fancy constitutional questions? Because if—"

"Renata, please. Please sit and be patient. You are disappointed
because I tend, far more than you, to subdue my emotional responses to a very different set of priorities. And there you stand,
hands on your hips, mumbling to yourself 'responses, priorities' as
though they are only my foul words. Well, you appear to me, to
be frank, to have the intellectual flexibility of your little baby
daughter, and I am losing patience. Surely we do not bring
forth the best in each other." She clasps her hands as though

she were shaking on a deal. "If you did not wish to confront
this question seriously, Renata, then why, may I ask, why
did you call upon a lawyer?"

At which I raise my head and look at the ceiling, showing her a
good bit of white of the eye: skepticism and disgust. "That's it,
that's what you are. You see yourself that way, 'a lawyer.' Yes?
Not my mother. Not a friend of Catalina's. 'A lawyer.' "

"Extraordinary." She joins her hands and beats them against
her forehead. "But where does my motherhood have bearing on
this case? It is very nice of you to remember our relationship
through all weathers. But you have not brought me *your* dead
child to weep upon, heaven forbid. You have, I thought I understood but perhaps I have been mistaken, brought me the facts per-
taining to the case of a woman of our acquaintance, and you have
begged my opinion on one question and one question only: is this
dreadful occurrence court-worthy? It is like a ship—will it sail?
Whether or not you *wish* it to, the only relevant question is, will
it stay afloat or shall you capsize or sink and drown if you set foot
on it."

She waits as though the question were intended to be answered.

"No, I have given you my opinion, and you are free to get another if you would like to, I can give you a dozen names of some
of my most reliable colleagues. Most of them, to begin, would
find this a grievously expensive case to pursue, it is the sort of case
in which—I hesitate to mention this to you, it is a reality for
which I know you have a dreamer's contempt—but most of them
would need to ask a considerable down payment, because the
chances of award are very slight and they would have to set aside
other work—competing work—to do it."

At the words down payment—I hate to be so predictable—I
gasp and get up from my slump on the sofa. I begin to walk back
and forth in front of the dark window.

"Alas, your taste for casual arrangements does not enter in, not
to this world which partakes of compromise and probability at
least as much as does the political."

This woman is dangerous. She is like some unstoppable disease
quietly, blindly ravaging upward toward what I, sentimentalist,

would dare to call my heart. Was it Socrates who felt the chill rise from his feet? She is my hemlock, then.

"Now, my opinion is that, even though any jury would be predisposed in your favor, and would enjoy awarding your grieving mother a million dollars against her tears—even they, kind and charitable as they might be, and guilt-stricken that their own sons thus far survive—they would be overwhelmed by the hospital's evidence in its own behalf. Beginning with the waiver of responsibility signed by Mrs. Huerta so routinely, and continuing through the legally weighty fact that this is not her own child we are speaking of, either by birth or by court ruling, complicated by the further fact that he was by no means a financial support, plus—"

"All right," I say in what I hope is a deadly quiet voice, "all right, but you should hear yourself."

She is bewildered. "And should I hear myself, what would I discover?"

"You should hear what kind of a machine you have turned into, did you know that? The rigor of your bloody mind, drip-dripping away in perfect order, you're so perfect I can't believe it, you're a fucking metronome." I shouldn't complicate our argument with those words, I know, I know, she hears a whole damn barbaric generation in them, we're all "fornicating" on the Supreme Court steps, and it distracts even her narrow little lawyer's eyes from the real issue. "You're like the worst damn defense lawyer I ever heard, I used to have to go to court in Woodstock sometimes for traffic stuff, and there was this one creep of a small-town shyster, he had the pencil mustache and everything, the whole ambulance chaser's getup, I couldn't believe it. And everybody had to hire him to get them off their d.w.i.'s and their violations for crossing the yellow line, and the courtroom was always—just smarmy with this horrible stink of innuendo and insult between the lawyer and the poor cops who arrested everybody. All this point shaving. Do you know what I mean? All this absolute literalism would take over everybody's brain, like a kind of paralysis. Like an Ionesco play, till you couldn't remember what real reason meant, only this fake courtroom logic and catching people off base if they breathed out the wrong nostril. And it was all for these lousy fifteen-dollar fines!"

My mother sits and watches me very seriously. "You do allow yourself to get wound up, do you not?" She licks her lips. "You yourself would throw out the adversary style and advocate nothing but passive feeling and tears, I take it. We are all to spend the day henceforth lying about on a couch, preferably naked, convulsed over the whole world's unapproachable injustices, and then we could rise with the moon, perhaps, and stir up a brew of hallucinogens and sing a hocus-pocus over it, and make what you call 'love,' and all would be saved. Do I misrepresent you, do you think? Do you know, you are a dangerous woman, such passions to spend with no control or purpose? You need a life of your own, my lady, an occupation for your energies so that you can leave other people's business alone."

Her look is a mirror of mine, I suspect. We are appalled by one another.

"Especially the hired help's."

I can see her deciding to say nothing, letting that go because it's beneath contempt.

"I thought you suffered. You used to rub that shit into my wounds all the time when I was little. I thought you had a corner on suffering: immigrant women, pulling everybody along by their hair, traipsing back and forth through Harlem, feeling, bleeding with the natives, sympathy on the other side of the fence. So look at you, you've got a hide full of callouses."

She sits heavily, looking off into space. As if on cue Tippy calls out from the back, querulous, demanding, she tries what small weapons of obligation and inconvenience she keeps under her pillow, who can blame her: I am here, Mother, if you drift too far into your own daughterhood, I yank the string and you shall answer, and I shall remember and hoard your words and use them against you when the time comes.

Then Tippy is dragging at my knees, whimpering. And she is my weapon. How I regret this, but those are tears on my face, too. We are both daughters. "Look, Tippy, you see your grandmother?"

Tippy looks up at me gravely, not at her. Maybe she understands that what I'm about to say has nothing to do with her at all. "You remember what a cruel face looks like, OK? You look at Grandma and hear me tell you she is selfish and mean and not a good mother, and you remember that. She'll try to buy your love back with candy and chewing gum, I never got that but she'll shovel it into you, but don't you forget—"

Tippy backs up till her heels knock against the coffee table. She is already more complicated than her damn fool mother, I don't doubt it. In this gypsy light she looks like a peaked little whore, lines under her huge eyes, tousled smoky hair. Confused and nervous, the poor child tries to smile at her grandmother, slip her a little smile, furtive. Or maybe it's only a nervous movement of the mouth that she's learned from me, whose pale face hangs before her, the single moon in her sky. She starts back toward her bed. This wasn't what she was expecting when she came out, a cockfight in the sawdust. Feathers everywhere and a terrible stench of anger. Helpless, I put my head in my hands and weep noisy declarative tears. God, they can feel good, you can collapse into them, it's like finding the john when you can't wait another second—crude, Mother would hate the image, but that's what it feels like, one of life's least profound necessities: the long letting-go.

I've begun to feel desperate: I haven't been doing anything good since I've come back—granted. But I haven't done anything bad either. No drugs, no men. *Healing.* She doesn't have any idea how terrified I am of trying to do something. Later, later, I want to tell her; let me pile some more foundation. Doesn't anything ever *count?* Is that what it means to have a mother, that there's always going to be somebody to remember what *you've* lived past to forget? That I'll always be a child? Oh, Jesus, I thought—like a child—is that how it works? Does she have to die? Will I have to die for Tippy to get free of me, free of the part of her history I carry around?

"Renata."

Her tone is faintly conciliatory. I cry all the harder. Out of control, let them have their control, it's an enemy tool, careening, it feels so good, telling myself it's OK, abandoned. Like lying down when you're exhausted: simple.

"Renata, might I take Tippy off your hands for a few days, do you think you could relax and go off somewhere?"

I look at her meekly, snuffling. That was meant to be humane, I know. When I was little I hated it when she blamed all my angers and petulance on tiredness or a cold coming on. I was always happy to take responsibility, if only she'd let me. Her look is like that now: she isn't going to be sidetracked with sympathy for irrelevant problems like death and fury and a tendency to soil myself with hysteria. I must be overtired.

This woman is my fate, that's all. Not my history only: my future. She won't die, she'll be waiting for me in the graveyard no matter what.

"Don't you think—" She looks impatient that her generosity isn't leaped upon with gratitude.

"No I do not."

"I could—"

"No you could not. You cannot touch her. You don't even know how."

"All right, my dear, I shall leave you alone to resolve this for yourself." She gets up. "I am going for a nice long walk." It's hard, she pulls herself up creaking, nearly falling back down again, like a rusty bucket out of a well, and goes to the door pulling across her shoulders her hulk of a thrift-shop coat while she walks. She is, by now, like me, breathing hard—what a huge physical exertion it is to grapple with anger. I thought digesting food was hard, how some people say you could heat a house with the energy it takes to consume a four-course dinner. My forehead's pink and sweaty, lit up from inside with the heat of so many unsaid words.

I shout from nowhere then. Already shamed I itch with the need to finish it off—finish her, finish me. I hope I can be heard on the upper level of the Brooklyn Bridge. "You know what you remind me of? You'll never guess what."

"I do not need your rhetorical questions right now. Of what do I remind you?" She sighs.

"One of those bastards who's always going around saying 'All you need is a good fuck.' You've got the same damn pinched mentality, you never listen to what I'm saying, you've always got to be two steps into your own diagnosis of what I need, only it's never never what I really need, and it never respects me."

She nods slowly and evenly: all right, anything you say, yes you certainly have caught my tone there, especially with my favorite of all words. She restrains herself from telling me that what I really need is a good sinus-clearing breath of intelligent hard work, caustic fact, commitment to the greater good, and a custom mouthwash by Mr. Clean.

"You are certainly a simplifier, my daughter. You can reduce the world to its primary colors and flail about at all the available surfaces with a dripping brush."

"Yes, I am a simplifier if that's what it comes to, to choose. There is such a thing as right and another thing called wrong. If you've got tools you should use them or stop tinkering, that's all. What's the difference between simplifying and"—I look around to get help out of the shadows—"and morality? Is your world too complicated for justice and cruelty, are those words all outmoded? Or they're only for amateurs and soap operas, maybe."

She shakes her head, which for her is the same as nodding—it dismisses. She opens the door with a yank, crudely, and is gone. But she's so damn cool she manages to close it carefully and try it once to be sure it's locked. Yes I am safe. No one can get in to hurt me but myself. Heaven forgive me, I made a terrible mess of a real outrage, realer than I am. Who would believe there is a fresh grave somewhere, after hearing the two of us? I try to see Alejandro's face, his crooked tooth, his long twiggy fingers, but I never knew him well enough, the familiarity is fake. And she's made him unreal for both of us now anyway. An issue. A taffy pull. What I see is my mother's angry face, her lips working. They are an old woman's dry lips.

I know I'm not blameless, only I can't find where the frayed and dirty string begins.

three

GERDA

So near am I, having left my daughter to her self-rightcous stub-bornness, to my friend Anna-Joyce McHugh, who lives a few blocks uptown near the river, that I walk over to see if her good cheer abides. It is one of the unforgivable facts about Anna-Joyce in the eyes of many that she lives in this lovely old house with its broad granite staircase. True, the stairs are unfortunate, in the way of chance, because the previous owner, perhaps for the sake of ostentation or of an incapacity to live in a rowhouse identical to its neighbors, had them replaced with a turn in the middle so that they go down from there as if in two branching flights and put one on the sidewalk at either side; and so, acsthetic though they are, it is true that they call rather unfortunate, perhaps queenly, attention to the presence of Mrs. McHugh, who truly would rather blend in with her charges—the entire neighborhood under her roomy wing.

But some consider residence in the house as though it were a continually repeated act, a conscious vivid daily violation of the poor, and in the end she is further penalized for her occupation among the miserable of the neighborhood than she would be were she a piano teacher or a stockbroker or simply a housewife. She is, you see, robbed continually as a corrective to her inappropriate idealism! It serves not to argue that were Anna-Joyce to live with a cot and a hot plate behind her community center she would not decrease by a single one the poor of the city; still, a month or so ago some wit relieved her of a brand-new tape recorder and, by way of thanks, sprayed on her front steps (as though they were a subway train) the quaint message SUCK SUCK SUCK SUCK SUCK all the way to the bottom step where, ingeniously, the message was amended to SUCKER. What is one to say. Hollis McHugh, A-J's husband, is a bilateral heir to the Jewel Salt fortune. Therefore is her house built upon her salt, you see—so goes the reasoning, one should assume—blood, sweat, tears of thousands. The salt shines in the granite of those stairs, except where the recent blacking has put it out.

This Anna-Joyce, strange to think, in a way stands in similar relation to me as I stand to my daughter. That is to say, I disagree profoundly with the direction she has chosen, in which her energies flow. I feel her to be childishly trusting, even absurdly optimistic because her profession, unlike the law which speaks into time, is one which must reconstruct its constituents daily, rouse them from their daily beds, which it must often *find* for them in the first place. Must shore them up against the ruins of their lives, give them a reason to stir and hope they will see fit to walk a straight line into the future. But the disagreement, you see, is bracing to us, it does not render us bitter. And moreover, I believe that each of us recognizes that the other's style and talents are well-served by the choice. We would not, could not change places for the world, but we meet with embraces and, in rather a jolly style, we spend much time in mockery of the other's elected futility.

She is, if you have not guessed it, a social worker. She works in a little storefront with not-so-fresh youngsters—dropouts, addicts, gang warriors—and with seasoned failures, depleted Puerto Rican wives and black prostitutes, old people approaching from the other side the birthdays of their childhoods. She is a valiant and foolish woman, Anna-Joyce, and without her kind of pastoral commitment the impossible slum she works in, works at, would be —what is worse than impossible, there must be a word appropriate? Yet I do not know how she arises each morning. Sisyphus was a satisfied man by comparison. I met her when she brought a tiny shoplifter named Tomaso to a sort of jerry-built court over which I was presiding—experiment 932 in the doomed effort of the city to short-cut the approach to juvenile offenders. Let me spare you the details only to say that I enjoyed the powers of judgeship and rather regretted never having pursued the kind of influence that would have secured a permanent place on the bench. Tomaso was a wrinkled brown waif, and before he was gone from the anteroom court he had not only abused me in language that tasted, against my tongue, like cayenne pepper (and Anna-Joyce's mouth kept popping open, either in shock or in preparation to silence him—as if she could—so that she looked like his ventriloquist!) but he had also, to make a point I had already grasped, pocketed an ashtray, wretched black plastic City of N.Y. issue, and three ballpoint pens with a tendency to clog, and had acquired a battered marijuana cigarette which Anna-Joyce swore he did not bring in with him. She is wise but her young charges are smart—all the difference that matters—and the battle of styles is forever joined. She sees me as my own kind of fool, you may believe, altogether beyond useful wisdom, all my coinage non-negotiable on the streets; I see hers as pleasant, palliative, absorbing but not basic, not structural. We need each other. Thus the angels of the underworld descend toward earth, their professions linked like hands: it may disgust my daughter but I am proud of us and how we fly through the atmosphere—yes, this democracy is an imperfect heaven but one can breathe in it, and find some fellowship.

I scratch at the basement window because, in spite of the grand staircase, the bell has never worked as long as I have known the McHughs. A-J comes to the door with a mouthful of pins, and in the course of our embrace, for a disconcerting moment thinks she has swallowed one.

"But what are you doing?!" I ask her, beginning to remember (and too late) the feeling I always develop here, of being empty-handed in the path of a volunteer fire brigade.

"Fixing Lily's dress," as though it were self-evident. "Here—" and she hands me, rather foists upon me a pattern for a most handsome lace wedding dress, which I then see before me, but more saggingly and in a cheaper lace, on the figure of a thin dusty-ish black girl with those large lonely-making glasses the children wear nowadays: owl eyes, eyes that say, if I am not beautiful in these, then let us have a laugh instead. In 1940 I had a pair like those, gold-framed if I remember, and always thought I resembled a farm girl.

"Ah, you are getting married."

She stares at me.

"Soon."

And stares yet more. Do I frighten her?

"To a fine young man."

I have begun to wonder if her wedding is to take place in a school for the deaf-mute, but when I have walked into the kitchen to scout for a tea bag, Anna-Joyce passes quickly through on no particular business and tells me quite matter-of-factly, "Oh, don't mind her, Lily won't talk to whites these days. She's a fool but very sweet really, and she's all but raised a bunch of little brothers and sisters—and, do you know, cousins and things—with only a drunken daddy around, so—" So she is excused.

"But you!" I complain naïvely. "Are you now a crypto-black?"

"Only an honorary," she says seriously, reaching on tiptoes into the cupboard for me and handing me miraculously one lone bag of Lapsang souchong. "Help yourself to those muffins there," she says and disappears, adding over her shoulder, sotto voce, "Wait till you see"—forgetting I won't see—"how many whites she'll end up having at her wedding!"

Which is the kind of inconsistency I revile, you see. No wonder I have lived to defend such scoundrels as I have; more than all else I respect consistency and a passionate rigor. Stubbornness, even, if it has its internal logic. I should truly prefer this Lily with her powerless shoulders and fern-curly hair to make no distinctions for as long as her separation of the races serves her. In fact she will get over it faster if she is truly confronted with her hatred in its purity and sees how many good people she excludes and then must yearn for. At this rate her half-baked bigotry could drag on forever.

I am sipping my tea, alone, and the phone rings four times. It is turned to its loudest volume so that Anna can hear it undoubtedly in her sleep. But she does not now hear it. I answer it. One time it is someone named Hjalmar who tells me to instruct A-J that he has the cage but not the oars. Another time it is Marie who is looking for Anthony and will look elsewhere (though in this asylum I should have checked under the beds). The third time Anna-Joyce's own daughter is calling to give her the message "Boston ivy." "Ah," say I, "Boston ivy, of course. How could it be otherwise, how foolish. Not Boston lettuce, Boston ivy." "Yes." "You are quite sure. Not bittersweet." "No, tell her ivy. Boston." She has a peevish quality I have never heard in her mother; also a house in Long Island and small children underfoot. Thus, as her mother would say, excused. At last, the only call that A-J comes to take herself, it is a deep-voiced man who says he is calling long-distance and sounds to me rather distraught. Such mystery is other people's business.

Anna-Joyce skids into the kitchen, she wears no shoes. Straight pins all around her collar, she speaks with the man in a series of small gusty exclamations. Someone is being made unhappy, apparently unfairly. There is a judge involved and his reputation for impartiality is impugned. A small wiry black teen-ager without a shirt looks into the room and Anna-Joyce holds up one finger to him to wait, she looks up at the sky imploringly, suggesting that she would rather be with him at the moment. She is mouthing words, cradling the phone and gesturing toward a pot on the crowded stove. Just as the young man, who has shining muscles in spite of his size, lifts all the lids and sniffs disapprovingly the contents of what appears to be a banquet, I say to him, suddenly apprehensive, "Are you by any chance Anthony?"

He looks at me sidelong and smiles that I should know this; as though it were a grand secret shared by all.

"Well, if you are, someone named Marie was looking for you."

"Where?"

"I am afraid she telephoned and I—"

"Fuck it," says Anthony most cheerfully, finding the cookie jar. "Let her look. I can't stand fat women." He disappears into the front of the house eating a Fig Newton. It must be the one great difference between people whether they can tolerate numbers of people coming and going in their midst. It appears to take a special metabolism which I decisively lack, and then on top of it, it appears to foster this breezy egocentric assumption that everyone knows everyone else or hang them all. "Well, they are my profession, one by one by one," is the way Anna-Joyce accounts for them always. "You figure, for every book or case or whatever you look at in a day, I have a person walking through."

Now she is saying on the phone, "I will, I will, I will, please promise me you won't worry." The poor worried man must be perjuring himself in answer, but she does not hang up until she is satisfied. "All right, Pat. Now please don't get yourself fouled up worrying about him, that'll make matters impossible." She grunts and puts one hand against her temple. "He is going to go out and get completely smashed now in the worst little neighborhood tavern he can find, where no one knows him with his big-deal reputation, and make sure his son ends up in jail."

Anna-Joyce looks straight through me with her clear, I should call them slightly prominent, gray eyes. She seems to me tired, her gray hair has slipped the barrette at her neck, her blouse collar is still studded with those pins. Undoubtedly she was up at five-thirty baking a necessary cake or stewing an indispensable chicken. She tilts her head a bit to hear into the front room. "They're necking in there, wouldn't you know it?"

"Who?"

"Anthony and Lily."

"Is that the boy she is going to marry? He seems so young—"

"Oh no," and she laughs at the very thought. "No, she's marrying a very large young man, absolutely a giant, named Jimbo, who's still up at the Tombs—down, I mean. No resemblance, he's very nearly white, one of these fellows with light green eyes? I'm convinced, Gerda, they're *the* most brilliant blacks there are, always look for the light eyes—he is an extraordinary con man who fleeced half of Brooklyn with a scheme about land speculation, he had all sorts of documents, you wouldn't have believed!—and they're even letting him get the marriage license in jail, and get his blood test and everything, I've fixed it, so that he will come out next Saturday morning and they will march straight to the church, non-stop, to be married."

"Before he gets into trouble again, I should think that would be a fine idea." I clear my throat, feeling rather cruel for such a remark. But I do wonder if things begin to lose their edge here after a while. Anna-Joyce spends a great deal of herself in the appreciation of what I should call raw material, as opposed to virtue or achievement, making the most, in her scarcity economy, of the only resource she can find. They lead her rather a race because of it: I believe they can intuit what she once told to me outright, that she condemns no one—only pushers, she said; only the ultimate witting corrupters of the young. Beyond that, Christlike, she forgives them all, she even appears to me to enjoy the occasions for her mercy. "Anna, you still go on living in a constant state of forgiveness, don't you?"

She looks at me with wide eyes, hurt. "Where does forgiveness enter in?" She peels a miniature pinkish banana, breaks it cleanly and offers me half. "It's not for me to forgive him—in addition to which I assume jail sentences, when they're just, as his was because he did steal a lot of money, no joke—but they're a way of paying back, aren't they? So he'll come out settled up, pretty nearly." She rattles her front teeth experimentally, muttering to see if they are about to break off into her banana. We are so young and beguiling, all of us. I believe Anna-Joyce was quite lovely as a girl, actually; I have seen a picture in which she has a quality of round-eyed forthrightness, a clarity that is a kind of beauty. She has always, judging by that picture, been the one who would not lie to you, take that or leave it; with her nearly comic earnestness any number of things you would just as soon not know will soon be wholly unfolded to you and perhaps to anyone else who may happen to attend to your business, for it is her conviction that purity, truth, honor can be so served. In comparison I, who feel rather more forward than many, appear to be calculating and small-eyed, dealing my tolerance here and my disapproval there on the niggling grounds of merit as opposed to love.

"No, I'm concerned much more with questions like what kind of husband he'll make for Lily."

"Well, what kind of wife shall she make if, truly you don't mean she is in there in the arms of that boy who—"

She shrugs. "Well, I don't know and I'm not about to tell you I approve. Only she's been there before and I'll be surprised if she isn't there again, everybody seems to like to kiss little Anthony, he must have some secret. He probably smells good or something."

laugh outright. I have a picture of all the girls lined
that shirtless young man and his catnip as though he
booth at a fair. "Anna-Joyce, what kind of goings-on are
allowing in your house these days?"

She does not answer that question but goes off for a moment in
thought. "Do you remember—" with a look so lyric on her face
that I know it is going to be a question about being a girl or a
bride or something that will embarrass both of us or make us sad
outright. I wonder if I would have disapproved of A-J as a girl; I
know she would have found me cheerless, what is the phrase I
once heard from a British friend, cheerless as a bed-sitter with
no tuppence for heat.

But there is noisy scuffling up in the parlor and the sound of
Lily's voice, which I am finally privileged to hear, a nasal whine,
shouting, "Serve you right, I got *pins* all over!"

"Today he must not smell so sweet." And I fold my hands.

But Anna-Joyce has left her youthful fancies behind. "Gerda,
you ought to be the one!" Her gray eyes blaze at me as though I
had aimed a bellows at her.

"The one to do just what?" Entanglements with A-J in this benign madhouse are not my sort of amusement.

"Pat who was on the phone—that's Pat Weirsma, who used to
be our lawyer here at the center, used to live on West End, a—I
don't know, a certain kind of courtly gentleman I truly loved. He
lives in Syracuse now, without any wife, she killed herself—it was
awful, you can't imagine, hung herself in the laundry room." Why
do all things sound faintly comic in A-J's unweighing Midwestern
voice? Singlehanded, she undoes tragedy by appearing not to comprehend it or to "let it get her down" when she does confront it.
"And now his son Danny is in just terrible terrible trouble." The
horrible facts with which my friend lives surrounded seem to surface as tiny islands of ineluctable seriousness in the ocean of her
volubility. I should find it strange to discover myself, sometime,
the object of her warm, slightly moist attention. Like Anthony's
kisses perhaps it smells sweet. Undoubtedly it would tickle at a
time when I was trying to be deadly serious. How can my daughter label me an optimist when there are in the world absolutely
non-principled ameliorators and continual uphill-walkers like

Anna-Joyce? "I don't quite know what Danny's problem is—are, I'm sure there's more than one. Oh dear, as fine-looking as any son you ever dreamed of having, and now there's this drug thing and he's just—sort of gone down the drain with all the others." She makes a gesture of dismissal with her hand, and shakes her short-haired terrier head. "Think how much of this you'd have seen if you were doing that judgeship business now, eight-year-olds hooked. . . ."

"And now, what is this about the judge?"

"Well, you know what's gone and happened, it's so inevitable. He and some of his wretched company began robbing, drugstores it must have been, and now he's on his way to jail. And his father a lawyer with an impeccable reputation."

I do indeed shake my head at the waste. Someone told me one time that I should be grateful my daughter is a few years older than these children who so automatically fling themselves half-asleep into the gaping mass grave of these poisons, these pills. It gapes so hugely it is apparently hard to avoid it, to be average seems insufficient, one must be specially equipped, and my Renata avoids nothing she can fall into for sheer slackness of will. I must say that I never thought to be grateful but perhaps I should have been: she could be dead or in prison, not merely lost and—limp. Sitting and watching soap operas is absolutely salubrious in comparison.

"But you see," Anna-Joyce is saying confidentially. "He can be gotten into one of these places, Odyssey, Marathon, Phoenix—"

"One of those marvelous-sounding houses named for the triumph of human will, yes—"

"Well, they are, you know, don't be snide now. I don't think it's easy to be a graduate of one of those places. Or if there is a special situation, someone he could live with away from his old friends, the judge has stipulated—this is, you know, quite frankly a favor to Pat Weirsma, he's a friend after all, a colleague, it's all been terribly embarrassing to everyone, and they worry about Pat too—I must say with reason." And she goes on about the lovely boy who is not rebellious and his suffering father who is not to blame. To hear her tell it the two of them are barely involved, it is two others who are in trouble. "And then," she finishes, breathless, "his sentence could be suspended."

She is smiling at me, her slightly crooked best. At the age of thirty-five I was put by some fool to read *Tom Sawyer*, whom I loathed for his complacent coyness, but here it is before me in the face of a seventy-year-old social worker. She is about to whitewash a fence Missouri-style. She runs a hand through her pepper-and-salt hair, her nervous mannerisms undoubtedly the only comb she ever has need of.

"And how long would this obligation be?"

She shrugs most innocently, which I take to be irresponsible under the circumstances. One would think this was all but a story she had stopped in to hear herself. "Two years at the most—that's the length of those programs, I think. Probably less."

"And what about your most famous house of influence here?" I ask, gesturing toward the parlor which is suspiciously quiet again, the obstacle of pins quite clearly overcome.

"Full up. You can't imagine—no vacancies. Anthony's in the guest room, don't ask me to explain, till he can go back to Birmingham, his family is in straits beyond belief, and Roger, you don't know him, is in Kevin's room" (Kevin being her one son, long gone to school and then to West Africa for some peace, I should venture). "There's a girl named Carmella sort of in and out—and that's all the beds we've got besides our own. I couldn't ask him to sleep on the sofa."

"But I—"

"But you."

"Have my hands full."

"But they are forever. Because you will not open them. And never full of people. With books. And correspondence. Let your secretary do it."

"Don't be simple-minded, Anna-Joyce. Shall I let my secretary do my life?"

"That's not simple at all. That's very complex. You have ideas and you love them, you love people, humankind, with too—too capital an H." She is looking all around her as though she will find the words for me walking around her table at lap level.

"Too capital an H. That is absurd. We have finished this con-

versation about your straw man years ago, I had thought. You
have positively a defective intellect."

"There is nothing wrong with my intellect, Gerda. If I'm not
mistaken it was Sartre who said that evil is making concrete
things abstract and—"

"I am certain Sartre has said a great many things, please not to
invoke geniuses who cannot be in attendance here. But there are
no such easy dichotomies as this one you make. If I were in a
movie yes, you would educate me, you and my daughter, you
would take me, roughly but kindly, yes? by the arm and escort me
through the underworld, the way I once so stupidly made a habit
of dragging her up through Harlem, the Lower East Side, and you
would make me bow, kneel—whatever—and admit that I have
been serving ghosts in the courts, changing one hypocrisy for another, while real people starve and die of overdoses, but this is
false, this is a Yahoo attitude, it is—"

"But Gerda," my friend says in a voice that would convince a
stranger we had been arguing now for two days without respite, "I
have nothing against the law, I think we all have to work side by
side on the same problems, don't think I wasn't delighted with
that ruling yesterday about affirmative action on mortgages, we
have a man who right now—"

I hold my head, quite literally. "Please may we try to keep on
one single subject, for sanity's poor sake."

She shakes the distractions out of her head like hair out of eyes.
"I'm sorry. Forgive me. I only mean that I am happy to have all
kinds of lawyers working on the same causes I am from another
direction, that's all well and good, but for your soul—the good of
your, Gerda's, soul"—which, judging by where she flattens her
hands and presses with great passion, is lodged in the bosom, far
back—"I wish you were not one of them. That's all."

This begins to anger me. "Anna-Joyce, I owe nothing to the
world that I do not give, you shall not make me guilty—"

"Of course you owe nothing." Her kindly voice, battering. "No
one does. Giving and owing are two different things. I can make
distinctions too." She bristles a bit, I know that A-J feels my perpetual condescension which (even in its muted, carefully
suppressed form) precisely matches her professorial husband's and

is perhaps one too many for her. One would never believe she has a degree from Vassar, she is so defensive. (As for her husband Hollis, he is a linguist who rarely deigns to listen to words as they appear in live, unmonitored mouths. He would hang meters from our tongues with our kind permission for the study of our adverbial clauses.)

The scene, here in this cluttered kitchen, is too much a, what is called a set-up, I feel my good judgment compromised here. I am to be overcome by the evidence of steaming teakettles, proletarian woodcuts, thriving plants, duplicate saltcellars. But I shall not be bullied into mistaking these for the only love there is. There is solitary love as well, painstaking and undemonstrative—why will no one let me have it without making public defense?

"Have you never heard the admonition to the shoemaker to stick to his last, Anna? You would like to push me into something, a commitment of great concern and energy for years at a time, and to a stranger, you realize—purely as a favor, and because it is convenient for you to have this matter dealt with. And so you will put me on the defensive."

"But haven't you always wanted a son, Gerda love?"

"Oh please." This is going too far. "Is this how desperate you are, that you will use this offensive psychiatry upon me? What I have wanted and what I have gotten I have long since settled up, just as you speak of the jail sentence of your giant groom, your emerging confidence man." At this I am prepared to leave Anna-Joyce's outright. "I suppose my daughter, your prime witness, has told you that as well? Because she has spent a lifetime despising some imaginary brother whom I have loved more?"

"Well, that's an interesting metaphor for your life, Gerda, a jail sentence. I hadn't thought . . ." But she stops herself and just as well. She lifts the depleted tea bag from my cup into her own and rises to get the water. Renata described the ungenerous point-shaving atmosphere of a courtroom; she is correct. This conversation has just that unresolvable tension, that parry and thrust of my day's work to it.

"You have never before been quite so—feline, Anna-Joyce." Because, you see, we are looking, both, at each other like aroused animals in a standoff. Our eyes are narrowed. Nothing, I see, nothing at all, no pain, no difference, is ever truly resolved, or even set aside; not too far away to be reached by a stretched-out arm when a weapon is needed. Scars pale but do not ever wholly vanish, one must know that and remember it. "I do not understand why we must be competitive about the dedication of our lives. Are we to spend our last moments, even when it comes to that, our deathbed moments, trying to convert each other?" Bless the Jews, I am thinking, and bless them well, my fathers, for being entirely repulsed by the idea of the proselyte. "Have I ever tried to make a lawyer out of you, Anna-Joyce? Come now."

She looks abashed, if that is the word, for one instant; then regrouping, raises her head in a clear challenge. "No, you don't think I'm smart enough. But that's quite all right, I imagine I can live very well without being a lawyer. What I worry about is how you can live without . . ." She dwindles off and stirs her tea.

"Ah, hearts and flowers, without people? Is that truly how I appear to you? Truly?" I have been attacked twice in one evening with the same weapon; I do not trust their testimony, Anna's or my daughter's, but I must feel myself incline toward some small humility in the breech. "Anna-Joyce. Again I go on record declaring that this is an absurd argument, the kind I thought only adolescents indulge: which is better, a—ballet dancer or a fan dancer? Your premises are wholly untenable. Do you attempt to take Hollis, who is a linguist, and make a jockey out of him, or a horse? Or a streetmonger with a cart? Where is the sense?"

She is stirring her tea round and round absently. I am astounded to see the woman listening, perhaps it is a skill she could develop were she often to sit in one place long enough.

"You see, there is a very veiled kind of bigotry in you against ideas. Principles. Abstractions. It is shocking but you believe that all I do is shuffle papers about, rather than hire myself out to live breathing people in trouble, whose problems are putting them in conflict with indefensible—why do you look at me as though I am digging for myself a deeper and deeper hole? Am I saying something terribly amusing to you?"

I feel that Anna-Joyce, in a kind of trance, her eyes fixed, is penetrating my face with some stern rocky accusation which goes far beyond this pettiness. I am judged and it is a wordless, reasonless, ultimate judgment; but unconvincing. My Kafka, what were his words to his diary, "Were you to come, invisible judgment!" But not in the form of Anna-Joyce's disapproval, surely . . . "Do you know, Anna, you act as though you are the world's only mother?"

She rocks a bit in her chair and puckers her mouth, nods her head. "Do I. The world's only mother?" She sighs deeply at my foolishness. "Gerda. You were a less than humane judge when you were doing that intervention business, did anyone ever convey that opinion to you? There were some people who were glad you were not a permanent judge." She has narrowed her eyes to deliver this blow, or not to see me clearly as I receive it.

I believe my heart has stopped with surprise more than with pain. "What do you know of what kind of judge I was."

"You had a reputation at least among my friends. You can be a very old-fashioned and stern moralist, you know. I had some friends who hoped they would go to court so they wouldn't have to be saved from it by your refereeing. The family court is the last resort of innocent children—"

"Or not so innocent, yes?" I am forced to say then, "Please not to look at me like that, I am not in the dock."

She runs her hands each up the other arm, briskly, like an athlete warming herself. "And you were not always their defender. You were harsh, you were punitive. If I had been a little child who came before you I'd never have seen behind your eyebrows. They never smiled when you smiled."

"So now I am to be held responsible for a lifetime of immobile eyebrows. No child ever cried in my office. Not once." Oh pitiable, to allow myself to be forced to such a defense. I blush with humiliation for having stooped to pick up the gauntlet.

"They were probably frozen stiff with terror. Let me ask you something. Do you like the people you defend?"

At which I explode in laughter. This woman is much less intelligent than I have been giving her credit for. "Like? Where does personal liking enter at any point into the legal profession? Or the medical, for that matter. Anna, you are a child at large in the world, a positive naïf in this, I am overcome. Tell me, and this is not even a proper analogy because the judicial system is precisely devoted to the cultivation of absolute objectivity—and that is an end I have never assumed for the profession, so-called profession, of social work. But tell me, do you like every young person who comes to shoot at the pool table in your community center? Or the older people? Those failures. Those harridan women and the boozy men, the deserters and child-beaters, the lazy or dishonest or whichever they may be or they would not in the first place need you? Do they come to you to have their characters approved or their difficulties assuaged?"

Anna is swiveling in her chair like a teen-ager on a soda shop stool. Her endless high-metabolism productivity becomes a twitch, suppressed. "Please, you make me dizzy doing that." I hold up my hand to her.

"There."

"What 'there'? If I am to be compelled to sit and look at you I should like to have you in one place, approximately."

"Gerda, if you could see yourself, the way you do things. You know, somebody who sees you on the tube" (How I hate that low-class expression, she picks up the tone of her young hoodlums as if it were a contagion, a social disease!) "said the other day, 'Good glory, she's so godalmighty earnest she would frighten a baby.'"

Do you know, I am beginning to wonder if there is a conspiracy tonight to undo my self-respect, to make it founder on pebbles and crumbs. Has my daughter put her on warning? "I have all my life done things as I do them now," I said to her stiffly as you may imagine. And? And, she might say now? And?

"Have you truly—now tell me this, think about it and tell me because I am in dead earnest and I'm deeply sorry about—everything. Gerda, have you ever, do you think, actually loved anybody?"

"There is that movie again, with violins swelling and big tympani sounding ominously. Anna-Joyce, how are we to have a conversation at this humiliating level? We are not fourteen years old, wondering what our capabilities for life shall be. Our lives are nearly over."

"Gerda?"

"Well, let me ask you then, wearily, the converse. Do you believe you can love everybody? Have you actually, whatever the word means to you and I quite frankly cannot even begin to imagine, have you loved all these hundreds and hundreds of people who have leaned upon you for one reason or another, or perhaps must you be asked the same inane question—loving all of them, have *you* loved any? Or do you love them merely because they need you?"

"Oh please. *Merely.*"

"Oh please." I echo mockingly. Well, where are we then? "What are you trying to do, Anna-Joyce McHugh? Since when do you deal with matters at this lofty abstract level, where words are degraded and mean nothing?"

"I do better on my hands and knees."

I nod. "You do. At the level of the concrete." That makes us smile. "But please. Seriously. Do leave the abstraction to me."

She sighs as I have done. This has been a discussion of sullying stupidity but I fear her point has nonetheless been made. I reject it but it has been made, alas, precisely as the prosecution makes insidious irrevocable points with a jury even while they are, technically, being overruled. I am apparently to stand accused of failure as woman, or wife, or mother, or judge; if not those, then at least I stand deprived of the friendship of this one woman. Ah, the universe is vast and may contain multitudes but either I am too narrow to hold within me this single friendship, or she is.

Why then, I wonder, should she wish upon me—upon him— the destiny, even on short-term loan, of this young man from Syracuse? Is he to instruct me in moral generosity, like the righteous poor in stories about spoiled princesses who serve, all unknowing, as teachers of humility and self-sacrifice? But no. While on the one hand I know she is a diabolical woman, a good witch making marriages, arranging new lives for her charges at their moments of desperation, even though I suspect her of many motives, of harboring her perpetual hidden agenda in the pocket of that red-checked mother hubbard she wears, still to be so she must also be one of those casual fixers who will often—arbitrary as a heavy wind—blow any two exigent objects together and see what shall happen. If she has a job and a fifteen-year-old boy opens the door to her community center, she combines the two and before he knows what has happened, aha, the boy is unloading boxes of borax for the bathroom or he is moving the pink and black up-

right piano with such bravado (however strained) one would think he had come just to volunteer her shoulders. She is promiscuous in her favors, demands, attentions. I have been told I do likewise, but it is in affairs that are not tangible; we should approve each other more than we do, if it is so.

"Why," I ask her carefully, having so determined that she is sloppy and arbitrary and that I had best take care, "do you wish me to take on this boy? You would very casually assign away his next two years."

"What boy?"

"Oh, Anna, you are irritating! The young addict from Syracuse."

"He's not an addict," she replies, imagine, testily. "No hard stuff. Pills. He was half asleep, apparently, and then speeding, then very down again. That's all."

"All right, I do not want the sublime details. Why should you entrust this fragile soul to me after this admission of affection and deep respect on your part. Tell me that."

Anna-Joyce looks more angry than pained but she will not be permitted to take back a bit of it. That much she shall pay for her honesty which makes her all alone feel so cleansed. Anyone who cannot keep her mouth shut is a fool; that is the first tenet of *my* business.

I am so pleased to see her rendered speechless. Anna-Joyce without words: like Gerda silent. An achievement for the two of us. "I don't know," she tells me. She looks rather battered and so, I am sure, do I. A tired kindergarten teacher in a gingham smock. How undignified. We are old ladies and the skin below our eyes is vulnerable to such cruel weather as we have just made. "I really don't know what possessed me. You're right."

"You don't know." So. Her honesty continues; she dangles me at the end of it.

Lily, the girl in the wedding dress, enters the room at the stage-perfect moment with a seam ripped and a veil of perspiration fallen across her shoulders. She sits wearily on a high kitchen stool.

"Gerda," says Anna-Joyce, herself smiling pain. "Smile. Laugh. Loosen your bones a little before it's too late."

"It always has been too late, Anna. And your encounter session is not about to change that. And so, my dear, the answer is an unequivocal 'no.' You shall have to riffle through your address book for another bad match. One would think you were trying to find a blind date for a dance the way you go about your matchmaking." She has no idea how near she has come to convincing me to take the boy on: one reason, had she given me one weak reason, even, for my surrogate motherhood other than my chance presence when she needed a live body, I'd have done it for her. But she is honest: I am not worthy of the match. She does not know what possessed her.

Hollis, her tall husband who has a wax-pink scalp and, when one is forced to touch them, extremely cold hands, pokes his head in, nods uninvitingly to me—even more jovial than I, you see!—and I have a sudden vision of Anna-Joyce and this man in their bed, wrestling for some pleasure all these years as did my husband and I. What must he make of her endless uncritical non-stop love? It must feel like a messy spill sucked up by the capillary action of the world, diffused everywhere. He is a critical man. Or has it been precisely what he has needed, has it alone kept his body temperature up to normal?

And so we make our stiff goodbyes and I go out, and when I am in the cold which withholds snow—the air is tight with it, ready to split its seam and spill forth—when I relax from the onslaught of words, I can begin to feel how I have very nearly been, as the phrase goes, with such contemporary forthrightness, had. How Anna-Joyce, wittingly or not, used upon me with skill the most blunt of instruments, this crowbar guilt. She ought to be convicted of breaking and entering. Or perhaps my daughter has prised me open with the dead fingers of this Alejandro, and A-J has merely leaped in, feet first, dragging this poor Danny behind he knows not where. She lies to herself and lies, a moral opportunist, until she actually believes her little rearrangements. Truly she tries to be a good witch, while I am here stuck with, tarred with, the role of stepmother. Is such dangerous desperate manipulation really to be called love? Such promiscuity? Anna-Joyce gives me no credit but I too live in the world, pulling apart its wings, separating it like chicken meat, dark and light, getting

my fingers messed and tangled in the strings that join the parts. Only sometimes do I think there is water pure enough for their cleansing; but surely, I do know this, the homemade soap of Anna-Joyce's kitchen shall do nothing, it has no grit, no grain, only color and perfume. It shall not avail.

Good Christ, I have come very close to having Renata arrested. Let her go and be turned inside out with the rest of the women. How in the name of heaven could a grown woman do such a thing as this? I return to the house after a very long resigned walk right into the open arms of danger—Riverside Drive, if you please, entirely deserted it is, and the feeling, the breathing of the invisible river strangely like a protection, an infinite safety, and solitude to the right in the silence of the buildings, villages of eyes and shoulders—and when I arrive at my apartment there is no one home but my granddaughter all alone, in her crib, trustingly, thank God, asleep, and a note on the table that declares

> TOOK YOUR ADVICE. PLEASE WATCH TIPPY
> FOR ME. IF SHE COUGHS, THERE'S SOME
> TRIAMINIC ON SINK—THE YELLOW GOO.
> DIRECTIONS ON LABEL. FORGIVE—MAMA—
> PLEASE. BACK WHENEVER.   R.

Insufficient. Mama, where does that come from? That unprecedented sentimentality. A child can get out of her crib. And the fires one reads about continually with such horror, unbelievable negligence that is never naïve—"Mother had gone down to store to buy a bottle of milk," "child was left unattended." There are no accidents.

I sit on my bed watching the baby sleep with her mouth slightly open, wheezing. She is uncomfortable, sweaty, her damp hair clings to her cheeks. This child is not receiving a full portion of parental love—it is not the absence of a father but the presence of a distracted mother, though what it is that so troubles Renata I fail to understand. She has health, intelligence, everything but what? Vigor? Enthusiasm? Concentration? The daring to interest herself in anything, to lose herself. She is what I should have to call devotedly, even passionately, empty. And I must admit this terrible suspicion that I have recently begun to have: I think she must have an involvement in drugs, which would account for this lethargy. How else to explain that sluggishness is her profession? That it is directed at me precisely as a suicide might be? I had not known we were to share but one life between us, so that the fuller mine is, the more empty hers. I fear this child would be well served rescued from its own mother and put in the care of a woman or an agency competent to give it an adult's undivided attention. She—dear God, my daughter—had best be advised to watch her pretty step.

Tippy stirs and coughs once, twice, a paroxysm that lifts her head from the pillow. Whimpering, asleep, she pulls herself up and stares blindly over the side of the crib. She calls for her mother.

"Grandma is here, dear." I come forth to assure her she is not alone. But she bounces and calls for Mommy, wails and kicks and punches at me when I bend to her gingerly. When I reach out to her, she pounds at my arm with both her rocky little fists and cries, "Don't want you, go way, don't want." Is this, must I suppose, the result of Renata's loving endorsement of Grandma as a witch, or would the child have arrived thus as an independent stranger? I leave her shrieking.

And it is craven but I do this. My stomach has begun again its cruel and unusual punishment, it leaps and bites, and I am again in a tremble as I was at the jail. This will not do.

I sit to steady myself and find my strength. Where in the world could Renata have gone to that could not have awaited my return? Is this baby a pawn to be offered up in our little battle? Granted I am impatient with the obsessions of others. I have only the one single passion which informs my life: order, some thirst for making the world conform to its best possibilities. It has made me possibly intolerant of certain weaknesses. I cannot personally comprehend, for example, a lust for possessions or—lust itself for that matter. Or drink. I recall the day perhaps twenty years ago I had to work with a man who was an alcoholic and I was forced to explain to him that it was not that I had no sympathy for him, but that I did not understand; there is a crucial difference. I sympathized in general, there are a certain number of points we are simply given as fellow humans—peremptory sympathies, let us call them. But shared feeling, empathy, which springs from some place deep in experience, not to be casually summoned or spent—that is a sadly different story. I did not have it for Howard Fitts, who, drunk, attacked a man and put out his eye, I could not find it anywhere within me to feel his passion, to be unmanned, relieved of the last vestige of good sense. Though of course I defended certain rights which remained his no matter toward what waste of his own life he would apply them. I did not have it for my father, who found his true depressive's passion behind the fan of a deck of cards. I would not have had it for the genial armed robber Anna-Joyce tried to wish upon me; nor do I feel it for my daughter wherever she may be, in the arms of a man or a drug tonight.

My granddaughter has hiccoughs. She is as lathered as a running horse, she flails in all directions almost comically, and intermittently she coughs. The snaps between upper and lower deck of her flowered pajamas gap and her tiny puffing stomach shows out a sheer white. I fear she shall be sick. When she begins to bang her lovely dark head against the slats on the far side of the crib, well out of my reach, I become angry and bark at her. But her mother barks more than enough. Distraction perhaps. What do I have for the distraction of a baby? I bring a dish of chocolate ice cream. She knocks it, directly, out of my hand and onto my knees, what would have been my lap had I been sitting cradling her. Does her mother give in more than she ought, or less? I must admit I have never taken notice. Which is the tyrant among them? She is by now in a rhythmic rock that moves the crib on its very legs as her head comes down on the anvil of the bars.

In time, apologizing silently to the neighbors, whose patience has already been worn overmuch by Tippy's presence, I simply close the door on her with a bilingual curse, and make my bed on the living room couch.

In the morning I wake confused because I am not in my bed. And when the memory of the previous night swamps me, I think, Ah no, she shall only be worse this morning.

But she is conciliatory. Whatever it may be that babies can think, she has thought, and come to her own terms with. They do appear to have more choices than we credit to them. I swing out of the bed and sit, feet flat, thinking blank morning thoughts, and hear clop-clopping in the bedroom. Her head again, banging to break upon some wall? But when I move quietly to stand in the doorway, there is Tippy trying to waltz in my shoes, and it is a merry sight. And a relief. She bobs and weaves, her toothpick ankles twisted as though they were on ice skates. Once she holds her hands together and attempts a Sonja Henie twirl that lands her on her diapered rear, but she makes a mean and valiant face, positively sets her teeth, and does it again, and then again. My kind of girl, Tippy, that is just what I would have done. I watch the set of her neck into her soft shoulders, a certain pitch of concentration in the bend of her head, and just so, she keeps her head inclined at that precise angle for three minutes at the least. I am spellbound. I do not remember her mother—I did not see her mother, I had not the leisure—at that age. Did she have a few minutes of deep immersion in the heel of a shoe, and what its holes are for, what one may stuff into them? I wonder if Tippy's concentration feels, from inside, like mine: a kind of—I am guessing—transcendental meditation, secular style, a modulating of all the body rhythms and urgencies? She rolls things in her hands, inspecting, learning their shapes and possibilities; she barely troubles to breathe. It is very pure, this attention, in a kind of suspension of air: like a baby's soft sleep.

In time the telephone intrudes. It always must. When I make a move to answer it, she looks coolly over her plump shoulder and sees me. There is an instant's recognition: oh, you are here. A critical up-and-down sweep of gaze, rather impartial. And, I suppose, an accommodation: be grateful that someone is here. Her acceptance, I am forced to realize, is something I could not have willed: a gift.

She is halfway through orange juice beside me at the table when she asks, casually I think, "Mama?" and when I say "We shall see her soon," she accepts it and sings into her glass and listens to the hollow sound smiling. Whether she is manipulative or accepting I shall not, for a long time, be able to tell.

Then I must face the question of where and whether to look for a someone who shall tend her while I am working. Another face?

This is not what she needs at this one calm juncture. I shall not reward her by leaving her. "Tippy," I say to her, nose to nose, which she enjoys, "we shall go out and buy some toys for you and then you will keep busy with them, yes? Can you do that?"

"Ya, ya, ya." She is pulling at my hand.

"But you must be dressed first. What do you wear?" For a child her age, I think she is dazzlingly smart, she finds clothes, albeit two undershirts and no shoes at all. We manage.

After our walk to the nearest five-and-dime, wherein she throws a minor tantrum precisely before each piece of equipment she covets, we go solemnly up in the elevator. She is standing very still with little fists before her, measuring—something. The air current? How different it is upon her skin in the closed elevator car? The sinking in her stomach as the car lurches up? I can imagine her sensing how every infinitesimal hair on her forearms moves with the different breezes. . . .

In the house she is on-again off-again, works as hard as I do for a while, then fidgets, wheedles, climbs on my lap, opens drawers, makes faces in the mirror. Her mouth is wide like mine. I allow her to take out all my shoes and handbags and she stays happily among them until lunch. She opens each and withdraws every tissue, every penny, and makes a circle of them, a fairy ring as though they are flowers. A good organized *kup*, head, much exuberance, and an unwillingness to take orders. I approve.

❀ ❀ ❀

I had the day at my dining room table in lieu of a desk. I shall admit to accomplishing none of my phone calls—what is the phrase, I have never understood it, I was woolgathering. (Am I too literal-minded or is not woolgathering work like any other?) What I did do, in my immense new distractibility, Tippy to my left, to my right, even beneath the table, was to see again and insistently again my daughter's absent face with a feeling of great but frustrated familiarity. Does she bring to mind my husband,

Henry? She does, but whether the resemblance plays on me secretly to her disadvantage, I do not know.

Why ever I married I shall never understand. Emma Goldman, rest her, told me that she considered marriage the legitimization in the name of our parents of all that can never be legitimized of passion and independence from them: a sop. Whatever it may have been for me, I cannot now reconstruct why it is I had to marry the man when I could have had of him precisely what I wanted—the slaking of curiosity more than thirst—without such ties.

Henry May was a most attractive and kind and unlikely man for me and it was his judgment that was as much at fault as mine in the entire episode. My own was for a short time suspended utterly.

I had been so late to law school, you know, that (being someone who does but one thing at a time) by the point when I came to men I was like those Irish farmers who must be thirty-five years of age and established on their land before they cast about for companionship. Yearly the applications had been sent forth to Harvard, which was the only place I wished to go, the impossible fortress whose broaching would at very least begin to approach making recompense. There was for me no question of "if," only of "when" they would tire of resisting. The first few times, I was merely too honest with them. Perhaps I was also self-righteous but I believe it was my air of claimant for old damages that most frightened them off, sex and religion merely the capstones on an impossible bargain. For what did I say but . . . "and if I am fortunate enough to be permitted entrance to the Harvard Law School I feel certain that I will do justice not so much to my sex or my race as to the entire earth-moving potential of the profession of law which I humbly seek to serve. I have, I think, seen considerably more of the world's inequities than many (having spent my childhood in a section of France painfully torn by differences too numerous to mention here, and all but unknown by the world at large) and I dream only of the opportunity to right the balance of justice some small degree in the direction of the hapless victims of greed and chauvinism." Can one blame the poor dean of admissions for fleeing before such a tidal wave of arrogance?

I would work on my application in the morning before I went to work. My legs would be drawn up under me in my bed and my sister Esther, who was in a thirty-girl typing pool and would not rise from her cot to prepare to leave for work one second earlier than she must, would toss restlessly as though my excitement glowed with a real light which disturbed her thinning sleep.

No fewer than four rejections taught me to keep my peace and my intentions to myself. I assumed by then that if anyone in the admissions office were possessed of so much as a crumb of memory they would recognize my name and reward my persistence without my making too much of a point of it. I simply said, "I have for five years, since college, worked as a bookkeeper and general factotum in a busy auditor's office, with responsibility at times for over twenty employees. I feel confident that my mind can handle detail, my concentration is well-developed, and my objectivity a skill I have cultivated with application. I think you will agree that these constitute the basic skills of an attorney." This is what my partner Loren would write of me today! It was the year of my acceptance.

And so I went off in my heavy gabardine overcoat to the nearly all-male sanctum, the genteel locker room and steam bath wherein we exercised and sweated the excess fat off our flabby minds. They were for the most part young men of houses already solid, which cast venerable shadows; as often as not they were busy crawling out of their lifelong expectations as avidly as I was crawling in. A few of them would have given all they owned—a considerable amount—to have fathers who worked in the iron mills. (Gambling fathers undoubtedly they had to excess, though no pinochle players among them.) I do not know that their tweed ranks were more rigidly closed against me than were the cashmere sweaters of Wellesley (where they had forgiven me my existence because the smartest "gel" must be forborne, but never loved my peculiarities —ambition, for example, and undistractibility; and not the least, an unfashionableness they took to be insulting, when it was in fact oblivious). I do believe I was more cruelly excluded by those lovely pearl-toothed, pearl-choked, pearl-naveled young ladies because I was theoretically, anatomically, one of them and yet was not and needed to be expelled by a kind of self-immune reaction, you know. The viciousness of the pack. "The narcissism of small differences." Ought there not, for certain purposes, to be more than the two sexes? The men of course had no institutions into which I could think of being invited, there was simply no precedent and no threat, and thus they did not exclude me so much as kindly go on about their business as though in my absence. And so they were no force against me, and I went on about mine. I was even then what Loren calls me today: a woman happy to have arrived where I wanted to be. *Shoyin. Basta.*

But I do well recall, at the end of my three years of utter absorption, wondering if there would be any end to the hunger, any satiety, and if there were if it would be a feeling of well-being or of bloat and uncustomary indulgence. I remember the night of graduation sitting in my mother's stifling kitchen. Her arthritis had kept her home from the ceremony; my father's dwindling vigor kept him home from the world in general. The linoleum was worn raw. Flayed by the mop just as my face had been flayed, for every *shabbos*. As was it all; it had taken a certain brutality to scrape the filth out of the grain of this place, this *eck* of the hallowed America. I had put myself through law school like a dog going through a window: as a salesclerk in a dark department store in Harvard Square called Appleton's. My professor of torts came upon me there one Saturday morning with his wife—he too being human, his educated fingers were running absently through the nap of an orange bath mat. The man was horrified. He could hardly meet my eyes. I do not believe he was ever able to address me in his class thereafter without visibly overcoming a deep distaste, as though on a flushed Saturday night he had met me on the streets of Scollay Square plying my trade.

All these years I had worked nightly at the chipped metal kitchen table, the light glaring in my parents' eyes as they tossed to sleep on the living room couch: centuries of learning had been mastered there, the clean knife of logic so carefully inserted between layers of filth and pulled out clean and radiant. As for me— nothing had come out, it had all gone in, I was stuffed and protruded with knowledge not yet assimilated. "Gerda, guarding her chastity with the lion of her tongue," one attractive impudent young man had told me when stiffly I had shaken his hand at that graduation game. Had he ever come to try me? "And how do you know such a thing, my friend?" I had demanded, called to attention after my years of intense concentration on obliterating, not encouraging, the differences between us.

"I've sat behind you in Proceedings," he said, "and I can tell by the way you hold your head." But he had walked away, leaving the question moot.

I sat at my scratched kitchen table waiting to feel some rush of hope, of conviction that I was finally there, at the place where one begins. It was the best I could do, to have got there at all, my own way, but the others had started long ago and thus we were not at the same place, nor ever would be. It was an illusion. I remember sitting with a burnt match in my fingers, turning it slowly, facet to facet, staring at the ash on my fingers, thinking, perhaps, mon ami, you have already had the flame, it was struck while you were committing to memory the twenty-nine exceptions to the rule of tenancy, and this now, smudge at the fingertips, shall be your portion.

Well. I had, at the top of Milk Street in one of the narrow corners of Beacon Hill, a badly paying place in the very WASP-British firm of Wadsworth, Wollward and Hyde, where I had the relative purity of my clerking years compromised daily by our attempts to protect and increase the holdings of wealthy men who were surviving the Depression. (There was, you know, a great deal of legal work to be done in those wretched years; no apple sellers among the possessors of divine wisdom: we warded off bankruptcy with our spells, when we did not outright suggest it, we put firms into receivership and pulled them out again, we took our words and with them made lassos to throw about the waists of men on rooftops, and hauled them in the window. The work was repugnant but I did not starve.)

And I had decided that I should move away from my parents' joyless spaceless deskless apartment and live at last—I was past thirty, after all—on my own. Esther, married by then to her good thick Ernest, pregnant with the second of her children, begged me to come to stay with them in Milton. Pioneers they were, out in the far reaches of *goyische* cow country where Ernest in fact drove a milk truck and longed to be a teller in the little brick mock Colonial bank in the town square.

But I truly lusted for solitude, for a chance to do my work at night and neither explain nor fail to explain; it is always, in company, the one or the other. And so I found a room in one of the tall narrow houses on the Hill, a rather sad gray affair at the forgotten end of its cobbled street, surrounded so closely by others that, shutters, gold knocker, and all, it appeared to front on an air shaft. That could not have concerned me less: I was rushed every minute of every day and it was formidably satisfying.

For reasons I shall never understand, the tweed-vested gentlemen at Wadsworth, Wollward and Hyde appeared to enjoy all my anomalies of sex and background. I believe they found me quaint, they laughed a good deal in my presence as though I were an upstairs maid with a special twist of Cockney they had never happened upon before. It took me all too many years to begin to wonder if they had their good and possibly corrupt reasons for wanting an employee who, in a sense, dared not enter the locker room of their personal dealings with them. I stayed out, on the far side of the threshold of WW & H's inner offices for what appeared to be obvious reasons of sex and social caste. They visited me in mine and sat rather too familiarly on my desk, smelling one of exquisite pipe tobacco and the other of a sort of metallic cigarette smoke which I have always associated with the sloppier class of shopgirls. Mr. Hyde, who was in fact the nephew of Mr. Wollward and the most pernicious kind of imbecile, the kind that does not wish to notice that his family is accommodating his witlessness because no one else will do so—that young Mr. Hyde attempted one day to seduce me after hours as though I were a common secretary, making absurd blandishments, promising gifts, sweetly averring that he could, undone by passion, overlook my being "a Jewess." But he had always preferred strange women, exotic types, this he confided in a daring whisper. I very nearly quit my job at that moment. I would like to have taken my desk full of papers and emptied it upon his defective head. But it was not a time for casual job hunting and so I had to content myself with a few words to the effect that he too was exotic: I had never before had the experience of conversing with a moron, not to mention a gentile one.

The house wherein I had rented my dark room was, I had decided, a kind of crypt which held only my bodily remains while my spirit lived elsewhere. It was owned by a French lady named Gabrielle Fanteuil who had the look of a music teacher or a high-class governess; someone vaguely rentable, though only to the better classes.

One evening, arriving late from work with a wretched dinner lying heavy on my stomach—it was the blight of eating non-kosher, which my reason resisted but which my body understood —I found a piece of fine pale blue stationery under my door, folded over. It looked as if it should have had a spot of sealing wax. MAY I, asked a spidery handwriting which had the same curlicues which I had been at pains to stifle all these years, REQUEST YOUR COMPANY AT A LITTLE SOCIAL HOUR. I AM IN THE MIDST OF PLANNING THIS FOR THE GOOD RESIDENTS OF MY APARTMENT. I SHOULD BE DELIGHTED IF YOU HAD A FEW MOMENTS TO SPARE ON THE EVENING OF SUNDAY, MARCH 11, FOR EACH OTHER. And it was signed illegibly G. Fanteuil.

Well, I was full of the intention to give every detail of this soiree, to which all the residents of the house went reluctantly, I suspect: the girl whom I had often seen *shlepping* a cello against the wind, how she sat at the edge of a delicate chair which I suddenly took to be a real Louis XVII, sign of a complicated past for Mme. Fanteuil. Gordon Chu Li, who had helped me down the hall when I came to live there, ceremoniously carrying my boxes of books and then standing against the open door as if he were waiting for a tip. How we sat and minced words, ate small crumbling cakes, could not relax in each other's coerced presence. But I shall instead go directly to the point: that there burst into the room finally a young man who radiated both chill and heat; he put me in mind of the occasional morning when you are under the blankets, cozily, but an ice wind has found its way in at the window and blowing over you tantalizes your face. He had been walking in the March chill, and his cheeks were very pink, spotted the way blonds are, but he himself looked warm and thoroughly at ease. He wore boots, like a Cossack's, and a grand dark coat out of Dostoyevsky, carrying cold in its folds. Something voluminous enough for Raskolnikov to hide in; but what a benign face he had.

"Mr. May—" and Mme. Fanteuil fluttered up out of her chair like a bird to do a discreet little mating dance before the young man. All her arms, her legs, her short dark discreet curls moved in tiny increments, and her petite nose, which sniffed at the dark outdoors he had dragged inside, was busy, busy. This was because Mr. May—a name simultaneously at cross-purposes with itself and with its owner—was indeed most delightful-looking, capacious, courteous-voiced, and sincerely regretful for having been so tardy. He was an actor, he explained to us—an actor in a city without theater (he patted his pocket sympathetically)—and therefore he was anybody's man. He hired out body and brain in return for the privilege of avoiding starvation, and today he had been rolling barrels of coal down half the alleys of Commonwealth Avenue. It was extraordinary to see the attention to which he had so unpretentiously called this roomful of strangers. I did not know what captivated them, or myself for that matter, but it was potent. I was not easily delivered over to handsome hulking young men who smiled with delight while they talked and who spoke in egregiously perfect Midwestern accents.

He talked, with much humorous self-mockery, to all at the one time, not for an instant to any one. He had been at Provincetown at O'Neill's playhouse, playing the most negligible character roles, usually drunken and unshaven, which in his case, being blond, meant two hours of making up for six unintelligible minutes on-stage. He was in Boston because of family obligations but spent all his time dreaming of Broadway and using his shoulders, and worse, to get along. At the word "worse," Mme. Fanteuil smiled amiably; I dare say she wished she had some spare change. At one point did this Henry May look at me, take me into the democratic circle of his gaze; then it swept past. I can only remember thinking that evening that it might be pleasant to be so pleasant, but that one must somehow have to be a child to look so charmingly and uncritically out upon the world, especially a world which did not appear to welcome his skills, however great or negligible they might be. I must have distrusted the trust he bore at the center of himself, the potential for contentment. Having chosen—having been endowed with the luck so to choose—to feel hurt at little the world had done to him, he was an innocent, and he made me feel entirely jaded.

And yet, and yet. This buoyant person accepted from me, from my fingers, in the kitchen, a clandestine nibble of M. Fanteuil's ham salad, which suddenly my kosher stomach did not reject. I was there to throw away the pieces of a broken wineglass, he was there—I do not know why. He asked me who I was, never having stood before or behind me on the bathroom line ("Oh, I never have to go," he had said, astounding me, "I'm sort of like a camel!"). We decided we were the phantoms of M. Fanteuil's, too busy to loiter and lounge. It was no wonder this meeting had the casual air of a conversation in passing, upon the subway platform or at the corner market counter. As I turned to leave the kitchen, though, he said to me something about dignity. Something like "You have the kind of weight I need onstage."

"This is not an American compliment, you know," I berated him. "Women are not admired here for their mass."

"Oh, I don't mean weight, pounds. I mean—sort of," and he bent his arms before him and made muscles; but apparently I was to see them as figurative. "Dignity. Solidity. I have a habit of floating around, I was a wrestler once, I even won a lot of money, but see, that's not the kind of strength I mean. I have trouble—" and he frowned, just the way children do when they wish to represent hard thought to their elders—"concentrating all my resources in one spot. Do you know what I mean?"

I believed I did. He took me to a play to show me an actor who did, it was Sir James Eades at Harvard, in Sanders Theatre, playing Richard III with a savagery that made Henry May's eyes glint with a fire built upon all the broken rinds and shards of a lifetime of unconsumed passions, which he could not find sufficient heat to kindle. Then he took me to see Maude D'Arcy, who was then at the height of her "allure," I believe was the word, most accurate, and how Henry denounced her for her easy charm. "There you see a non-existent woman, an invisible spirit. If you put a hummingbird in that hat"—which was feathered by at least a hundred nests—"it would come down harder on those boards.

Cleopatra!" He gnashed perfect teeth, teeth with complicated facets one demanded to touch, like marble, to understand: whiter than eggshell and shiny with the moistness of his busy, happy, generous mouth.

And what shall I say of where this Henry May took me and why—it is the chief bewilderment of my life. One evening, after perhaps three weeks of the most demanding theatrical education, he followed me into my room rather than, in his brotherly way, giving me a peck on my cheek and removing with great flamboyance his high shined boots at the door and pantomiming his way on tips of toes down the hall to his own end. We had met friends of his at the theater, had drunk white wine with them; they had tried to hypnotize me to make me laugh, Henry had introduced me as the *au pair* girl of his sister Ronda Juliette. I had, especially abetted by that wine, a distant sense that this was how other women went about feeling all the time, this strange weightless quality in which nothing mattered very much, in which almost any word could emerge from my mouth, the guard who sat stationed at my lips long since having gone to sleep. And my English, you know, becomes so easily irresponsible, I have the feeling it is the same phenomenon that would overtake your hand if you kept a clenched fist too long, so that when you opened the grip your fingers would tremble, they would drop things.

Now I can see that I accomplished then the same bargain with myself that I did when I leapt upon that doctor beneath the culvert, for Rosie Jo. One time, one episode—which in this case lasted perhaps a month, two at most. My curiosity was unbearable. The possibilities for change—a leap into everything I was not —were so palpable I could not endure it. I cannot calculate now which was the most intriguing freedom offered by Henry May: his body, of which I found myself dreaming, or his differentness from everyone in my life, which I found strangely touching. Something in his attentions flattered me but there too, was it that he wanted me, this journeyman body, these dull breasts I had lugged around forever uselessly; or that he wanted *my* differentness, my gravity alongside his buoyancy? And so I melted and then I froze, and thereafter the melting point was too high for any man to approach with his little candle. . . .

And so he vowed to take me to that place where I should not be burdened with a brain, only a great disintegration, a glorious splintering, and I was fascinated, I was cowed. The wine helped, and when I was sober the sense that I had to know to understand something crucial about the behavior of the world or I would be forever at sea. It was not for me, I assured myself: it was an inquiry so that I might know why women killed and men left families high and dry and the world went on generation upon lustful generation.

Let me not be graphic, let me only assert that in time, with much more effort than I would have deemed necessary, Henry made a toast to me, against the pillows, with a cheap champagne: I had become myself. An interesting conception of the self, is it not? Abdication. Beseechment. Helplessness. How pleased he was with his potency. If he never again found a job would I not be content to keep him like a courtesan? "What a marriage we're going to have, Gerda," he had said and kissed the cold tip of my nose. "We can do that every morning, every night, imagine, that's what marriage is for. There's a law that says that if we don't do that, if one of us refuses conjugal rights, no, duties—it's a duty, what we just did is a legal duty!—the other one could get a divorce. Did you ever imagine they would legislate that people had to keep a bomb in their bedrooms. That's what it is, babe—"

Perhaps. But it was not the kind of law I did. Oh dear poor Henry. Simple Henry. My episode of discovery was so quickly terminated and I felt toward him, thereafter, precisely as one feels in the aftermath of that gigantic neural explosion he had worked so hard for: numb. Incapable of arousal, emotional or intellectual. Physical, perhaps; I drank deep and guiltily, knowing he was to be my final lover. But this prolonged willed blind farewell made me all the more abject. And I discovered one picks oneself up, satiated, tidies one's hair, goes on, and returns eventually as hungry, as thirsty as ever. One is never truly finished. I contemplated a lifetime of thralldom to my body and his, and I was limp with shame. To be so needy, so easily desolated, to be so dependent— should I not have known that Gerda Stein would never want to live the life of a turtle on its back?

And so he was, he felt, should I say, abused by my withdrawal into the parts of our marriage which I thought could be conducted with that dignity to which he had originally been drawn in me. (Had he loved it only to master it, to strip me of it when he stripped me of my dresses, my suits of shoulder pads and shiny linings?) But I could not abide his friends: they preened, they compared publicity photos that amounted to perjury, they were petty and vain and hostile to anyone skilled enough to gain employment and thus bear public scrutiny. I could see that most of them, and perhaps my husband as well, were doomed to a life of demeaning stage-door pimping, and of insignificant roles when they did approach the stage. Henry was a far better soul—what is the line of Pound to the effect that honor in a man is only a partial virtue—yet sacred. . . . Sacred, necessary, but not sufficient, I must add, except in the abstract. I do not trust poems; no one has ever had to inhabit one. Put simply, I did not need my husband. I had loved his body and his triviality for a short season, but we did not serve each other's truest purposes.

So. We moved to New York City a month after our marriage. I had many reasons to want to remove myself there and Henry had great hopes that, if he were only working, I should somehow find again the respect I seemed to have lost for him. He found a job— he was a page in *Dr. Faustus*, a representative of the devil. He was a better actor than I had dared hope, indeed he bore more psychic weight than he had himself imagined, because all the complexities and deviousness of his part seemed to run counter to his sweet beaming farm boy's face—evil took him entirely by surprise, it seemed. Had he played Iago it would have been with an air of pained bewilderment as though he had indeed been seized by an alien brutal spirit and shaken into malignancy. At the same time, if one were not in such a generous frame of mind, there was something pathetic and absurd about this large healthy young man with his peaceful brow and honest nose whose eyes could not be cold or arrogant, attempting to appear the initiator of the most calculating depredations of the spirit. His dark parts, if such he possessed—does one trust all to Freud's pessimism?—were inaccessible. Size he had, unfilled contented spaces, but no force. Even his good men lacked the quality of will and complicity in their goodness. Perhaps I should have schooled myself to trust in natural goodness, in satisfaction born and raised and butter-fed. Perhaps I should have but I failed him.

Yet if I take into my most intimate chambers this diagnosis of Henry's innocence as a kind of vacuity, might I not be left with the hint that another man, a man of more mature or troubled spirit, might have had power to hold me? Less vulnerability. More charisma. Less infant need, more masculine depth, more command, more of a shared terror at the heights and depths into which our bodies and our minds thrust us? More darkness, let me say it; more darkness, less light. This good man was wasted on me.

As for our child. I cannot say I desired a child. Nor did he. But in that passivity to which I had allowed myself to be consigned, I deserved whatever was wished upon me, and babies are made even without anyone's wishing a thing: one must, vigorously, wish not to have one. Compulsive my whole life about the disposition of every soup can, every phone call returned, still I lay back in the fogs and mists of my—I still thought of it as temporary abdication, mere business between two consenting adults and thus without consequences other than moral (if those). He was desperate to impress me with his maturity, he thought it must be his impulsiveness that failed to satisfy me and so he loved to, shall we say, play the Frenchman, to amuse me and show himself master of himself. (I was twelve when we lived in France; he hardly brought back memories to me.) But you see he was no good at the game, victim and not master of his physiology. Hence Renata, her father's jest and failure; and are not his preoccupations, this dedication to the sensual, his legacy to her as well?

The discovery that I was bearing a child I had never willed and could not want—that was the blow that stood me upright and finished our marriage. Sad to say, I cannot deny that by the last, poor Henry had forgotten most of the lines of his best performance: he was, in bed, I should have to say a casualty of my rather focused indifference. I believe he sought solace elsewhere. At one point I even suspected he had brought home a mild disease (undoubtedly from some ingenue, or someone who played the virgin in *Measure for Measure*): he was in some pain and would not undress before me. But I was not any longer involved. I had had my honeymoon, my mind was in gear once more, I bore him neither love nor malice.

The last of it was when I was still in hospital with Renata Johanne. She cried when they brought her to me, and cried when they took her away, an irritable child. I pleaded with the doctor to stop my milk, which was staining me, staining my hopes to go back quickly to work where I belonged. He did so, with huge pink pills and then with an unforgivable medieval milk machine, but not before Henry came to visit his child. Then, seeing my night-gown wet with huge blooming flowers of milk, he bent his head and with a look of such intentness one would have thought he was actually setting down at last to work at something, he removed one strap and put his pink soft mouth to my dark and swollen nipple. His favorite place, the very seat of our marriage, of which nothing in the world corresponded for me, and it was actually full for him this once. I was afraid to slap him away from me though I shuddered with disgust; but imagine, I hated him with such extremity—I hated *him*—that by displacement I was certain that if I pulled away he would bite me till I bled. Such an agony of joy he suffered, there behind the closed curtains of this crowded room, I thought I should be sick. He suckled at that breast expertly—a breast my baby never saw—until with a moan of completion he had what he wanted, and I think I understood most clearly then why my dignity had attracted him as no chic or youthful bravado could have. My substance truly was, to him, an unthinkable dream; no wonder he had been so astonished that I had "saved" myself for him, a queer maternal virgin, a willing contradiction. So in all his sunny health in fact he had tasted flesh otherwise forbidden. He had always been content to see me busy around him, yet cared nothing for the details of my work. He had watched me go through those mysterious motions with as much awe as he must have brought to his own, the first and widowed Mrs. May, who ran a house and a small real estate business in Flint, Michigan, and addressed her son as Chickie.

Now in the hospital, flustered, on his knees thanking me, nearly in tears was Henry, and the nurse entered with Renata. He smiled his most disarming grin at her as he took the baby in her blanket, his mouth damp all around with my thin blue milk: a milk mustache, as children have. Had we stayed married (and he thought we would, he pleaded, I had stripped him that much of his own integrity and face-front, straight-up-and-down dignity) I wager he would have kept me pregnant like a cow had he needed to mount me in my sleep, so that he could have suck. Figuratively. Literally. I would have been undone. I would have been undone and so would he. I sent him away before I could hurt him more, to be healed. He tried, fitfully, to see his daughter, to bring presents to her, all things very pink, in the Flint, Michigan, style; better than Broadway, I must grant. But eventually I suppose he found for himself an Ophelia, a Cassandra, or perhaps only an Irene, and they made a sunny future for themselves. He had had his Gertrude and, just as it is written, we had made a bloody scene of it.

RENATA

The problem is, you can't fake it. "An interest in life." Men's bodies have interested me profoundly, but really the career possibilities are limited. I knew a girl with a Ph.D. who worked in a massage parlor but it turned out she was writing a book. I'm no poet. I'm not intuitive enough to do some social thing—and anyway, what's that but shuffling around responsibility for people? A game of hot potato. What would I do if I worked with Catalina, say? (With? "At" is more like it.) Refer her to an agency to help her "deal with her grief," explain to her why it's worth having kids and raising them and chancing the next day's pain? Or if I was a psychologist I referred her to, and she came, would I know? I suppose doctors who keep you alive have a sort of absolute good they do, but can you see me as a doctor, really? I know my limitations.

Who have the friends been that I've admired? I try that on myself, crossing Fifth Avenue near the library. A dark block—the park is just a missing hunk with a few chalky white lights. Leon there was—the kind of friend who gives you whatever you need when you need it, no questions, no obligations: sympathy, sex, beer and laughs—and then goes back to himself and his work and leaves behind no garbage—emotional garbage, I mean. A crumbless, stainless bed that stays warm a long time. He'll never belong to anyone. What Leon went back to—he lived in the Mission District in San Francisco as far from the Haight as he could get, so that he could do his work—what he loved as he loved no one, and just as well, there are lots of so-so lovers in the world but not enough artists—was the most beautiful silver jewelry I've ever seen. It was linked stuff, heavy as chains, I told him it looked like medieval torture equipment, only the metal is buttery-looking, it would be kind to your wrists and ankles. Every time he finished a piece he brought it over and I got to watch him smile on it. That was a nice sight. He had a lot of black hair and a huge doggy mustache and a face that went horizontal instead of vertical. He'd hold the bracelet or ring or whatever it happened to be in the palm of his large hand, but very loosely, as though to give it room to jump out if it wanted to, and he'd settle his shoulders down, his jowls down, his big clumpy boots down, and sort of breathe gentle satisfaction over the jewelry. A blessing. I think he softened the silver by talking to it when he worked, like a father to his child. His face moved the way cellists' faces do, all the inhibited action and the suppressed singing coming out at the cheeks and eyebrows.

There was Miriam who made pots shaped like real objects—matchboxes, cans and baking soda tins, huge stone clothespins. She was like Dickens, her stuff made her laugh and cry. And Jasmine Warren, a dancer I met at a Muni stop on Market Street, who was so often "between jobs" and filling in at a typewriter at NBC that she was in their goddamn pension plan. Once I gave her a lovely glass hash pipe just to remind her which side she was on. Jasmine I liked because she was straight and clean, somehow, without being priggish: very Midwestern but nothing fazed her, none of the shenanigans of the do-nothings I hung out with. Only in the end she sank back into the ordinary again, she married a space salesman, or time salesman, or whatever the hell they do with ads on television, and I saw that the dancing had been *her* craziness, she didn't need the rest of our insanities to feel free. To have left Butte, Montana, to be a failed dancer was insane enough.

But none of them, none, felt this lethargy when they wondered what they were going to do tomorrow. Defeat. I'm a case for a Forty-second Street movie, maybe I ought to be on screen and not in the audience: wearing a black band across my five-pound breasts on the sign out front. I stand on the curbstone, swaying with indecision; fifty of your typically urgent, bent-at-the-waist New Yorkers stand around me ready to beat the light for the sake of beating it. I am a rock and they wash all around me like water in its bed. I sway a little against an overcoat with a man inside, who smiles, wonders if I'm inviting him. That opiate, that oblivion—I think the only time I know where I'm going and I'm sure that *this* will lead to *this* and then inevitably to *that,* is at that first touch of a hand to my hip or a warm mouth to the side of my head: an arrow leading home. Certainty, Mama. You are ballasted by the goddamn constitution and I by the nerve switches in my body opening and closing. Laws of nature! Each to her own, as you like to say.

Actually I don't want any more friends. Dolores was my last friend, fat amiable Dolores like a pill-soaked slow-moving Rubens. The long baggy dresses and endless incoherent earrings tugging her thick lobes down. Dolores patient with women and men in equal numbers. Each new love glowed for a while on her pale cheeks. I lived with her awhile in San Francisco one summer, we walked around naked all the time, me a scrawny chicken, all my bones showing, Dolores a sort of live and moving bowl of risen dough, boundless curves, flesh penetrable anywhere by anything: if you poked her with a finger she'd hold the shadow. Till the day I woke up and found her with one hand on me here and one there. No anger, I understood her, how it all flows together for her, even her syllables moist in that loose mouth. Half out on her uppers and downers, rounders, flatteners, sharpeners, if you shouted orders to her she'd blink like a cat at a candle flame and smile vaguely and do it, just about anything. No conflict of edges, unmuscular, unresistant. She lay there next to me and I looked at her breasts, how they flowed off under her arms, leaving this great blank in the middle. She closed her eyes in a preparation for ecstasy that made me laugh out loud. I tried to explain, I liked women, looking at them, we had such wonderful variations and I was glad for all of us in our bodies, but men were really enough to keep me busy and happy.

"Not happy, Renata, since when are you happy?"

"Happy enough. Busy enough."

"Try," she said. "Look how you can hide in me. Look." She rolled to me. I could always use another hiding place. I tried. I tried. It was too easy, though, like loving myself. I like hard edges, I decided. Sharpness. Intrusion. Otherness. If you're empty inside, you want to be filled . . . could that be it? People have said profound things on the subject, battles have raged, all that goes on in another world. In my own world it meant she wasn't enough for me, she was soft and essentially gentle and I didn't want to kiss those upholstered breasts, I felt absurd when I tried. But I couldn't really make her understand that I had preferences: she didn't make choices.

The only decisions Dolores had to make she let the I Ching make for her; she went nowhere under her own power. I admit it, when I was deciding to leave Joe and come home I told Dolores and she offered to come and throw the Ching for me. "But I think I've already decided to go." "Doesn't matter," she said. "This will say what to expect."

She came with her yarrow stalks, her lovely rough green-gray pickup sticks. We sat down on the dirty rug like kids with a handful of jacks, only this kid was nursing her baby. She did her elaborate counting with her head bent over, grave as a child. Her profile was made of soap, someday she would just melt, float off and be gone. . . . Her lips moved without sound as she doled the piles and when she was finished and looked at me she had to refocus her eyes. They came in to rest on my eyes as though they'd been let out on a long long string and were drifting back to a heavy center.

She shook her head, rocking a little.

"What?"

"Oh dear, Renata. Shit. There's no way out of that." Her simple little girl's voice. In spite of all her folds of flesh, she has no pockets to hold, let alone hide, a single thing.

"I thought this thing helped you make choices."

She shook out her hair and put her fingers wearily in the inside corners of her eyes, thumb and index, where she leaned on them. She was upset.

"Some of the choices have been made, that's all," she said gently and ran her finger slowly up and down the margin of the book, stroking it absently, thinking, she must have been thinking, poor Renata.

"Well, should I not go? Is that what it means? Don't play with me, Dolores."

"I don't know what it means that way, hon. It only says losses, terrible losses. Your cow, your house."

"Shit, I don't have a cow and I don't have a house."

"Of course you don't. It doesn't really mean that."

"Well, I've got plenty of losses here. This fucker I'm living with cuts out my heart and sucks it for breakfast."

"Fine. Then you made your decision a long time ago."

"But what does this thing mean?"

Dolores shook her pale curls at me. She patted Tippy's bald head absently and then gathered up her yarrow stalks and said goodbye.

I'm on the traffic island at Thirty-third and Broadway. Gimbel's behind me, those hedges of fence down the middle. When I was little, shopping in those stores, Gimbel's and Klein's with their wooden floors, it was like taking medicine.

I can't. I hate this kind of coward I've become. *Is this a vocational problem?* I must look drunk. I was taught to despise healthy people who waste their possibilities. Cars going by like horses in a stampede, tempting: if you lose a foot what do they expect you to do with yourself? Your life. Do you get to lie down or do they expect to see you up and around and overcompensating? If I lose a foot I'll become Queen of the Work Force on sheer rage and pain and because no one will expect it of me. *Ingrate* was the big word in my childhood. Better to be sick and poor and helpless than fine and well and helpless. . . . Saturday morning in the museum with Mother, holding onto her coat in the crowd. The title of every photograph read out dutifully and explained: "This one is *Child Labor*, 1902—you see, these machines here are being run by little children, smaller even than you. Can you imagine that? They spend all day every day and sometimes the night too in this dark hot loft for only a few pennies. Look, here's mother and daughter, oh, a miner's family. And here, an out-of-work miner." My mother crouched to read it, then straightened squinting. They were a terrible pair, not as dirty as you'd expect, and the house behind them, what you could see of the little porch, was clean as new laundry. But their eyes looked as though they'd been eaten out by insects who couldn't take the sockets; they were cups full of shadow.

My mother's face had that distraught flush she wore when she was waking to some outrage. "They look like they don't get enough sleep," I said. I stared at the picture desperate to figure out what I was supposed to be seeing. That the girl had a neck of braided string? That the mother had the kind of nose I'd seen at Aunt Esther's funeral, or not the nose so much as the face sunk around it so that it was big and pointy in a funny new way, and the mouth like a badly taken seam? What was the right answer?

"What?" my mother asked, leaning down. I swallowed hard and pretended great interest in the next set of pictures which showed the porches of old country stores stuck all over with Coca-Cola signs and a woman's face three times over with a sickly smile and the word CAMEL coming out of her mouth. "Here is the bed of the Biloxi fisherman." His pillow was like a rock in a deep sea of porcelain and old lace, hard in the midst of soft hearts and tin medals, a churchful of crosses. Mother was making a distinct "tsk" over and over again, without explaining why. I was trying. Was it the crosses, did she find it pathetic or disgraceful that somebody would live all surrounded that way with a religion she didn't approve of? But what was Biloxi? A kind of fish? There in the next picture was the iron bed (flies on the clean blanket) of a sharecropper whose ornament—the only one—was a gun high on the wall in Alabama, shining.

There were people jostling us on all sides, Mother guided me by the shoulders of my coat, which I had stubbornly refused to carry: I was always refusing to be comfortable, making her threaten me with my own best welfare. The last photograph in the gallery up nearest the archway to the next room was a small one. There was dirt, all crumbly and dry, and set into a mound of it was a toy tea set, cups and saucers neatly arranged, a Coca-Cola bottle at the same angle a feather would take on a lady's hat, and a milk bottle with a few inches of scummy rain water standing in it. There was a large stone, a few feet down the tilting mound a small stone, and in the headstone the unclear picture of a baby. The baby dead? Or sleeping? She was overwhelmed by a white dress which had spring and life to it: probably stiff as a thornbush. Her head was a small rock totally still and heavy, just leaning forward, about to tumble. On the stone the words were carved by such bright unobstructed sunlight they were easy to read:

We can't have all things to please us,
Our little Daughter, Joe An, has gone to Jesus.

My mother gasped, that's what I remember, and put her hand to her mouth. I took her other hand and held it. I was embarrassed with all these people milling around; she just stood there stricken. I tugged experimentally at the hand I had but my mother turned and gave me a blind warning look. I pulled away and stood looking at the picture over my mother's stiffened shoulder.

It was a pretty stupid kind of grave, I thought, but the stupider and stranger and farther from home, the more my mother would stand and sigh. If I was in that grave what would it mean? But some stranger who's poor enough to have snot on her nose. I stood in the flow of traffic and was cuffed with overcoats and umbrellas but my mother was still stuck, her head at a pained angle. Was she trying to touch the grave in her head? To see all the way down into the dirt, to lift the child out of there with her love? (Is it any wonder I thought I could bring her Alejandro newly dead and have her *do* something about it? "So what you really want is someone to bring him back alive?" she said to me.) In the museum I tried to muster up a few tears to contribute, she'd have been pleased if I could do that, but it was worse than trying to pee when there was nothing there.

It's Thursday night and the shoppers are on Thirty-fourth Street. The marathon runners. Two giggling teen-agers in jeans so tight they make mine look baggy; wedgies so high you can watch their ankles wobble, asking for it. A girl in a good obedient plaid coat, hair made tolerable on Saturday mornings by her hairdresser. *True Love* under the dryer, and every other week a manicure. Next year she'll marry the office manager, now they're still necking in his car parked under a tree in Flatbush. Next year the honeymoon at a couples resort in the Poconos. Should I envy her? Instead of the bridal suite I think of the places I've been to—is it all the same? Do I have a handful of anything left, or does none of it last, hers or mine?

It is not a vocational problem. When was the last thought I had that was useful? Impersonal? Catalina. Alejandro's face was stiff but now it's softening. Imagine Catalina thinking of his face. That poem, what was it about the child in a fire—after the first death they are all—there are no others? After Mother's death I'll be ready for anything. A voice behind me, half-whisper, and I turn to the smoothest cat in a dark red suit, with blue and white lapels. The bloody American flag. I wonder what it's ever done for him. He has a flat-out konk that makes my head hurt. "Hey, little sister." I must have turned shameful eyes on him. He takes my arm and leads me into a dark store entrance, looks into my face for something. "I'm going to kill myself." I think I said that. I may only have thought it. "Ah no," he answers gently, though, so I must have said something. "Beautiful girl like you, what you want to lay a hand on yourself for?" I smile blankly. Dreaming. He lays his hands on me, right there, under my coat, cold hands. Not taking me anywhere, just obliging the both of us a minute. He presses one dark red thigh between my legs. Why does he keep his eye over his shoulder? Somehow he gets bare hands on one bare breast under my shirt, wakes one nipple right on Thirty-fourth Street while the girls up the block at Ohrbach's are chastely keeping their underwear covered in the dressing rooms. I want to tell him that nipple's bent all out of shape, Tippy did it. "A little life in you yet, sister, say you won't do yourself no harm." I keep smiling. He thinks I'm high. He fingers my hair, lifts it high over one ear and drops it strand by strand. "Not enough little blondes in the world, honey, you take care of it." He whispers under my hair, "Blondes all I take to bed these days, know that? Mmm, blond all over I bet." I lean heavily on him, I'll go anywhere, lie down, to rest under the certainty, the only thing I know, then sleep. But he's dragging something out of his pocket. Yes, yes, he's got a fucking camera to sell. "Ten bucks for you, hon." His words are hot in my ear. "For me?" He jiggles the camera. "Give it to somebody, he take a picture how pretty you be." A funky Dale Carnegie, Jesus, I must be going crazy. He stuffs the camera in my hand in a paper grocery bag with an oil stain on it.

A couple of hundred bucks' worth of machine, poor bastard. I'd like to smash it against his shiny head, but I'm not strong, I push the camera back to him, we look like a couple who wants to pay each other's dinner bill. Finally he shakes his head and walks away fast. A cop with a pink and white face goes by, looking me over with his jaw set, just wondering.

So I walk and walk, afraid to stop again. There aren't any benches to sit down on in this city. When I get tired I have to go down the escalator at Port Authority and hoist myself up onto the first bus I can find, parked in its angled bay. It's nearly empty except for a few disheveled sleepers. I think it's headed for Morristown, New Jersey, or Morrisville, Delaware, or something like that. I don't want to go home and I don't want to disappear forever, so I sit down and I lean back and pretend to rest, but everything's going inside me, my motor could run the damn bus. When I close my eyes I see bubbles dancing, a shadowy pink and blue passing in and out of the blackness. They look like what I used to see on slides of flowers and hacked-open seeds under my microscope in college botany. God, I remember how my teacher used to terrify me, my freshman year, by telling me I had talent. "You move around among the works in here with comfort, did you know that?" The works. Good Christ, I said to Duffy, save me.

But I liked the lab, that was my nasty secret. If I let myself like it too much I'd be Dr. C. L. Johannsen before I knew it, with her chapped cheeks and her short fingernails. Or if not that, then off somewhere alone, my own mother. (My history professor had written a book in which some of my mother's cases figured, he had been to talk to her, he made me writhe in class listening to the respect and the significance, that was the word, everything about her was significant, he wasn't the least embarrassed to gush on about her, and he simply assumed I was going to law school; divine right demanded it. Shit.) But why not be the first beautiful botanist on your block? Buried in a white lab coat, my hair shorn like a nun's with no wimple to cover it. I leaned over the microscope to see a cross section. (Can you see angels on the head of a pin? Can you see bubbles? Don't be afraid to look into these deep hidden kingdoms, *Ranunculus, Allium cepa, pedidipulae*

188

caniaster, Dr. Johannsen said in her first three minutes of class, with a ripple of sensual innuendo. Who knows what evil lurks in the heart of a buttercup?) And I could see them perfectly, the nuclei danced for me in their garden borders and I drew them beautifully with a set of colored pencils, a near flunk-out from Music and Art with all my talent still rolled up in my trick hand. Bubbles was right, they were a world of unrepeatable bubbles, or sunflowers maybe, that multiplied but never broke, and I always had the focus right. My friend Duffy was going out of her mind, in tears, slamming notebooks around, because her glasses made it hard to focus and her mirror always played at the wrong angle. But I didn't want to be good at it, Jesus, I remember what a drag it was to watch that scrawny woman in her lab coat admiring me all the way from the big sink up front, calling on me to document the treasures I'd brought up from the depths of the onion skin. Why did she matter to me, why weren't the lovely undersea sights enough for me? If I'd chosen then and there, why did I think I'd have a career in being Dr. Johannsen and not in doing botany? All I remember of the rest of that semester was going up and down the dark steps to Giuseppe's apartment. Eventually I guess Dr. C. L. Johannsen got what must have been the point.

I close my eyes on the bubbles again, queer pale colors that turn bright when I move my head toward the little bus-light. I feel like I'm high on something, just hovering over a real pit. The bubbles are like dye spots on dark cloth. You know what I'd really like to do? If I could close my eyes and have a wish come true? I'd like to have a tie-dye store. Really. When I was in San Francisco I thought about it but it took too much—sort of straightening up. Dolores and I used to do all our old clothes in pots of color, we'd do great sunspots, all in primary, kindergarten reds and yellows, or deep purples, like angry flower hearts you could go down into and be trapped in forever. The extraordinary thing about the designs is how they repeat and repeat but never more precisely than ripples in water; you can't count on them. You know what you're making, more or less, when you fold the silk or the simple crude muslin, and you mix the dyes to make the depth of color you want. But then—you're not a painter holding a brush in your hand, you know, controlling it, making it go; you're trusting to chance and—

well, it's not approximation, it's a sort of *half* control. It's like a natural phenomenon and it gives you feather marks or footprints or wind stripes—all of it a gift, a shock to unfold. I'd have a big shop, wide open like a loft, with all these gorgeous dreams hanging up like banners, and people could buy them as is, or they could just buy a big hunk of sheet from me and tie on a smock and I'd show them how to use the dyes and give them ropes and rubber bands and they could flabbergast themselves! Like little kids forever. Make great bloody messes or tiny precise folded-up margin notes and spider webs, and they could pay me a little just to keep me in fabric and colors. Why not? I could get a cheap place somewhere—some part of the city where people walk slower than they do on shopping night around Macy's, so they'd have some time to come in and feast and groove on themselves and their inside colors. And I'd get a great name. What? I'd have a contest for a name. Living and Dyeing? Or Dip and Dye, something like that. Cowards dye a thousand times, there's so much to get off on! I think the idea brings out the best in me. I'd need to be staked a little till I could begin to make something out of it, and then—well, that's the end of it, right? It begins to seep away and the idea dries pale and wrinkled. Who would stake me? Who in the world? If I go to my mother with a half-assed kid's idea like this . . . a laugh. When will you grow up, Renata, remember your projects when you were seven? You were going to build a circus in the apartment house lobby. You were going into the fudge business. You were taking out a patent on every other daydream. . . . A laugh, a laugh. Can't you hear her?

A young man is sitting right across from me in the deserted bus. He cocks a finger at me, smiling with no teeth showing. I know what he wants to do with it, no one will see. Maybe this is the bus Portnoy was so busy in, the Portnoy Memorial Seat with its vintage collection of gism, all that fantasy turning to real unstoppable juice that oils the leather. "Get lost," I hiss and turn my body toward the window. He has a sharp nose, mean eyes, he looks cheated. Have I promised him something in my sleep? "I'll scream," I tell him quietly and he looks all around as he moves down the aisle and scrunches up to a dark window near the driver's seat. Why in the hell would he want me anyway? I'm all out at the seams, it's all disheveled, everything. Did Alejandro have a chance to get to know a girl, a woman? Catalina would say no, no matter what. Imagine my mother helpless on her back getting me.

All day I'm busy, bus after bus. I choose them carefully as though I'm going somewhere. I sleep, I walk in shopping centers, I think, in three or four contiguous states. The morning drags, I check my watch every ten minutes and we haven't moved. Then the afternoon speeds right past me. There's nothing I want, that's clear. Once I thought Tippy was autistic but it's me: no will, no need to move my arm, my leg, my lungs. Looking in windows, seeing mannequins, seeing handsome boys with obedient short hair, with ponytails in rubber bands, with baseball hats, and unzipped parkas, seeing children and glass reflections of myself under a cloud of wild white hair, there's nothing in the world I want. Spilled dye, wet muslin, there's a life. I see myself spread-eagled on a sheet, right in the middle of a huge blue and purple rose, inflamed flower the color of a bruise, waiting, open, for something. I doze before I can see what it is.

When it begins to get dark and the sky is an unfriendly snow-gray I've had enough, and I go find a cop. "You better take me home, get somebody to take me, I'm going to walk into a truck or something, I'm sick." He asks me a dozen questions, one stupider than the next. I feel like I'm waking up from a thousand pills. Coming back into focus slowly, surfacing. I feel the way a print must feel in the darkroom, bobbing up in the developer, taking shape. I'm coming together again out of darkness and shadow; then into light. Into sharpness.

I only ask him where we are. New Jersey, that's all I've managed in all this shuffling. He calls in on his whosy-whatsis and gets somebody to come for me. I won't get into the cruiser until he promises me he won't tell my mother. "I did this once before," I tell him and cover my face like the criminals you see in the newspaper leaving the courthouse.

GERDA

I am at this moment, while this baby paddles around me turning her ankles in my shoes, preparing a brief for the Supreme Court. Wonderful incongruity. At one time in my life I should have been desperate and distracted if I were not alone: I am learning some new tricks. But by now this work is almost routine. One does find that preparation for the oral argument eats up a colossal amount of time. No cut corners. Once and only once have I allowed myself the luxury of suicidal impulses the morning after, when they caught me utterly unprepared on one entire arm of a case, a wing as it were, a jurisdictional question to which I'd given not a thought. The shame in that discovery—it could be no worse for a surgeon to discover that he has brought the wrong knives and scalpels while the patient faints upon the table. Well, suicide is considerably too kind for anyone humiliated twice, so I am now extremely cautious: I do homework and homework and more homework. The world narrows to a point and I swim slowly and evenly toward it: a thesis and the full support thereof.

The more impatient I am with the case, and the less in love with the technicalities on which I used to sharpen my teeth gladly, the less will I brook interruption. Time is running out and I am dyspeptic, and the brief must go to the printer's. Tippy appears to understand something of my seriousness. Or she possesses her own.

But the phone rings. My secretary has told Catalina Huerta where she may find me. "Yes," I say, continuing to copy out citation page numbers. She is shy of the telephone, I should guess it is rather a face-to-face life she lives. She abounds in guilty silences. I have many uses for silence on the phone, quite frankly, however few I may have for it in the rest of my dealings: it is the single most persuasive instrument I know for making people leap into the breach and tell you everything you wish to know, and more, or make fools of themselves, hence delivering themselves up to your mercy without a self-indicting word from you. But Mrs. Huerta introduces herself as though she has never set foot inside my house, let alone swabbed down my bathtub. She would never be able to imagine the family crisis she has occasioned.

But in fact she does, in her way. This time indeed the silence renders me the uncomfortable one. I put down my pen. May one ask a bereaved mother how she is, *azoi?* There would seem to be a regrettable casualness in such a question. And so, rather irrelevantly, feeling just as must my victims in the web of silence, I ask if she and Renata got home satisfactorily yesterday.

"Well, Renata got hit by a cab almost," she tells me—a wonder I was spared the details last night, let alone the responsibility— "and she wants to, you know, put in a charge—what do you call it, a citizen's arrest, against the driver, she got his license and all."

"Renata appears to be in rather a litigious mood these days."

Again an awkward silence. This time I shall not crumble.

"Look," she begins, "Mrs. Stein. I'm sorry we took up your time yesterday, I only wanted to tell you it's Renata that's upset, not me. I got enough already, you know? I don't get nothing I need out of courts and papers and this and that, what I lost. You know what I lost. . . ." She dwindles off to a full stop. "I got to tell you just one more thing, Mrs. Stein. No, two things. One"— her voice folds in the middle, nearly Talmudic in its scrupulous separations—"is Renata. I—she got so upset about this thing with Alejandro, I don't know—I mean, he died and anybody that ever knew him would cry about that, even if you didn't." A modest sigh. "You know what I mean. Only see, I told her what happened, you know, and I didn't have nobody I could go to and she, you should have heard her shouting and cursing, she says, 'Why you couldn't call me? Why you don't trust me all of a sudden, and my mother she's a lawyer, she could help.' I mean, I don't even know her except to talk a little sometimes. So you know—" And her voice is confidential as though I will share her view of the unseemliness of Renata's behavior—"so I say no, it ain't trust, I didn't think of you is all. I'm not going to apologize, I mean I like her and she like me but I'm—you know." The polisher of your sink, my dear, the duster under your bed. Her connections are her connections. A certain distance only the arrogant can forget. Quite right. I respect Mrs. Huerta for understanding, with the wisdom of the seller, just what it is Renata and I have bought of her and no more. Who sat to talk and who wiped mirrors and polished the stove during their "intimate" conversations? Carlotta and I, all those years, saw the glass wall and never flew headlong against it, we indulged none of that absolutely hypocritical "closeness" of the mistress who confides in the servant or, worse, who subjugates herself to the servant's wisdom, however greater it may be. It is a commercial relationship, and proof is that the buyers are the only ones who are ever privileged wholly to forget that. "Anyway," adds Mrs. Huerta as an afterthought, "his side was all rotten by then, so who could help him? I don't care who, what were we supposed to do?"

Her voice is breathy with her most unapproachable memories. I believe I do them honor by not so much as attempting to come near them, let alone appropriate them or attempt to change her sorrow to guilt. Grace, I am thinking, grace growing anywhere, weed in a crack in the sidewalk, Fifth and Union Street. She should be left alone to heal.

"Anyway, see, I'm a fighter in my life, you know, with the people I got close up in my life, but them out there—" She gives into the telephone what can only be a shrug. "Your business, you do a good job, I figure if you tell me they don't give up so easy, the hospital, I better believe you. I know I couldn't prove nothing against like that nurse I told you, that bitch and her clipboard? I couldn't get near her, all I do is stamp and say I know what I know and all she got to do is smile this smile with a, what she got, a nurse's diploma, whatever she got in her pocket of that uniform. But your daughter—" She sighs, very close into the phone, one of those phone-gobblers who make sticky sounds in your ear like children; so does Anna-Joyce. "She's saying now it all happened because I can't shout and make trouble. She said—I tell you only don't tell her what I said, she'll get mad—she said if I only threaten somebody, the right person, or call the cops upstairs with me, my son could be alive right now sitting here with me. She said I work for a lawyer, I ought to bring your name in, you could scare them." The poor abused woman. Her statement ends in a terrible real question.

"Renata told you that?" Renata who can barely ask permission to go to the head of the supermarket line when she has but one stick of butter?

"Oh, she's blaming me, Mrs. Stein. Nobody ever made me cry so much before, I swear, she put both her hands right on my shoulders, and she shaking me, she say, 'Damn Puerto Ricans just like the Jews, just only Jews in a different language, they can't stop crawling, never going nowhere, filth and dying, and then if they get money they piss it away and they don't ever look back any more.' She say, if they bring the cattle car around right up here on Fifth Avenue, if it stop right where the Mr. Softee truck pulls up against the curb, and said to, we all hop in and be dead."

I let out a long pent-up breath but can think of nothing but gross disloyalty to say to her. My daughter's unique skill is that she can with her good intentions and her inept love affront so many victims in a single breath. Is there a full moon? There would seem to be an astonishing amount of virulent language being heaved about this week in the name of moral correction. We are all proceeding by insult and not by logic; certainly not by compassion. I thank Mrs. Huerta and wish her well. Shall I see her later in the week on the day she comes to clean? Of course, she assures me: being sad don't mean you can stop eating very long, especially growing children.

When I hang up, shaking with anger, but literally, I am a planet away from my Supreme Court case, this question of free speech.

Free speech, free speech, our tongues go before us into battle. Wanton speech and no distinctions made. See how it kills.

I take Tippy to the office with me and she naps, while Loren and I again are at each other's necks.

"What is *wrong* with you, Gerda, your absolutely deadly final insupportable limitation, is that you are only interested in getting this shit done—" My entire desk is the shit he magnanimously includes in a wave of his hairy hand. "I've come to the conclusion you do not care a thimbleful about changing a bloody thing, you will not think about leaving any impact on anything you touch, you have made yourself a clerk, do you realize? A damn clerk, a supernumerary of the courts, trying to work your way through the calendar."

"Loren." I am seated, trapped behind that swamped desk, he has all the freedom to thrust and move. But I am too weary to stand and deal with this advantage of his. "You and I have a different interpretation of our roles, I wish you could appreciate this and stop hurling brickbats at me. If you wish to make history and change laws, you should once and for all run for legislative office. We are caretakers—"

"Right. You got that into your head when you were three years old and you're fixated right there. Gardeners, vine-clippers. Why in hell can't we *plant* anything?"

"Because it is hard to be both, love. Because one is forever forced to choose. I too want to make good law but there is difficulty enough simply protecting—clearing up the overgrowths and obliteration of the perfectly good laws we already have."

And so on. I repeat this, which is our endless obloquy for one shocking reason. Not because it represents me as housewife of the law, rather than as master builder (and, believe me, Loren barely restrains himself from attributing my style to my sex, however many men there may be who play this game by similar rules), but because it becomes evident to me now that I am to Loren what Anna-Joyce is to me. Ah, our tiny conservative hearts, our refusal to batter at the large structures. There is some aspect of the status quo that appears to content us, we have vested interests, we are happy with our little work. Perhaps my daughter would be less intimidated by me were she to see me in the perspective of a critic so unimpressed. I think it must be a gift of age to see us all impaled on flow charts with little pins stuck in our middles, indicating that I am to her as she is to them as they are to us. In the midst of our conversation I begin to laugh and Loren nods knowingly. I do not have any idea what he thinks he knows.

My afternoon is spent wrapping up a case more routine than the sensational six o'clock news would have it—*pace* Loren—and gay liberation shall have its social club at a college campus on Long Island; the bigots who would prevent it, protecting their threatened selves, their assorted latencies with biblical quotations and mailed fists, were at the courthouse in great numbers. If I were a cartoonist I should depict that crowd as a conglomeration of spear carriers, only they are truly hoisting half-raised phalluses wearing hard hats. They called me the most interesting concatenation of names since my short but vivid Mississippi days and, surely to confuse them utterly, the student in whose name the suit had been filed descended upon me like a parachute to show his gratitude. I was simply engulfed in arms and sleeves and sweet-smelling cheek and non-stop verbal fervor. Tippy stood beside me laughing as this perfumed gentleman reached across her to embrace me. She grabbed his leg and he gave an alarmed hoot as though stung by a bee.

Again, of course, the point is lost; it is remarkable how invisible it is to a majority: that one need not be one—one anything—to champion its rights. Perhaps they talk of it too much at school and thus obliterate the chances of such a doctrine's actually influencing anybody. *Disinterest remains the world's implausible diamond, its inexhaustible mystery.* It is only out of fashion in these times when advocacy, prejudice, single-minded "sincerity" is all: the new Romantics.

Think of the fascinating life I would have leading my Nazis and my communists, my gay butterflies and my rightist incendiaries, my prisoners and their ladies carrying files in their fingernails—the Queen Mother takes them to an open field and we dance and plot nuclear ambush and make love and subvert the third-grade library list all at the one time. We sign no oaths, pledge no allegiance, pray no prayers. We incriminate no one, least of all ourselves. We sleep, a day's work done, in the Sheep Meadow of Central Park, for which we have a proper police permit; some unclothed, though with all dogs curbed. No one urinates in public; nor fornicates within sight of community standards. We smoke anything and suffer minimally for it. We bear no arms but we carry Mace in legal doses, which we use upon each other if need be. I am the mother who has won permission from the father. They all sleep, but I have too many bad dreams. I shall lie awake tonight and wonder about my children and my children's children, my Tippy who dozes weightless against my arm returning home, what they shall inherit because my skill has bought them such freedom.

Tippy again has worked her way into a grief-stricken tantrum. Unpredictability appears to be her invincible weapon: her needs, to me, are an untranslated language I can only guess at by hints and colorings.

At bedtime I make what I must presume is the mistake of saying to her—gaily, because I do feel a peculiar unfamiliar delight in the day, "Have we not had a fine time today, my little lady?" I try, awkwardly I grant, to kiss her on the warm top of her head.

"Now Mama?" she asks quite eagerly into my chest.

"Dear, I do not know for a fact." Honesty with a child, possibly it is a mistake however much I would like to respect her integrity. I was more honest with Renata than ever she gave me credit for.

"No Mama?" Oh, so she has had me on sufferance. I have taken her care in good spirits and have protected her from yet another stranger as guardian while I worked, but there is no credit there either. And so she goes off into a snit and I am angry, only then, wondering in whose bed her mother has found solace without a backward glance.

The key is in the door, Renata is here looking unspeakably distraught. Unaccountably I go to her smiling, my arms so recently warm around her child. She weeps without a word of explanation.

RENATA

How in the hell can you get pneumonia in the spring? Tippy has
it. No blame, no blame, the Ching says. I can never find her
sweater, her hat, her gloves. "But she never goes out," I tell the
doctor, "how could she get such a—"
"Never goes out. Well, there you are."
Tippy coughs once to confirm the problem.
"Don't even wonder what did it, though; it's not worth the
speculation," he goes on. I want to make an appeal for consistency, I've got to know whether it is or isn't my fault. He can't try
this casual business with me. "Events are not really to the point
in this kind of thing, you know. There was a study recently where
they stood a bunch of wet people, absolutely soaked through, in
front of open windows and let the cold air blow on them and of
course they had a control group with no wet feet, all bundled up,
and guess what happened?"
I blink.
He looks merry reporting the results. "Well, you know, the results shook their finger at all our mothers, the whole galoshes and
mufflers treatment, there were no more colds—not one—in the
wet group than the dry. So there you are."
Where? "But resistance—"
"Yes, well, resistance is another story." In case I thought I
could slip out of it. I didn't mean to be angry with her. She had

cried, though, had been made to cry, and said, "Mommy, I'm sorry, I'm sorry I got sick."

I had slammed a glass of apple juice—there was no orange juice and I was afraid to leave her and go downstairs for some—on the little bed table so hard that it splashed up over the top. "Get a sponge," she said very seriously, "your mommy will be mad." I didn't smile.

"Enough," I said and pushed her rather roughly back against her pillow, then smoothed the blankets much too gently. I am sure she looks condescendingly at me when I get like this.

Of course the room was hot. The bitterness of the medication ate the good green air and left only the veins behind, like leaves that have been munched by beetles. The walls were pink with candy topping. Tippy loved it, her treat was to be sick enough to have a hundred spoons to lick.

When she is sweet as ampicillin then I'm like this. When her patience runs out she's left with a ferocious unfamiliar thrust-out jaw and the whine of a buzz saw and the saw divides me in two. Then I am sweet and juicy: when she's at her worst. We are out of phase. But I don't like to be helpless. She wakes at night, hacking and hawking and my fists clench. I try to keep a door closed between her and my mother in case she coughs, or there's hell to pay. I don't like the way my mother looks at me.

The doctor taps her narrow chest.

"Cold!" Tippy breathes when his stethoscope touches her. "Ouch." She doesn't know whether to laugh or scowl at him. He makes her breathe huh-in, huh-out, mostly in. During the out he looks up and around, listening. Then he bangs the stethoscope against his palm. "Well, you've got a good bronchial clog there, all right. Call it pneumonia, bronchitis, severe—all the same—" and he begins writing out the cures vigorously, slashing, pulling the sheets off his pad into a neat little pile.

Tippy is sitting so patiently I know she has to be very sick. And I cry. The point of all this: I cry. Her lungs labor and her infinitesimal pale shoulders rise and quiver under her cough as though under a whip, and I cry for shame, that I could allow such a thing to overtake my baby. Sneak. Sneak. It all gets past me. When I let down my guard I'm back on the bus to nowhere; to New Jersey. Of the two of us, I'm the one who has no resistance.

"Now Mrs.—" the doctor begins. But I wave him quiet with his own prescription pages. "It isn't serious," he tells me, lowering his voice, playing preposterous comforting bedside music on it, worse than the way he talked to Tippy. "She'll be better than new in no time at all with this, don't skip any spoonfuls, that's all. It's just a bother and a discomfort, but . . ." He shakes his head at me.

But I can't see him through my cloud of sentimental tears. Of course she'll be all right, I have no doubt of that. Will I?

Later that night she is screaming awake, as though somebody has his hands around her throat. I run to her barefoot. I hold her to me in the dark, pajama to nightgown shoulder, remembering her softness a little that way. How can I abuse her, ever? The feeling is like a frostbitten limb beginning to wake up: that she is smaller than I am. In my care.

She was walking, in her dream, through a room crowded with people, losing my hand and finding it again. She was looking in store windows crammed with dollhouses and big dolls on bikes that went in circles and came close, almost crashed through to her, and when she turned and reached up next to her to catch my hand somehow she saw it wasn't me. "It was another mommy!" she tells me, outraged. I can feel her forehead lifting above her eyes, those single-line eyebrows arching, though I can't see them. "A big mommy—" gesturing for girth, gasping as if at the memory of something that has really happened. Well, I guess she feels like she's confessing a betrayal. She thinks she's hurt me; also she's scared herself to death. It's the first nightmare she's ever been able to get in words.

She is choking on tears of shame and fear and I will never know what else. Then she begins, inevitably, to cough. Big Mother's in Chicago this week, I think, thank God, and then at this college and that, gathering degrees *honoris causa*. *Ms.* has her on the cover this week: Heroine or Uncle Tom? Tippy can cough if she has to, there's nobody here but me. All I can do is murmur and murmur and not help her, and feel a dreadful fear cracking open in my chest at all she knows about me already.

Outside Tippy's window the sky is a huge black egg, beginning to shatter. Morning will seep out. Both of us sit on the bed and watch it flow slowly toward us, tears on our cheeks, our pale flannel shoulders just touching.

❦ ❦ ❦

A better day. Tippy sleeps and every time she wakes up she smiles at me with a little more conviction. After a day's exertion at being depressed, I'm the one who dozes like an invalid on the living room couch.

Once in the government store in Mexico City—I was there with a whole crowd whose faces are blank for me, eaten away except for this guitarist named Arnett something who was my reason for being there (and it isn't his face I remember)—I saw a box full of hundreds of Mexican—amulets? magic tokens? Little paper gods in pale colors with their hands up beside their heads, half like Tippy, the way she sleeps with her wrists up on the cool pillow, and half like they lived surrendering or warding something off. The cut-outs were brought by the Aztecs to Montezuma, originally, tributes of these things by the thousands, they slaved to make the paper and then to cut these precise little triangular eyes and mouths like the nicks in snowflakes. And then I think they buried them.

My daughter Theresa Stein this day, recovering fast, faster than I am, has sat up and cut out a circle of dancing paper dolls, their arms up similarly, shielding, but with hands sweetly joined. I wake from my mindless doze to find she has gotten out of bed and laid them across my chest as I slept, all green and empty of features or wrinkles or imperfections. When I pick them up she comes and dances them for me and I think, you shall learn to dance, she will teach you patience if you can only give her a place to penetrate, to take her in. Could my mother have been as helpless as I am against these beautiful distractions? Her life was too full, mine is too empty, but it's all the same, it doesn't leave anything for sharing. . . . Tippy brings blue dolls and crosses them over the green ones. "Make you pretty," she promises as she works solemnly on my chest. "Pretty pretty. Making you smile, Mommy, don't be sick."

So: everything is self-fulfilling. Is that a reason for hope or despair? Bad mothers make bad daughters make bad mothers. Poor Tip.

When I drift back into sleep I have a wonderfully funny desolating dream. I am in store in a dusty square in Mexico. That figures. I am looking at the postcards and there's a huge one like a poster and it's a picture of a place I've actually seen. My mother in all her modesty has it, clipped from a calendar, a painting of some Hawaiian place called the City of Refuge, where wrongdoers went for safety and were protected no matter what their crime. I suppose Mother sees herself as one of the gods in the great circle. In the dream there's this ring of totems, greenish-looking, ungraceful, and a big sign in Coca-Cola writing that says Taxatlac or something like that, and a figure barely visible at the bottom of one to give a sense of their extraordinary scale. I pick up the card, which takes both hands and much lugging, and I bring it up to the man at the counter. He squints at the picture through tiny bloodshot eyes, and then he laughs, his chest a pot of phlegm stirring itself: a movie Mexican. Then he wheezes to me something like, "Hah, nobody knows this place, it's a—how is it, a fakery. A fake. Sí. One day this thing appears like a mushroom out of the ground and some bum is sitting in a chair there, he is charging ten pesos to see it, it's all—" and the old man looks all around him and my friend Arnett is slouched down behind the counter whittling a stick, "they're big, big, but there's still just big shit. All their history is—" and he snaps his stiff old fingers. When I look at it the card is gone, it's all pretty pictures of the tallest building in Mexico City, and carved wooden phalluses against velvet.

Anna-Joyce McHugh is on the phone. A *yenta* with an Irish name, but her voice is just like Mother's: more comfortable talking than shutting up. *Teach these people to keep quiet, these fucking do-gooders.* I swear their voices are like these giant skeleton keys, they go around fitting them into every empty lock they see, to turn it, just to feel the power in their hands whenever something clicks. With men you've got the macho toughs, the cocksmen who lead with their superior power, their superior pricks. But I'm beginning to see these women have their own round-shouldered macho when they want to bear down on a victim.

Which is to say she's calling because she and Mother are old friends, she this, Mother that—yes, I used to be subjected to her regularly on street corners, for Sunday brunch. How is my baby? Fine, no baby any more, do you think the rain'll hurt the rhubarb? She's been put up to it: would I like a little work, part-time only, no commitment, and bring the baby (she doesn't listen). Advising teen-age girls.

My laugh is a slash through her curtain of amiable bullshit. "Me advise teen-age girls?" Tippy is about to throw one of Mother's folders out the window. I watch, mesmerized. "What do you want me to advise? Use myself as a bitter example of waste and spoilage?" Oh, I perplex the lady. "You want me to tell them everything's safer if they keep their legs closed? Or their eyes closed? Or—" It isn't possible. I tell her, "Please don't try, please, please," and lay the phone down next to its cradle where it lies like the head snapped off a tulip. Black after the growing season. Tippy kisses my eyes. She shouldn't have to do that so often, I'm going to make a fucking little nurse out of her when she needs to be a soldier to get through.

four

RENATA

The famous parents show. We are Les Levine's televised "Confrontation" this week. Yes, I have said I would come, months ago, I thought it was the funniest thing I'd ever heard. My sense of humor was more elastic then. Somehow in my continuous immovable—it's not a high or a low, more a *mist*—I decide to come along and "do" the show. It'll be all right.

We are met at the studio door by a bevy, I think it's called, of girl graduate cocktail waitresses with clipboards. *They all know my mother.* It's as if I've confirmed a secret vice of hers, a perversion I'd only suspected. They are programmed to be very earnest; they are stewardesses with ambition. They move us here and there to be smiled at and then take us in to be made up—Mother's face gains twenty pounds and jowls under the stuff they apply, slogging it on like mortar between bricks. It exaggerates the image of solidity in her, though: when they're done she looks like a rabbi. I get whiter and whiter, perfect for my state of mind, until I feel weightless. The rabbi and her daughter the paper airplane.

There are two other couples: one black, one white. What are we for balance? The Jews, I suppose, maybe a little yellow. One is a son behind glasses thicker than prisms.

We come before our "host," Les Levine, to be briefed. His cuffs and his teeth are blinding—wouldn't it be interesting if someday they could find somebody who annihilated your stereotypes? For all I know he started out that way, I believe he was once a college professor, but this—this fraudulent charm and high-powered excited low seriousness seems to come in the pay envelope. "Let's hear, now, what's the kind of image you can project as a team. We picked you because you're so—so very different." He makes it sound like a compliment, in that husky oversincere actor's voice. What a trial lawyer he'd make with a delivery like that, Mama. It's all in the pauses.

The black mother and daughter are dancers but, wonderful: Mama, who is ponderous and hung like a sacrifice with golden earrings and tinkly necklaces half of which they take away from her, the stewardesses, shaking their heads—Mama used to be with Martha Graham and now has her own company, Olivia something, "very innovative," Les Levine says, "I believe they can walk on the ceiling." Pause. "Barefoot." But the daughter is into classical ballet. She talks fast, in a high-pitched girl's voice, but she turns her long emaciated hands slowly, slowly, very deliberate and musical. "I am in love with my work, a marriage," she says in her junior high voice. Nothing is visible from outside—no wonder I can't see how my mother, for example, ever achieved me. Everyone says a banality or two. I am informed mine should have to do with the wonders of having the freedom to choose. "You know," Levine suggests to me brightly, discovering the pitch as he goes, "you can tell people, really, you can even be ordinary, you know, just a nice plain private person—mother, of course, bake cookies and tend the home fires and all—exactly because of what your mother did a generation before, right?" He waves his tailored hand. "What does your husband do"—pause, while he checks my name on his card—"Renata?"

"No husband," I say, smiling brightly back.

"Divorced."

"No."

"Ah—then—" He doesn't want to say widowed. Or he's got the point. I smile relentlessly. He's thinking, goddamn, we pulled one, didn't we, where in the hell did we get her from? Gerda Stein is in their files, such a personality, and they *assumed* . . . It's all right, I'm thinking, Mother will use up our talk and decency quotient without a blink. . . .

The leather sofas onstage are disconcerting, they've been silenced somehow, they don't squeak or make sticky sounds. The dancers do OK in the heat of the lights, it's not their first time out. Their postures change as though at command, their heads flick smartly around, birdlike and precise, their smiles are quick and stagy. The thick-lensed boy is a post-doctoral biology student, son of a famous biologist father. "How do you manage not to feel —competitive—with your father, Sidney? You work in the same lab, I understand, shoulder to shoulder."

The question that could justify a suicide emerges smooth as Cream of Wheat. Les smiles encouragingly.

Sidney mumbles in the familiar endearing vowels of the Bronx that they are serving truth side by side, something like that. Christ. Picture them in an ox yoke, padding forward slowly in matched step. I'll bet, I'll bet. Where does your incessant blink come from, Sidney? He looks like he's got a perpetual cinder in his left eye; a wound got in the service of truth, I suppose. "I've learned everything from my dad," he volunteers and looks fondly at Father, who is youthful and pleasant and aggressively short-haired, neither tyrannical nor old-world. An astronaut. They played Little League ball together, they still go camping. Daddy broils a mean steak. Either I don't believe what they're saying or there are fortunate people in the world. (But father's wife and son's mother, where is she tonight?)

And in my time, Les turns his smile to me like a klieg light: a command to heel. "And another kind of response, interesting in its own way, here is Gerda Stein's daughter Renata who has been —correct me if I'm wrong, Renata—freer than most girls to say, 'Well, our family'—the way you would tell the Red Cross when they come to your door, 'Well, we already gave, down at the office. My mother gave—to society, I mean.'" He smiles with pleasure at his wit; nothing like watching a man enjoy his work. "Now please, folks, don't take it out on the old Red Cross, uh, give twice, will you, once for you and please, uh, once for me." Casts eyes to heaven, mock horror at his *faux pas*. "But I mean, you're free and can pursue some of the older, more traditional, let's call them pre-women's lib, activities, and you have a daughter of your own. Is this an accurate picture? Would you say? Or is it more complicated than that?"

I open my mouth to answer. Beside me I feel my mother shift in her silenced seat, she is hoping I'll say it well, and grammatically, and not mumble. The camera in front of me waits about the size of a bear but a bear leaping. Off the ground with both feet. Shadows on its shoulders, moving around, flicking switches. There is a lovely young cameraman in a khaki uniform, one-piece like a baker—signaling time; after a while he is slitting his throat with his finger, smiling so wide I know it's a grimace.

"Well," says Les coaxing; he'll cut my gizzard out backstage. "I hope that's not your answer." Dead air, stifling dead expensive air. Will sirens blow when my time is up, will the cameraman come down and carry me away?

"Yes, I can imagine"—glancing at Gerda provocatively—"there must be times when a woman who speaks so—very eloquently as this woman here, one of the major advocates of our day—she must make it hard sometimes to—" He laughs. "I hope this isn't a comment, Renata, we're going to have to read volumes into your—ah—"

"Nerves," my mother mutters, whether for publication or not I don't know. "She is our stay-at-home, after all."

"Nothing to say for the defense. Or the prosecution?" He is trying a little more harshly. "You mean you rest, the case rests, we can send the jury out."

I have regained my composure while he's flailed and fluttered, trying to make something out of my nothing. It's very strange and satisfying. I watch them jump. Everybody talks at once, covering up the silence like a stain, and I lean back smiling. They get busy then, sorting out the differences between work as a means and work as an end. They live on words, they eat them, sleep them, shit them, spend them to buy everything they have. The dancers talk less, they move their swan heads around from those heights of theirs, muscles taut, and I can see how good that feels to them. The biologists I don't know anything about. They're not wordy, they seem to use their hands endlessly, cleverly. But silence—see how easily you can throw it into the word machine and make it falter and fail. A cross held up to the vampire's face. Ah, Mother: learn it. Learn it.

At the end of the show, Les—who because he is known to be well-educated and therefore allowed to be literary even without writers—says when he gets to me, "And her daughter, here—Bartleby the Scriveneress—no, Scrivener-person, I guess it is these days, I can't be too careful after I've got the Red Cross down on me—who prefers not to. Ladies and gentlemen, a comment in itself, you might say, and an eloquent one, on the peculiar tensions of being a child of fame."

We all rise when the camera lights go out, and straighten our skirts. I am elated, you can't imagine. More weightless than I was before. Mother murmurs into my face in a harsh whisper, "Thank you for the humiliation. Do you know you shall be a victim all your life."

Levine isn't even going to acknowledge my presence. My absence, I should say. He walks away as though he's got another show waiting outside.

But I don't feel like a victim. I feel like an aggressor, with a fine shelter to go to. Nobody owns my tongue, or even hires it.

Mother is chattering away very fast with Levine, noisily, apologetically, too late. So I can make her jump, that big cat running free. How lovely. So I have a thing or two to teach.

"I am so glad to have come," the dancer mother is saying, pumping Levine's hand, nearly curtsying. Her daughter stands in her dancer's duck posture, stomach out, rear high, knees locked.

"Me too," I call out, very gay, making for the door. "Your makeup!" somebody shouts who still cares about me, but I don't mind if I look like a whore or a clown. I lose myself between the cars on Fifty-second Street. *Survival is always different and always the same.* I learned that at my mama's knee. *And nobody ever said survivors were pleasant to be near.*

GERDA

My daughter is punishing me with silence; she is wasting. I would like to find some help for her but I do not enjoy the idea of therapists, of spilling weaknesses out in hopes of being repaid with strength. But less do I like the self-indulgence in which she appears to drown. She has crossed a line of rationality, or so she would have me believe; has positively made a resolution to be absent in my sight and to take pleasure in it.

I talk to Stanley Balch in my office about Renata because he has a son who was a depressive, so-called and clinically certified, and had much electroshock therapy. Of course Stan has his own problems. He is nowadays a large fine-looking man who has a face that appears to hang on by sheer luck alone, so eroded is the character behind it. He has the suppressed quiver of a drinking man and the abused eyes of a failure eager to abash himself. I mean those self-deprecating eyes that flinch at kindness far more than most men at cruelty. He has many fine wrinkles and a few premature gross ones, and having known him twenty, ten, even five years ago and not having seen him since, one would be terribly pained to meet him now.

About his son, Stan shrugs. "Jeff . . . all right, I suppose, you'd say he's doing all right. He never did go back to school. He works in Altman's in their better shoes. Their better shoes."

"What—was it, then, Stan, did his psychiatrist tell you?"

He laughs gently at me. "Oh, Gerda, 'what was it?' Do you have a germ theory of psychological illness? You think it was a virus, maybe, or a bacteria he picked up in a crowded movie, the way the kids used to get polio? I mean the way we thought they did, remember?" He rubs his hands together as though there might be something to be savored in his argument. "He had a bunch of hang-ups, I don't know, I'll never know, they went way back. I had a lot to do with them, his mother had a lot to do with them. But what good are the post-mortems? They put a hell of a lot of money in his analyst's pocket and I don't say I'm not grateful, he's alive, he's functioning, and I've learned a lot about keeping my mouth shut. But all that's after the fact, and the fact's buried by now. Water under the bridge." He screws up his face like a small boy. "Sorry, it brings out the clichés in me. It seems that every time I touched him I mangled something, so I was told. Well, I never knew I was doing that, you know." He runs a hand through his classic hair. "It's a little better now, I suppose. But—people like Jeff, they always have bad spots, you know, like rotten planks, you can't afford to forget yourself and just run around on them anywhere like you can with healthy kids. They just *give* in the damnedest places."

"You call him 'people like that,' do you not feel any identification with his problems?" I can hear Renata on this subject; Renata when she spoke to me.

"Oh—" He shrugs. Stan's hands perpetually shake: they did all those years ago. No, I do not know him, for all we have worked together. Quick to anger, quick to forgive, apologetic beyond the call. "I suppose I try but it's hard, I've never really been very good at family life, I guess. And then when you feel blamed yourself, it's too frightening to take the other side. The offensive."

I do not tell him that I understand, I only take his hand for one surprising moment and hold it. How casually he says he is no good at family life. Another sport, is it. Golf, lacrosse, fatherhood. Or he is covering himself, he is keeping it back, hiding it from himself. He looks astonished at the touch of skin in something other than a handshake. His heavy bloodhound eyes positively widen, I should say he looks frightened. Somehow, I suspect it is my little granddaughter and her easy flinging-around of her bones and soft skin in embraces necessary to her as milk, that now makes our abrupt touching less of a shock to me. I can understand how the advent of children in a marriage would shift the balance of sensuality somehow from husband and wife exclusively to a general, available, non-complicated warming at all that rump and back and smooth fat thigh. This many men resent, I should guess, it takes a part of their wives away from them. It is cleaner than sex, surely, all the touching, smoothing, stroking, gathering handfuls. Carlotta got all that of Renata, she was well-practiced at taking it, like a farm wife who knows how to get even the last drop of milk from the cow. I look forward now, after the evening class I must teach, to going home and hoping that Tippy is awake, Tippy-of-the-little-face, so that she shall fling her arms over my neck and impress herself on me bone by bone. It will warm me so it shall be like a bath for smoothing out the kinks of the day.

As for her mother, my best stories are wasted entirely on her. I cannot bestir myself to regale a corpse, and so I shall before I know it begin to meet her angry silence with my own. If this is a battle of wills she shall win by default because they do not weigh equally: you cannot put up against each other one silence and one endless conversation with no one to hear it. But I swear she shall regret such a victory.

Nightly I arrive from work to the silence of an empty apartment. But no. She is sitting on my worn couch, feet flat, hands at her sides. Her face is apparently at peace, she appears to be meditating but that would hardly last so long. She is erasing me, you see; or erasing herself. Consciousness tricks, a sort of informal catatonia. I greet her and put down my briefcase, hug Tippy who is full of affection and can be surprised, talk as casually as one can to a post about my plans for dinner.

When I place her lamb chop before her tonight I say, "As a ploy, Renata, this is not very interesting."

She spreads the napkin in her lap with great care. Such fine and empty features, this American pleasantness. Think of Baudelaire, Rimbaud, drugged and sinking and full of self-hate, and they did not look unlined and self-satisfied as this sweet daughter of chaos. Her face has closed back over her sins, her griefs, like water over flung stones. All the junkies who swallow the little bags when the police come to the door—I have a picture of this, how Renata has swallowed it, swallowed the wrath, the fear, the disgust, and now she is going to drown it with lamb chop and peas. That, or it is not true, any of it. I do not believe her: that is the upshot. I am unconvinced.

She continues to smooth her napkin. Whatever else she may have learned of me, I taught manners in my house; her manners must have made her a laughingstock at many a "rock and roll" festival. She raises her eyes, holding her fork and knife like ski poles, at their ends, and looks through my face.

Once, do you know, I saw and touched an Eskimo statue in an exhibit; it made me strangely uneasy. The wind had made it, I think that was to be the implication; had violently punched it in at the stomach, then sanded the sides as gently as need be, and could now pass through untroubled. An open passage for the wind, a natural convenience. So she looks through me, through the passage made by, what shall I call it, my irrelevance, and I see that it takes no effort. She goes about cutting her meat into perfect squares forever.

Tippy is in my lap. She plays us against each other shamelessly, like the two blocks of wood she has which are covered in sandpaper, and we make just that kind of rasping music.

When I return to the kitchen and put down my amber bowl with a few peas rattling in their butter, it is with a feeling, let me say it, of empty panic. I turn on the stove for coffee and I look at the swaying blue flame which contains no voice, no face, and think: what can I see but my own concentration here. It puddles up like gas, enriching the flame. I see how it is my own death, but first my obsolescence, then my death that is coming toward me, that makes me so penetrable suddenly to my daughter's contempt. It is prophetic: if she looks through me long enough soon I will not be there. My posterity? Sooner and sooner. Silence is a corrosive. It eats at my solid parts. *I am not accustomed to having no effect.* What have I if my reason is denied me?

People soften in so many ways, their eyes, their logical powers, their firmest resolves and antipathies become so much salt: they forgive. Am I merely getting old? My mother before she died swore passion for my father; swore delight and was not lying, only remembering a few minutes of her life, a few hours at most. Addie sat swallowing silence until he could be said to have choked on it. A dear friend, Clara—my only friend in the wretched high school in Boston where I was perhaps as silent as Renata, only in timidity, not contempt—a girl so quiet herself one needed to lean forward to hear a single word of her—she died talking, talking, through the last weeks of her cancer, endlessly jabbering out all the news on the radio, Roosevelt dying, the OPA investigating, a whale washed up at Laguna Beach, A-bomb tests that made her cry and curse, her son's fraternity sending an orchid for her bedside, on and on, not even in a monotone but with a lifetime of suppressed inflection coloring her voice, desperate to hold on by words alone. Gerda. I am sad for myself as though I were a good friend. I am Clara Chaimowitz preparing to mourn for me. Obscurely I am thinking that I cannot be suddenly drowned in this self-pity, I am like my daughter. Perhaps it may be my newly acquired friendship with my grandchild, with its indulgence of feeling, feeling all the time, so alien to the concentration of my life outside myself, that has actually weakened me? Has become an influence upon me, has changed my metabolism? I have let my guard too far down, the thick skin I know has saved me is crumpled around my ankles, sagging and useless. To be vulnerable is to render oneself inefficient, a blunt object. *Why must she answer me to make me feel I am truly here?*

Now I must admit that I have been cutting up a pear throughout this poor metaphysics, and raking the cheese with this very modern little gadget like a tuning fork with a wire across its tines. (I glimpse my mother cutting a huge rock of cheese toward herself, and I in a panic as the knife thrust through toward her chest! How even our tools have withered and thinned.) And I find I have slashed my third finger, so deeply it was done without pain, like a paper cut. And so I hold it up, only slowly unfreezing, pain begins to seep into it gradually. A kind of mild chagrin: poor finger, poor bird, do you know this detachment? Poor Gerda. At last the blood begins to roll into my gray cuff and branch up into a thousand nylon capillaries, and I have to turn from my tranced contemplation. Third finger up I look as though I am offering an obscene comment to heaven. Imagine, so quietly I shall go, feeling myself other, distant, unreachable: just so even your cattle cars came, Renata. They came for strangers and acquaintances, but never for one's children or oneself. Don't you know that?

"Renata." What would she do if I were dying here? "Renata? I need your help, I have had an accident."

Nowhere so much as the rustle of curiosity. "Renata, I am here bleeding."

But she is not here for me, I am to learn that. She is no doubt glad of the occasion to so instruct me under the stress of blood. I shall not forgive her callousness, however. There are times when the rules of such little games are suspended.

I walk to the threshold spilling blood. "You are, as I have suspected, a spoiled child," is all I say, quite evenly, for my anger tends always to restrain me and drive me to a minimum of elucidation. "I do not believe you are so out of your own control that you cannot come when you are truly needed. I put you on notice that what pity I may have had for you this minute disappears."

My granddaughter has been ripping old magazines into precise shreds. She looks up, calibrating the tone of my voice, I dare say, and leaps to her feet. She comes running, all the faster because her mother sits tight. Child on a string, I should like to save you these cruel distortions of love but I do not know how to begin.

The telephone—forever the intrusive voice of my real, my other, life. I speak to Jack Tenney and forget my bleeding hand, which is not so terribly serious at that. (And I am left thinking, guiltily, that I am the first to say there are no accidents.) When I am finished with Jack and return my attention I see that dear Tippy is trying to bind the wound with her dirty pink sock. She winds it as far as it can go, leaves it, and it unwinds itself and drops like a petal. Again and again, her small face angry, "Grandma!" as though I am making it happen. Look how she tries it, though: it would not occur to this delightful terrier child to abandon a thing she wants. I embrace her so hard she cries out in pain.

RENATA

Another morning of TV. They are peddling detergents. Lady, they really want to say between acts in the endless seeping soap opera, think of the mess of your life, all in the family wash: your husband spills his beer, your son jerks off alone listening to the Stones, your daughter spills her mascara that she's forbidden to use till she's eleven, your dog craps at your feet, a gift—and we can help you get your whole life clean! Magic purity, linens like they have at the castle.

The phone rings. One of the eradicated ladies is calling in to report it doesn't work, her husband's collars still have rings, he doesn't hug her in the laundry room. "Hey, Renata." A strong buzzy voice, no lady, the iron kind you can hear through closed doors.

"Sam Eisenstadt. Look, Renata, I need help."

"Do you." A little low-phosphate soap, maybe?

"Bad. Yeah."

"Who is Sam Eisenstadt?"

"Listen, can I—are you busy, could you meet me and talk?"

Another of my mother's jobs. In which case he knows damn well I'm never busy. "No, look, I haven't been feeling well, I'm not—"

"Let me come over. I need some . . ." He dwindles off. Suspicious. "I really do."

"Well, you come over here, then. I'm not going out much. And my little girl."

"Be over in less than an hour." He has supreme unmitigated affronting confidence. Who the hell is he? I shouldn't let strange men in, haven't I heard that somewhere?

The want ads are propped on the table. Not exactly subtle: she leaves them beside my breakfast coffee cup. What was that about being a mother, one thing at a time done well? SEC/RECEPT. No trng. req. Good voice, typg. pref. No fee. CASE WORKERS NEEDED. Curiosity, flexibility, no exper. nec. Well, why not what I'm doing, is it worse? I could write IMMOVABLE OBJECT. No trng. req. Patience. High frustr. threshold. No touching req., no tmptations, dirty past ok. No salary, no fture.

I get the buzzer. Sam Eisenstadt turns out to be the junior partner I saw with my mother the day I arrived all that empty time ago, before I grew into this clinging vine I am today. Too many teeth, he must have half a set of extras and he shows them all at once. His mouth reminds me of a deck of cards spread out for a trick, and I hate card tricks: they're designed to make me feel stupid.

"Can I have a drink or something?" he asks when he comes in, rubbing his hands together.

"Are you allowed to drink on the job?" I feel vile and mean and I don't think he ought to drink. He'd better keep his guard up with me because I'm going to get this little messenger of my mama's in trouble.

But I bring him what he asks for, a double scotch. "At this hour?" It's eleven or so.

He raises it against the window light. "I can take it." And licks off his long lips. "Where's your daughter?"

"Asleep. She's been sick."

"Ah."

"What, ah?"

"Nothing. Just 'ah.' 'Oh,' you like that better?"

I narrow my eyes at him. He's still around that office. I remember thinking he'd be off into a political career, all tooth and cuff and sharp crease in the pants, straight to the knee. He looks smart; maybe he's not lucky.

"You like my mother's office."

"You learn a lot. Everybody there sort of represents one of the eight or ten deadly sins of legal advocacy, sloth or greed or whatever." I wish he wouldn't give me that crocodile smile.

"Yeah? What's my mother's? Isn't she what Dick Cavett says she is?"

"Oh—" He spreads his large hands, wondering how much he wants to say to me. "She's the mother superior, she got religion before all the rest of us and she spends a hell of a lot of useful time down on her knees, you know? I like her in spite of it but she's—"

"Out of date?"

"Well, it's more complicated than that, but maybe that's what it could come down to. Anyway, there are higher jumpers around, you know, and some seven-foot-high guards who never miss a shot, and she's down there counting how many times she dribbled the ball."

"You like to talk."

"Sure. Don't tell Gerda I said any of this, though. I have a way of—" He shrugs, suddenly boyish, at my mercy, all helpless charm and impetuousness. I want to get down to it but I don't remember how you flirt. I feel tighter than a virgin, fear layered on fear. All my time alone has done just what I wanted it to, and now I'm about to undo it all.

"Listen," I say, "Sam. I don't know what you came for but . . ." I'm hoping he'll get some idea of what I mean just because I stop and look down modestly. When you can't look a man in the eye he ought to guess why. But I'm crazy and furious and he's not, so he just looks at me, eager beaver, bright boy, blinking. I have to stand myself in front of him, between him and the window light. Brazen, I have to touch him.

"Renata, no, look, honey," he finally says, "don't vamp me, that's not what I came for."

"I'm sure it's not. It better not be. But—" I put his large lumpy hand on my breast, which disappears like a pebble in his grasp. He looks confused, a little flustered. He had no orders from Gerda about procedures in the event of seduction; she lacks the proper imagination. Nice to make him lose that polished cool.

"I don't have many surprises like this in the line of duty." Long breath. And another.

"Smile, Sam. Nobody's looking."

"Look—" He moves back a step.

"Look yourself." And I move his one hand slowly. "Don't do my mother's errands, do your own, Sam." I feel like a teen-age tease, awkward and absurd. But it'll be all right: some rhythms have to come back to you. "Don't you ever want to think for yourself, doesn't my mother make you hand in your balls at the front desk? Don't you have to check them with Cornelia to work there?"

"No I don't, why the hell do you say that? A law office isn't a gym, you know, we're not playing against each other." But I'm winning, I'll bet he thinks that, he's breathing that into the hair over my right ear. Vain. He enchants himself. He's wearing the nicest smoothest grayest suit. No cat food on those fingertips. Good wine, expensive sheets, percale, not even muslin. No screwing in sleeping bags, on shag rugs full of cat hair, on mattresses stained with the map of the world. A little money from somewhere else, I'll bet. Girls with clean long hair and no pins in their underwear.

I tell him I've been alone a long time, a recluse waiting for something but I haven't known what, some accident to save me. But I don't lie the way a man would, I don't say, waiting for you. I couldn't do that. I describe it a little: everything blowing around in my head like papers in the wind. "I need some weight on me, Sam," and then I watch the way a methodical man, who will someday be an assistant district attorney, gets ready to make love in broad daylight. He folds his pants. Takes the change out of his pocket so it won't roll when he folds his pants over the chair, to keep the pleats. Puts his socks in his shiny shoes for safekeeping. Wristwatch stays on. The meter ticks. He should be Mother's lover, I think, as he brings his long tanned body to me finally, all the housekeeping tasks done, everything in place except his reason for being here.

He slides his hands lightly over my stomach, which is the only rounded place my self-pity hasn't eaten away. "Is it true you get a stripe down your stomach when you have a baby?"

"Yup," I tell him without smiling. "Except blondes, I didn't have much of one. But a little, yes. How did you know that?"

"My cousin had one, it was wild—it gave away this baby she'd had. Her parents wouldn't ever have found out but she came home from college and they saw her in a bikini and they said, you know, what's that?"

"And?"

"And 'that' was already out for adoption and they all cried and said all the usual horrified fascinated things. I was about fifteen, I remember, and I couldn't believe there was this sort of mark of Zorro, this brand, that could give her away like that. Nobody with a baby ever showed me her stomach."

"Oh, they could see it if it was still new enough." I look at him as hard as I can: I haven't seen a man close up for so long it makes me want to cry. He looks back, asking questions. "My mother never said anything. But then, she never saw my stripe."

"Well, your mother probably never stopped talking quite long enough to notice you had anybody with you." He laughs.

When he finally stops talking and begins to move, and finds his way inside my deserted, my abandoned, my faraway body, I taste copper, rusty tin in the back of my mouth. I was prepared to have my motives ruin this. I was going to hate him when he was done, I was counting on being numb with calculation. But I find myself in tears. I can see he can't tell whether I'm crying from pleasure or disappointment; the tears of a crazy woman must be less readable than others'. "Renata, did you like that? I'm sorry if it didn't—"

"Sam, no need. I can't explain. Just sshhh."

"Why did we do this?"

"You wanted to."

"No." He shakes his dark hair emphatically against my neck.

"I wanted to."

"No. No, you didn't."

"Well, what's left. My mother wanted us to."

"Jesus." He pulls himself away and springs off the couch abruptly. "That isn't very funny." And just as he couldn't read me, I can't read him: is he offended or just efficient, is his little alarm set for five minutes of *post coitum triste* and not a minute more?

When he is coming out of the john, Tippy is waiting in the hall on tiptoe. She is making a face for innocent evil: Mama, what mischief I'm doing, spying! Sam comes out, fast, and there she is watching his lean hairless ass. She's never seen a naked man, our traffic in lovers is a little thin, Mother's and mine. Her eyes widen. The poor man, towering over her, goes pink all over, his hips, his chest, he is rosy with astonishment. He covers himself like a maiden. I should be restrained, I think, but I only say, ignoring Tippy, "Now why don't you tell me what you came to inveigle me into doing."

Efficient indeed. He is dressed in about thirty seconds, tying his tie in gigantic tugs, like a bell rope. "Typing." He slams his feet into his classy shoes. "I heard you could type and I've got an article I needed done. A book review."

"Ah. As you say: ah. Well, I'm sorry."

"Me too. Renata—" He wants to ask me why I did this, and why I was crying because those were not the tears of ordinary relief he likes to bring his women to. What were they, he wants to know but he's afraid to ask, and there's my little daughter, here now in the doorway, poking out her dark head once in a while to see if the coast is clear.

"Renata, if you care to know, I'm not the shit you think I am—"

"I don't think you're anything of the kind. Please. Don't worry about that. It never occurred to me. Actually, if you want to know, I think you're very obliging."

I suppose he's humiliated after the fact, the way I was when I was a pushover; only it's worse for him, he isn't used to it.

"Sam, look. Take your typing back to the office and forget this. I'm a lousy typist, but anyway I'm working on a career of—transparency. Nothingness. It's what I'm good at. Giving displeasure and adding and multiplying up to zero. And I can't afford to catch myself enjoying that."

"What?"

"What we just did. Being with anybody and liking it."

"You're going to live a life of mortification of the flesh?"

I am still naked; appropriate, that, and not very appealing. "I'm vanishing, see, I'm disappearing a couple of square inches a week."

"Renata, you'd better get some help. You're a very scary lady." But he's on his way to the door.

"My mother and I love each other through a window, you know, glass in between. No touching."

"The hell with your mother, what does she have to do with that? Jesus, you're obsessed with her, she's not obsessed with you, you know."

"Right." I turn over, then—see, I can dismiss people the way she does, voilà. "Right you are. She's not." And I put my head down on my arms and wish for blankness. Whiteness. This stranger's babies are white, swimming and flailing around inside me, bobbing in their milky medium right now. I lie there and try to feel them lurch their tails and buck and crawl, desperate, straining upward in me, random as bump 'em cars at the amusement park, thank god their power dying as they go.

GERDA

It came upon me that this was June, the fiscal year at an end, another season begun and so little accomplished. How many seasons shall a woman of my age have left to her, with which to feel dissatisfied? I am so fortunate, always, to have more to do than time in which to do it: I think again, I think so often of the outworn passions in the outworn bodies of the *bubbas* and *zaydes* in that hotel in Long Beach to which my friend Tavistock retired to sleep forever. (And does he still? Clients do not return for annual checkups.)

I was on the plane to Washington when I met a dear old friend. It was Nahum Simms from Gillespie, Mississippi, and I was more astounded than he at the meeting: so much, I think, has astounded Nahum in past years that in him the quality of surprise is worn quite flat.

"Where have you been, my friend, and where are you going?"

He had eyes crossed at such a severe angle it was uncomfortable to look straight at him. But such eyes, and his glasses, gave him the face of an uncommonly serious man. "Oh, Miz Stein, I been goin around, you know, I get sent ever which where for the county program, comin from a housin meetin in New York, now I'm goin down and breathe a little on the body of the OEO's. Then I get to go home awhile and see how none of it don't make no difference." He stretched his clasped hands before him to act out his ennui.

"Why, so am I, Nahum. I am going to testify about the cuts in legal services."

"Yeah, we got them too, they leavin us crumbs and expect us to fill up on 'em and have the strength left to salute the flag." He looked grim, smiling his gold-toothed grin. Ah, Nahum. I remember him as a farmer, with small holdings like his neighbors, making do for a considerable family in a grubbing inefficient way. But you would not find him ever in work clothes at the end of the day. You could not so much as picture his hands covered with radish dirt or the green slime of the okra he planted and harvested. I should guess he preferred to look sedentary. He would show up at desegregation meetings in dark sport shirts, buttoned right to the neck around his slight chest. You had to admire him for not going the next step, though, and becoming what some people called a white shirt man. It was a fine line but he respected the side of it on which he was born and lived.

I should say I recalled him as middling smart, middling brown, only middling bitter for a man from Horace County, Mississippi. Perhaps things had changed but there were worse counties and worse times. Possibly now, ten years after we sat side by side in our interminable meetings things were more bleak, not with fear or apathy but with resignation and defeat: so much and so little have happened. "Well, look," he would explain most patiently. "I growed up in the middle of nine, and I seen four die deaths that wasn't none of them pretty, and none of them nec'sary either. So I know how the man do us. Not just me, I'm makin out all right, I mean all of us." Whatever the reason (if one is the kind who needs the better things explained as well as the worse) he never really was afraid. Perhaps he made up in genuine fearlessness for his lack of stature, of size and charisma. He was one of the first men in town to vote. His tool shed or his barn, I have forgotten, was fire-bombed. He lost his credit in the town on Saturdays. "But," he would say, "nothin so bad if you ain't started out scared." He helped some of his neighbors try to work together in a farming cooperative, getting some practice with the account books, learning as he went. I taught him a good deal about double-entry bookkeeping and he caught on without much humor but with a slow unsurprised smile over his mistakes. I could recognize what it felt like to be Nahum, you see; not that I am not a bit more flamboyant in my demands, my ambitions, my expression, but that we both of us have at core a certain faith and a heavy balance which costs us the ability to fly.

By the time I met him Nahum had run for Congress, because there were so few faithful freedom party people above him who were trusted and did not also have a pocketful of enemies to unbalance their friends. And then he went to work for the poverty program in Gillespie. He looked comfortable in the work; unsmiling he kept the little office running. If he had vices they were dryness and a certain unforgiving quality. If I am to be honest, I should say I recognize these as well. Solemn the two of us over our accounts. And we forgot nothing. What a run on honest competent men there was—well, perhaps there always is, at differing levels, always the same run. I too have looked for them, from office custodians to senators.

Nahum, whom you would most surely have missed in a dark room, because I could never induce him to bring his voice up beyond a modest whisper, showed up well in a hard noon light. You can recognize this, how people whose flesh is pared so close to the bone do not look as though they have many places on them, quite literally, in which to hide anything. Standing, short, pants buckled high, before a dusty gray blackboard on wheels, he would move his lips, wetting them often while he scratched in the columns of votes or spelled out the name of someone slowly, with a first initial and (never omitted) a fat white period, like a swollen tick, after it.

"How are the folks at home?" I asked Nahum, still holding his warm dark hand, shaking and shaking it with delight. His veins were hard as bone.

"Oh, Miz Stein, I don know. Good enough, I guess. Sanka been drinkin a little but that ain't nothin new. You remember. And my little ones all out of school now, they finish, the baby gettin married in a week or so. Nice boy from Vicksburg. But Eddie—" He looked all around the cabin of the plane as though for an unmarked exit all his own.

"What about Eddie?" Who was Rosie Jo's friend, who had

tried to lead a bunch of his friends with lit torches on the day of Rosie Jo's funeral, while I was in jail, in trouble.

"Eddie in Springfield, Illinois. I be honest, Miz Stein, he what they call all strung out these days. No good for nothin. Since he was over there he push dope, he smoke dope, he done things I wouldn't know what they was if I seen him up close only they all against the law's all I know." He sighed from the depth of his shallow chest.

"He's been away for a long time," I said, as though by way of excuse.

"Oh yeah. Yeah." He fixed his poor crossed eyes on my face; on my ears, I should say. "What there to hold a able-body boy down home? He been in the war. Ain't no poverty money no more. His daddy keepin on cause if I stop I be sayin it was all for what? Keep me in pencils and tight collars?" Had there been a place to spit, he would have punctuated his speech then with a rough thrust of his tongue. He smoothed his hair, which could not need smoothing. Perhaps he has been studying the senators with the great crops of photogenic curls.

Together we went to the hotel when we arrived in Washington, and strolled out Connecticut Avenue through the spring heat toward dinner with half a dozen others, ambling along. He still walked very straight, stiffly in his bent-over-backward dignity, this sweet man who seemed to me a triumph of will and the decency of ambition. He spoke little to the others, but listened, listened, his head inclined downward not out of humility but for the sake of concentration and, I think, to keep his crooked eyes from showing. We sat in the restaurant, a bunch of old poverty warriors thumbing sadly through our memories, warm with wine and the immediacy of younger days and hopes, until they asked us to leave. They were casting sawdust around the table. When, once, Nahum and some friends and I sat together in the Gillespie Hitone Diner, a woman walked angrily round and round our booth with an atomizer spreading deodorizer on the air. . . .

Perhaps it was two o'clock in the morning when my telephone rang. It was Nahum, or a pale voice nearly like his that said, "Miz Stein, come quick, I think I'm goin, I'm goin."

In my robe I ran, he was on my corridor. His door was locked. I summoned the man at the desk, I ran to him feeling as though I were on a ship and it was sinking, the narrow halls endless and sloping beneath my feet. He was reluctant to leave the lobby unattended. Similarly was he unwilling to give me his key. I nearly picked the man up by his lapels. He considered and reconsidered and came with me, running.

We came back to unlock the door and there we found poor Nahum lying half across his bed, his head toward the floor at a violent twisted angle—Addie, again that yielding by the human body of all its order at moments of extremity. Why must I be haunted regularly by such visions? Do I somehow make them recur because I *believe* in recurrence? Such a thing cannot be!

"Oh he's bad, he's bad," the man from the desk kept murmuring to himself as he set Nahum's head and shoulders back on the rumpled bed. "He's bad," he kept on as he dialed for a doctor, his eyes on Nahum as though he might take it into his head to escape. But he looked at me without hope. He hummed as it rang, absently, without remembering to be sad. But how nice, how very kind, was all I could think, grateful only not to be alone, that this stranger who did not care to come in the first place could then care about the skinny black man half fallen from his bed at two in the morning, with his professional anonymous concern.

The doctor came quickly with his own more educated hopelessness, he said we were lucky he was nearby so very often. He seemed in fact so pleased by the coincidence it was a wonder he did not ask us to agree it was good fortune that had seized Nahum by the throat, and not death. In a discreet voice he dialed for an ambulance. Nahum lay now in the corrugated sheets which I was forbidden to straighten, and his eyes were on me. They had swung out nearly straight. Why must ironies be always unkind? So he shall have fine straight eyes to take to his grave with him, which in another man would be at this point on the walls, out of control. He looked at me beseechingly, though nothing of his face moved. Yet I could see he felt like the little boy who gets sick at the school picnic. He looked shamed and defeated, his eyes too frightened to move. I held his hand and murmured meaningless words to him. "We will take you home to Sanka," I told him in a calm voice. "We will bring a plane and take you quickly home to Gillespie. Down the street, down Central Street, around the bank—is the bank there still? I'll bet it has mushroomed up branch windows in all directions—and we shall go down to the Esso pump and there will be that dog—what was his name? Spark, Spunk? Or—he would be quite old now, wouldn't he? And up to your end, where the blacktop stops. . . ." Whenever I ceased my speaking, what rose to my mind were the flotsam, jetsam of my own silent disordered language, it is the voice aloud that keeps me at attention, but the silent voice dozed through all its aberrations, *langsam, begonias,* I thought, *bilateral fenestration.* The hypnogogic dreams that wait just beyond reason. *Put a cassava stick in his hand and he will punish the murderer. Put the names in a dish and pour sweet oil on them and burn a white candle each morning beside it for one hour, from nine to ten. They will destroy themselves in court at your bequest and honor. Langsam. Sadakah means charity. Abandonné.*

When I woke they had closed his eyes and pulled the sheet up over his modest mustache but not his nose. A new technique, to aid the breathing of the deceased. . . . Heaven rest him. Two thousand miles from the county line, Horace and Blue, two such beautiful ugly places, an administrator of nothing, whose fifty-five, sixty years, smaller than some, not so small as others, had cracked open in his head. He did not linger to see the entire kingdom desecrated. He predeceased his son, his junkie, whose friend Rosie Jo was predeceased before him. Spared. The world, turning, shook Nahum from one longitude to another and so many, his world, had stayed behind to receive him when he came home. They would follow the very route I traveled from memory but would stop at the funeral parlor and leave him with goldmouth Frank who wore a rubber apron and a diamond chip on his pinkie. Where will Renata bury me?

"Oh my dear lady," said the doctor gently, and clicked his tongue at me. "I believe I should give you something to take to put you to sleep."

"Nonsense, why should I sleep," I demanded of him, this very young man dressed up for the party from which he had come running, "when soon enough I shall be sleeping the way your patient sleeps? And please do not look at me as though I pity myself, that is fact, not pity."

I should like a funeral at which weeping would be allowed: the kind Nahum will have.

I felt as must have Nahum, unable to speak, as I stood before the doctor and the desk man. I wished to be a small girl who could weep into my mother's skirts with no apology. So I made myself stern and thanked them formally. "To whom shall this bill be sent?" I asked, to see how far this doctor's regret would extend.

"I don't know," he said, glancing at the desk man. Apparently this is a question most are too discreet to ask, but I am aware that doctors levy their fees to the vanquished as well as to the victors of their illnesses.

"Only be certain not to send it to his family," I instructed. "Put his on my bill, if you will. And let me notify his next of kin, please."

And I left them with Nahum to return to my room where I lay panting, breathless, until dawn. I begin to see the many little ways in which one conspires with one's slowing-down. I shall begin to wait, now, for signs until I make them come.

At seven I called Mrs. Nahum Simms, née Sanka. I could barely imagine the woman, having seen her rarely. Nahum, so efficient in his fields and in his office, liked to give the impression that he was, at home, merely tolerated: feet for sweeping around. By reputation his wife was violent and unresponsive to her husband's work. Oh my, she did hate "white folks," too, in utter abashed silence. Just so would she now confirm her hatred, when I bring her this news.

She answered the phone with a kind of scowl and I introduced myself as best I could. Yes, she grunted recognition. "Mrs. Simms," I said to her gently, "I am afraid I am the bearer of bad tidings."

"Say-*what?*" she asked, impatient, that so-familiar old phrase breaking upon me like a warm wave. It is nearly a one-syllable word, and must be sung out skeptically, head cocked to one side for better hearing and a kind of better vision.

"Bad news." I bit down upon it, loud. Reduced to bareness: well, so it should be. "Nahum was taken ill—he was—" And so I told her, "Mrs. Simms, your husband has this morning died."

"Say-*what?*" Her voice only rose higher; it had caught some inkling of my tone if not my message. Was she deaf or stupid or merely unbelieving? It would be too intimate a thing to allow me to know. There was a commotion and one of her children apparently seized the phone. And so I repeated my message and there was only a little "huh" to acknowledge its receipt.

"Do you understand?"

"Yes'm." Obedient and cowed. Wherever did Nahum come from? There is no gene for bravery. Or might her silence, even her mother's silence, be brave on their terms.

"Do you wish to hear the details?"

"Yes'm."

When I had done I said, "And now what will you do?"

"I don't know, missus," said the husky-voiced girl. "We go wait on him to come home, I guess."

"Do you know that he was a fine man, and much loved?"

"Yes'm," she said again. "He always was." Indeed. So I hung up at last reluctantly—I would like to have made certain they knew what kind of father they had had. But they knew him too. Let me not romanticize. We are none of us what we seem straight on. Who are the egotists who order the tombstones that say MOTHER or BROTHER? Merely the ones who are paying.

So I hung up, wholly unthanked. Perhaps I mean unforgiven. All I wanted was to hear them weep. I wanted to hear, from someone, proper mourning.

All that day while I dozed through eulogies for legal services for the poor, health care services, educational services, I thought, so many ways to die, my friends, to dry up or be squeezed to death between pennies, or to be rendered invisible, erased like a pencil line. The great stage lights shone on us where we sat, the dome of Senator Javits's head reflected as though it were a diamond, many-faceted. Under the table the feet of half a dozen senators danced and twined and only in the most riveting of personal cries, agonized appeals, did they stand still respectfully, shamed. We most dutifully spoke into our little microphones and were dutifully applauded, and as I talked I watched the little tap dances commence again, the points of shined shoes disappear over the rungs of their chairs. It was nearly hypnotizing. Our words went outside the violent light of the hearing room stage, and they too died.

RENATA

Mother brings home éclairs for Tippy; shamelessly they share
them. One sits in the plate for me, looking forgotten. She is excited, she has taken a case that has something or other to do with
migrants. She hugs Tippy and dances around the room with her.
It is real joy, she is capable of that: the kind I used to have when
the phone rang and it was the right boy. Little girls are always
jumping up and down with it. Tip puts her feet on Mother's and
they do the giant walk.

"The growers," she says jubilantly, "will be brought to bay once
and for all, no more equivocation," and she is off into the particulars—for me? for Tippy? How she loves victims to remake into
victors, forever grateful. Imagine, my infinitesimal daughter sits
and looks into her face, nodding, pretending to understand. She
licks her lips now, just like her grandmother; one of these days
she'll start developing an accent. Well, there's something for her,
the music of that excitement, the vigor. She has plenty of reason
to be bored with me; I'm boring for two.

She needs friends, I decided. So did I but I couldn't even begin.
I want some nice normal happy houses with clean space to play in
and straight kids who sleep so far off the floor maybe they have
big chunky maple bunk beds with blankets on them their mothers
got for opening bank accounts.

Monica is as far as I got in my search. She's a nice enough girl.

She invites us right in. Obviously she's had her eye on me, in an apartment house the neighbors whisper in the elevator to give themselves something to do. I feel obligated to sit down and be friendly. She has four children, three of them girls, and so she says she won't even notice an extra. "Leave her, leave her, go out and have the afternoon on me. Go to a movie or something," she suggests. I think of the way one child, quiet, grates on my open skin. Tippy goes right down the hall with some or all of them. Why is she so trusting? She's never played in a houseful of kids but in ten minutes they'll be arranging Barbie and Ken dolls in a circle, they'll knock them down with their dodge ball and then they'll play doctor and see where they've been hurt. I sit down over instant coffee in the kitchen. It's sunny. Yellow curtains and a thorough spice rack.

Monica, I'm thinking, if you only knew why I'm here, if you could see me floating nowhere on the couch all afternoon while Tippy makes do arranging and rearranging the silverware, the books, all the empty time.

I try to begin. "Hey, your chandelier is great. Doesn't your husband hit his head on it?" It is a wagon wheel with little tulip-shaped bulbs.

"Well, not if the table's in the right place he doesn't," Monica says. "But if my kids move it one more time. They get under it, see, and they put a blanket over it and—" She waves her hand; amiable disgust.

Enviable Monica with her so lovable problems. Half her grievances her kids will grow out of, the other half will be changed for shiny new ones. She goes running suddenly—I barely see her go—down the hall, around the corner and back: somebody was yowling. "Sound like dogs, they really do." She sits lightly, poised for another quick intervention.

Her virtues she keeps modestly hidden: fast reflexes, patience with perpetual disorder which I suppose she turns into order after each and every meal: the kitchen is crumbless. I have a picture of my daughter's face peering at me, tearless but desolate, somehow, over the greasy bones of a chicken quarter that lies on her plate like a canary; an apple coated with crumbs like something out of a Halloween bag; the kitchen is cluttered but essentially empty.

Lord forgive me, I have no respect for anybody, I'm like my mother, intolerant and nasty and snobbish. It wouldn't hurt if I were more like Monica. So I turn to her, weary. On the counter-top behind her there is a kitchen knife, brown-handled with those big brass studs. It is standing at an angle in the heart of an orange. I like Monica a great deal suddenly, I feel a rush of some true relation that's chemical. The lives I see etched on our faces by our days and nights alone or with our husbands aren't to the point, they're only the distractions. Here and there our lives are going to leave some perfect frames behind, like Vermeers, Bergmans. The only time I've ever come close to such a feeling— knife in the heart of the world, hard and sloppy at the same time —was when I've been very high, when complicated things get very simple and simple things all tangled and impenetrable. High on instant coffee and evaporated milk.

Monica confirms my good feeling just as it disappears. She asks, turning to look at me, "Have you ever thought about a psychiatrist?"

I laugh. "Thought what about a psychiatrist?"

"No, I mean just generally." She talks eagerly. How much has she changed since high school? "I went for a little while, just sort of short-term, crisis therapy, it was called."

Well, I suppose I am being invited to probe a secret. I probe. "Were you having a crisis?"

Her children look just like her, I realize. In spite of their father's hair and eyes they look like Monica because she has the more logical face for giving to children. They may grow out of her but now she is like their older sister. Where has she put her years?

"Oh—whew. A crisis." She smiles brightly. What she has, I decide, reversing myself, is the face of a fourteen-year-old girl who has aged a little before her time. Short pert middle-color hair, narrow Shirley MacLaine-cute eyes. The lines are all silicone-stuffed: is that what "putting a good face on it" means? Only my mother is the exception, she who has learned to make the most pained face possible, the complaining mouth, the weary voice, and yet is full of her strange joy.

Maybe you smile this way in the aftermath of a lobotomy? "I had a couple of shock treatments, you know. Boy, did I feel with that Eagleton, the poor bastard. What a rough deal. He'll never know how many just plain people know what he went through. . . ." She shakes her bouncy hair.

"No, I didn't know," I say. So I've underestimated my neighbor, we could have gone off the deep end together like pals if I'd known. She's like someone who commits suicide and thereby rises in your estimation. What was it like, I want to know.

"It was the house. We lived in this brownstone in Brooklyn, Cobble Hill? That's where my husband's office is, you know, this is very inconvenient, where we are now. Among other things. Well, when the house was first getting done, I mean, what a syndrome, boy. It dragged out everything in my whole life, can you imagine that? You're lucky you don't own anything."

"Well, nobody's ever put it quite like that before."

"Believe me," she insists. "Can you imagine we just picked up and sold it? That was a very uneconomical thing to do, let me tell you, I thought Frank was going to leave me he was so mad, but it was either me or the house." She laughs. "I think he had his moments. Did we take a loss. . . ."

Out of the corner of my eye I catch the rumpled wink of the orange reflected in the shiny knife. Those are the things to watch. Don't listen to this house story, I prod myself, it's an alibi. Some people know how to parlay an itch, good fortune, a good mortgage, into genuine angst. That's where Monica happened to be when her real life fell into shards and timbers—a convenient spot from which to view the ruins. Her foundations go steep and deep as anyone's and can rot and stink. And mine. I sell the world short, I see I sell myself.

"You've got a woman, at least, I see her come up. You and your mother." She is mopping the table with a sponge where it wasn't dirty. No wonder, the stains are overtaking her while they're still in the glass. Tomato juice is rising on all sides waiting for her children to stomp it into her carpets. Ah, she is my laundry soap customer made flesh. She will never get ahead of the dirt.

"I've got a woman?" Incredible.

"To help with the cleaning. There are a million good women around, don't listen to the complainers, they wouldn't be happy if God himself came and washed their windows. But see—the best

241

ones these days are all Spanish, is yours Spanish? You can't get anybody black, they're all too angry, they'll spite you every way they can. I hate to say that but it's true. Whether I blame them or not." She smiles shyly at her sociological certainties. "But Puerto Ricans are gentle and they're terrific with kids. . . . Isn't yours?"

Mine. I lay my spoon down in the saucer and consider: Monica in shackles, electric wires like silver necklaces all around her, sprouting from her plated head, attended by a cooing Catalina, shapely in a maid's uniform. Pedigreed. Certified gentle. I am overtaken by a need to laugh, but when I stifle it, it aches and glows in my chest like hot tears. So I laugh. I laugh so hard, so wrenched, like that Fred what-was-his-name in *Treasure of Sierra Madre* when all his money and his life blows away into the desert, that when Tippy comes bouncing in to get a cookie, what she sees is her mama and her friends' mama embracing helplessly, locked like dolls, laughing right over each other's shoulders. A pushme-pullyou. Tippy takes a cookie out of the jar solemnly, keeping her eyes on us just in case—I wonder if she's thinking, I figured my mother was crazy but now I know—and then remembers her new friends and takes four more.

GERDA

On the dining room table when I return home from my saddening trip I find a note propped on my topmost folder:

MAY I PLEASE BORROW $200. IS THERE ANY WAY? IT ISN'T
FOR ME, IT'S FOR A FRIEND WHO CAN'T ASK YOU FOR IT.
PLEASE DON'T TAKE OUR QUARRELS OUT ON THE REST OF THE
WORLD. WHEN I SEE HOW THINGS ARE FOR MOST PEOPLE WE
ARE (BOTH OF US) SELF-INDULGENT.   R.

It is interesting to see how my daughter's argument with me has become ours, ditto to the self-indulgence; also interesting that she has broken her strenuous silence for someone else. There may be a sign of life there under the self-pity, though *I* am quite free to bleed to death. But no teardrops on the note? Such control she is practicing. Now who can this friend be? Whose need would so embarrass her that she cannot utter his name full-face?

I go to her where she sits in her uniform lethargy watching television. A pity there was no TV in Addie's long stupefied day. All they are doing on this, the "education" channel, is raising money. The annual dunning. Phones ring, we see—dramatically—a mystery hand extended to catch it, and then a pretty long-haired girl's face rises up like a small sun and she is smiling and nodding and writing down a name and a sum, and the day is—piece by piece—saved. It is like watching an earth-moving machine, or an ant, transferring crumbs from here to there. Some people are fascinated by it, apparently. It is the story, behind the scenes, of Stein, Weisbacher, Tenney and Balch: perpetual money-grubbing, and no dignity anywhere in it.

"What a pity not to be able to hold out your open hand to these people for your friend." I sit on the arm of Renata's chair. What costs $200? An abortion—possibly. A month's rent? Unlikely. A month of Seconals?

"You are quite correct that we are self-indulgent, you know. Better if certain of us managed a tighter rein."

"That's both of us or neither." Her eyes stay on the screen, on that financial high intrigue. She would, if she swept out her head, make a decisive administrator; she can be as resolute as the next one, and as devious.

"Who is it, Renata? I don't care to discuss our behavior, I have come to wonder only why you so delight in haunting me that you will give up your own life to stay here and attempt to make me guilty and uncomfortable. Until I can understand what pleasure you take in inertia and entropy I have nothing to discuss. Only now it is a question of hard cash, correct? Then you shall specify just as though I were a bank or a loan company, please, precisely why you need this money."

"You are not a bank or a loan company." A tiny voice.

"Oh, this has a familiar ring, this conversation. You do enjoy putting me in this position to refuse you so that you then can be outraged."

"It should be familiar, it's about Catalina. Tico—"

"Oh my."

"Which means—"

"Which means, they never do stop, do they? Nor do you."

Her head is bent on one hand, her broken-stemmed look. "You're right, there's no reason to talk. Do you know, you would have a fit if, I don't know—if Jesus Christ was sitting here because he doesn't have a lousy college education. And you'd say, uh-oh, he's in trouble again."

"Tico needs bail. His mother's heart is again broken just where it was last cemented by your tears."

"Five hundred dollars. Catalina's finding three. Somehow or other. I don't know how she can see straight."

"And undoubtedly her daughter shall be next week pregnant and you shall begin again. The week after that her husband, her whatever-he-is, this common-law man of hers, shall be laid off. And then—"

She is gritting her eyes closed, and her mouth, making them tiny drawn seams. One foot leaps and leaps as though beating time. "I think this is the least you could do, considering."

"Considering." I slump in resignation. Considering. "Well, my friend, you still will not understand, I have no guilt to assuage in this other matter of Catalina. What strange ideas you persist in having. I am not abject with regrets, it is you who wants to crawl. Even Catalina has no desire to see your belly in the gutter for her son. Nor her own." Remembering her gratuitous cruelty on the subject.

She does not answer.

"Well, then, tell me, are we running a competing charity?" I lead with my chin toward the TV, which rackets on name after name and gushes thanks and gives away tokens of gratitude which no one who can spend such money could possibly need.

"Just let him stay in jail and rot, even with what you know about jails. For a couple of hundred bucks you wouldn't miss, just let him."

My impatience makes it difficult to contain myself. "What I know, Renata, includes some monstrous details, yes, of jails, of the bail system, of many sorry realities. But I also know that from this particular distance I cannot help, nor can you. Charity is the most destructive meliorative there is. Fool's gold, you shall buy off your conscience and feel free to go back to sleep here on this sofa until the next crisis rouses you for an hour. But the crises are, why am I forced to instruct you in this, symptomatic. You must understand that. This is not moral repugnance at the boy's criminality. Do you see the distinction?" How she and Anna-Joyce would get along! "Only the weak and the lazy can feed money into this machine that gives back bubble gum that will rot the teeth and plastic charms that will break in a day."

She is smiling at me and shaking her head.

"Well, come to my office and I will show you what can be done. Get off your *tuchis* here and do something besides throw good money and good pity after bad. Money is not even a Band-Aid, you see. If the boy bleeds, he bleeds. Let him acknowledge his wounds and learn to walk more wisely, help to teach him that. But if he shall die of internal bleeding, invisible, you will have helped him."

She again smiles, self-satisfied. "Did you ever in your life give a quarter to a blind man?"

"No I have not. Even when they were asking for nickels. But every year I buy wares from those Lighthouse people who are blind. Brooms and aprons, whether or not I need them. Some self-respect has built and sewed and tacked those things and they make me actually proud."

She nods, not with acceptance or comprehension; with weariness. "You and William Buckley," she mutters.

"Well, get a job, my love, and pay your way into whichever zoo makes you feel most comfortable. I shall hold no sway if you will put some of this random effort you waste on pity into buying your freedom. You choose. If you think I care too little about live ambulatory cases, then I think you care too little too. If you think the salvation of the world is a spectator sport. But either way, you see, it is unnatural for a grown woman like you to care so much what your mother thinks. It is worse, if you will ask me, than giving over your autonomy to a man, it is more immature." Because, you see, I do not wish any more to be blamed for her misery: it is hers alone.

She is staring blankly at the televised dénouement. "Over the top, ladies and gentlemen, you have been so good. We have $500,000 in pledges and that means—"

I raise myself slowly from the arm of her chair. She is very frail and frightened, I have eyes, I can see that—this solitude and isolation have weakened her, it is herself she has hurled against me as a weapon. It is as though her bones have softened from disuse. Every day she must ask herself like a centipede, how is it that one *does* walk? And so she cannot move. But to forgive with no sign of equal effort that she is trying to walk would be from me but another form of charity. Let her rise up, however blind, and make a broom for herself and need I say, I shall be the first to buy it?

❀ ❀ ❀

Tippy and I take a long walk to the Museum of Natural History on Saturday morning. There are thousands of children there spinning like flies on the marble floors, they assault my ears, they run into me, Tippy once is knocked against a glass cabinet by a small black boy, laughing, his jacket open on a shirt that says UNIVERSITY OF CUERNAVACA. Really. My shoes squeak on the marble. Tippy needs the bathroom endlessly, I hope she is not infected. (Why do I cover the toilet seat with paper, she wants to know, helping me to unroll it. Imagine, her mother has never done so, it would be—besides being superfluous in view of her conduct—entirely too much a capitulation to the bourgeois values that left in Europe unshaved legs and unshorn hair and a contempt for contact-borne bacteria.)

When she is hungry she whines unendurably and I can find no solace. And so as though it were our prime purpose in *shlepping* ourselves over here, the first thing we must do is devote ourselves to lunch, which costs a great deal and introduces to Tippy's yellow collar an ineradicable dollop of ketchup. I rub it with water while the child squirms and nearly upsets the glass. The stain is now large and gray with a red bull's-eye. She has her mother's gypsy slovenliness. Today I am decidedly too old for mothering. I scold her, she wilts, retracts her head between her shoulders and glares angrily. "You don't like Grandma," I prod her.

"I want Mama."

"Doesn't Mama scold you for doing things like that, dropping things?"

She thrusts her lip at me, thrusts upon me a gross ugliness as a punishment. "I don't know." The child glances all about her. "You smell like a raincoat," she tells me sweetly. "Like a shoe I once had and put it in the fire."

248

"A what?"

"Why do you wear a net?"

"To keep my hair where it should stay, in wind it—"

"How did you get to be my grandma?" She looks at me sharply, a pinprick in the eye. She has very beautiful eyes, this child, none that I recognize, undoubtedly from her father's side: gray, with brown-gold spokes. I pray to God she is not beautiful: spare her that. Or if she must be, and I fear she must, give her the strength her mother never had and which I never needed. "Because I am your mother's mother, *maidele*. I am—"

"My friend told me his grandma doesn't got teeth or anything. They come out and you just float them and they could bite in the water. But only—"

"What, dear?"

"I wish I had a lot of grandmas anyway."

Well, you know, she is right: she is deprived of an entire half of her family. My daughter's easy freedom—she spreads her legs like wings but what freedom has her flight brought for this lonely and bewildered child?

(Though, to be fair: what kind of family did my marriage bring to my own daughter? I have never thought there was a single similarity between our positions.)

"I want to go home now, Grandma." She looks weary.

"We won't go home quite yet, dear." Straining for gentleness. I look at her to see if her eyes are as cool as her little piping voice, she is not trying for poignancy. She has one long delicate eyebrow. I feel myself menacing from this vantage point—she must feel sometimes like an insect beneath a great rolling wheel.

"I didn't see the deer!" The way this child changes voices, she is like a knee that goes in and out of joint! "The ones like Bambi, I want to see."

"You have seen fifteen animals that did not in the least interest you."

"But I want to see Bambi."

"Please hush, then. Do not shout."

The child delivers to my shin a kick, not so hard that I must cry out but muted: saying, I would like to smash to bits your bones, dear Grandma, but I am afraid to do that for the obvious reasons, because I know already one thing or two. Within an instant of her kick she kisses my arm at the elbow where she can catch it. Her kiss is hard, teeth are in it far back, the child is altogether like a stone hidden in a snowball or a mud pie. A terrible force, a fury lurks behind her little fall of bangs and the down cheeks and it emerges in this unpredictable affection. I believe she contains the same sullen kernel of energy my brother tormented us with as a child: we, my mother and I, conspired to think it was a masculine syndrome learned of peasants, but I see how incomplete was our cosmology. It is, in fact, undoubtedly an admirable aspect of early childhood, that a child dare to assert her unpredictability and untrammeled aggressions before she must learn the kind of control she will need to be an adult. But I am not constrained to have to like being kicked. She shall never lie about the house slack like her mother, but still my ankle aches.

She is dragging me to Bambi and I go because were I to resist I should be dangerous to her. So my hidden force meets hers, they skirmish out of sight. Nuclear deterrents! Running before me on this veined shiny floor I see this child and feel my daughter's shadow stretching out even farther beyond me: out of my power where I cannot touch. And with this child my blood thins to water. Tippy-Theresa of my own blood, with her Catholic name, that saint who swooned with passion for Christ. Certainly her naming completed, ensured the distance between us, and was meant that way: a sign that I had no rights in the matter of her mother's obsessions. A child born cut adrift. Do you recall the famous monkeys in the experiment who moved things with sticks for tools, to great applause? The extension of intelligence! Well, now I feel I can only prod Tippy with a stick held in the crook of another stick dangling in my fingers. What force is left after such extension?

"All right. Bambi. Do you like her? See the little white star on her."

"Where's the daddy?" Tippy hugs at my dress angrily as though I had suppressed something.

"What daddy?" I do not know who is male and who female. "Here, let me read the card." Tippy stands with her tiny face turned up toward the fluorescent glow of the showcase, as though to the rain. "Why do you like this deer so much?" I am scanning the Latin, the breeding habits.

"She's soft." Tippy looks down modestly. "I think like a pussy willow. And her babies love her so much."

"They do," I find myself foolishly assuring her. "They do."

"But then she dies so I hate her when she dies." She looks at me warily. "She's not old so why does she have to get dead?"

"I do not know this Bambi story, dear, I'm sorry." This is a pity, I must do my homework for her, but where to begin?

"You know my daddy went and died too." She says this with wide eyes. She is only a little child, Gerda: to be afraid of her!

"Oh no—Tippy, no, he didn't die." But I do not so much as know his name, Renata has never spoken of her lover—was he a man she had cared about over time or one of her atrocious acts, her "one-night stands," and Tippy the outcome for a thousand times a thousand nights? This is privileged information even from Tippy.

I cannot believe my daughter ever had such fantasies about her missing father, I told her so clearly why he was not with us and she seemed always to understand. I bend and embrace this child who is so complete to the naked eye. She is smiling, her little picket teeth are showing.

"Would you like to see him?" I ask her.

"Well, I don't know if I'd like him much." Rebuking. "Only maybe that was Daddy that time, coming out of the bathroom."

"What, coming out of the bathroom when?"

She laughs. "This big man with his—" and she gestures at her lap, approximately so.

"What do you mean, dear, what did the man have?"

"A funny thing, a dumb swingy thing but I don't like it."

"Tippy—"

"Don't kiss me, come on." She wriggles away. Halfway across the huge dark vaulted room, looking back at me, squarely she bumps into a fat teen-aged girl who staggers back. Well, she has barely been hurt but she appears to be affronted nonetheless. "Watch where you're going!" she shouts in a huge cracked voice which even Bambi must hear behind glass. Her eyes become quite tiny, disappearing into the troughs of her cheeks. She is a sad young girl, straining her clothes tight across her thighs. One can see how easily such a creature might be bruised, all in the gaping place between her look of inviolability and what is no doubt an ego the size of a pea. She shouts at the child and seizes her wrist, jerking her right off the ground like a small doll. Tippy shrieks.

"Please! Leave the child alone." Tippy dangles horribly, crooked, like meat upon a hook.

The girl glares at me. And while she looks to see if I am a stranger, for I am certainly not the mother, Tippy gets her tiptoes on the ground and punches this girl in swollen breast and stomach, a succession of blows for which she summons, clearly, her whole small valiant strength. She is like, what is it called, a one-man band, everything goes at the one time, barely connected, her feet quite decent weapons (as I have discovered) at calf level, her hands tearing and pummeling at the groin and hips. The poor victim, nonplussed, stands with her legs apart absorbing blows in all her quivering parts.

And so I must stop looking in wonder and separate them. As in my own more subtle battles with this child she is well-matched with any adult. However pathetic, she is not helpless, she shall prevail.

"Jesus," the fat girl says. She has tears on the jutting ledge of her cheeks, they have been squeezed from the hidden raisin eyes. "Jesus, lady, you better keep her on a leash."

To which I must smile ruefully. Secretly I am very proud of this performance—she is what I believe is called a feisty dog, and I like this far better than the fraudulent quiet, the sullen helplessness of others I could name who take the easy refuge of tears and a delicate bruisable blond body. But Renata loves her bruises, honors and keeps them; she erases her own footsteps. And I? I talk, I should guess, I keep hostile silences at bay. I know. Each to his own.

❀ ❀ ❀

On my buzzer I call for Sam Eisenstadt.

He enters smiling as always, because he enjoys being ingratiating and he is vain about the luck that has put his long face just, just over the line of homeliness into some kind of ethnically indeterminate style. Greek, Lebanese, Italian, but oh not Jewish, Sam? It is all part of his technique.

Our preliminaries consist of a hasty review of some depositions he has in hand. They are well done: no complaints. He smooths, lovingly, a corner of that air-blown hair. Then he sits, hands on long knees, expectantly.

"So, Sam," say I, glumly. There is such a gray and weary word: "glumly"?

"So, Gerda."

"You have, a few weeks ago, made an interesting but rather loose interpretation of a simple request, haven't you?" This is fishing. The man Tippy saw could have been anyone; it could have been ten different men on ten occasions, coalesced into one nightmare. Frank who lives down the hall and comes incessantly for signatures to his petitions. The delivery boy. Catalina's surviving leather-jacket son, whatever is his name. But I can feel how the water moves when I bait my hook: certain ripples. Confused light and shadow reflected on the surface.

"What in the hell is that supposed to mean?" He is very quickly defensive, the dark hair bristles, I suspect, on his boyish neck. In turn it bristles on mine.

"Oh, Sam, the day I sent you to Renata." I spread wide my hands. "What foolishness."

"Gerda, this is—" He rises, tugging at his tie, does all the things we laugh at when they occur in court, turns his back, paces a bit, chooses to come back and sit frowning and determined. "We're adults, Gerda. Although I'll admit I wonder about myself sometimes." Quick smile, which does not disarm. "You shouldn't send other people to do your dirty work if you intend to complain about the results." But he looks down at his fingers, studies the cuticles; he is not feeling quite in the right.

"My daughter isn't well, Sam."

"She seemed pretty well to me." He gives me one daring look, the brow lowered as if to menace me but not truly: to pretend menace. "No, really, Gerda, this stopped being between you and me and became my business, and Renata's, very quickly. I didn't have a contract, you know: perform such and such a duty, achieve these results by sundown. Whatever I might think about what happened—and I think a lot of things I don't intend to tell you—thank god life's a little more unpredictable than that."

This is not a line worthy of pursuit. Therefore I come to the only point that matters any more to me.

"All right. I personally believe you had some responsibility to me, some honor to maintain, but we shall let that alone. I want to tell you that I intend now to work to remove my daughter's child from her care. When she has no small baby girl to influence, then she shall be free to do as she pleases, and when and where. Then the two of you may take whatever advantage of each other most pleases you."

He opens his mouth and closes it.

I have trouble with my hands which I can only clutch with: a pencil, a rubber band. Each other. "You tell me, young man free as a bird of all responsibility, do you find it a salubrious atmosphere for a child to meet in the afternoon her mother's lovers, whoever they may be, and in what numbers, walking naked in her house? Do you think this constitutes a proper curriculum for a baby?"

Sam churns in his armchair, whose leather clicks and settles beneath him. He crosses his long legs and uncrosses them. His socks appear to extend to his armpits. "Well—you think this happens a lot? I can't imagine—"

"No, dear, I am sure you like to fancy yourself one in a million, irresistible and such. Well, I have no concern for the vanities of your love life, you know, you could—when it comes to numbers, no, I have no idea. I do not know what scenes she has allowed, or even perhaps invited, her daughter to witness, I cannot think about it. I know nothing about Renata's life. Less than nothing. She lives in a world I do not even care to penetrate, it makes me sick even to contemplate, let alone to imagine the particulars." Tippy in the doorway watching the rise and fall of bare flesh, watching her mother helpless there, crying out. No. "But even without such disgraceful events, she is keeping this child in solitary confinement. She deserves to be more disturbed than she is."

"Is she disturbed? Tippy?"

I lick my lips. "No, I do not think she is. Arbitrary. Unpredictable. Possibly a bit unstable, but nothing for which she can truly be faulted, considering all. . . ."

"Gerda, are you sure you're the one to think about this? You really want to initiate proceedings and do some formal kind of thing? Because I get the sense you're punishing her—" Sam is relieved that he is not the butt of my anger. His color has returned to his cheeks. Now perhaps he shall help me.

"I should not be." I chew on my pencil: that sourness I have tasted every day of my working life. "I know I ought not to be, it violates my principle of impartiality, of course it does. But tell me, then, what am I to do? Who shall protect this child for me?"

"Has she ever gone for help?"

"Help. What help. Look, my friend, this is her passive form of suicide, you see. Who is to intervene? I have known for a very long time that to live there with me was the worst stimulation to all her fantasies, her—her nothingness—that could be. But how can one evict an invalid? And with a child to care for? So I have got to the point where I say, 'Fine, my dear, you want to slit open your young life and let every hope and talent spill out and wash down the drain? I myself may wish to spit on you, repudiate you, but fine, that too is your right, if you wish to call down such curses on your head.'" I myself was the attorney, in 1934, for a young woman named Harriet Malma, in Floral Park, New York, who slashed her wrists into a bathtub—unlucky and inept, she lived only to be arrested for the attempt, and charged with a criminal offense. And eagerly I took the case—it was my first of significance—and won for her full disposition rights to her own spirit and body, let the church howl as it may. "Narrow and obsessive let her be, Sam, but I have a life I am still in process of enjoying. Let me not drown with her and let her daughter who is defenseless not be dragged down between the two of us."

Sam anticipates me. "What can I do for you, Gerda? I'm not bearing witness against anybody." He stretches his legs, relaxed and in the clear.

"Well, I wish to ask—this is difficult for me, Sam." I put my hands before my face so as not to see him. "Is there, perhaps, any chance at all that this is a relationship you would be naturally inclined to pursue with Renata? Because—"

When I dare to look he is shaking his head very far to this side and that: a total *no* involving every neck muscle. "She's a fine woman, Gerda, I like Renata, you know, but no way. No way am I getting involved. She's got her agenda and I had an afternoon on it. An hour at the most. I don't even think she intended any more than that. She just wanted me to find where she had it hidden." Which makes him smile. I am not amused.

"You are not about to—"

"Thanks but no thanks. What I've learned from you, old mama, and there's nothing you can do about it now, is: you make each mistake once, right? Your whole life makes enough of them over and over again that you can't control, so you've got to go on the pretense that there are a couple you can handle. Have I got that right?"

Alas, he is a capable student, however smug. I am on my own. The court shall have my granddaughter. If they allow it I shall raise her. Second motherhood at a time when I should be preparing for second childhood. Anna-Joyce shall be delighted.

Her right to annihilation extends no farther than herself. It is admirably simple. Renata's madness, be it real or feigned, receding or reviving, shall be brought and laid at her empty doorstep. One does not trifle with any life.

❀ ❀ ❀

I phone my daughter to begin to make this rescue happen. To her I say, "Tomorrow it shall be hot again, Renata, that is what they are saying. I would like to plan for all of us a trip. You and Tippy and me. To the country somewhere. Will you be so good as to count it one of your days on terra firma, sane enough for some rudimentary conversation? There are some things to be discussed."

"But it's Thursday," she objects, quite sanely.

"No matter. If I get out of town, Friday perhaps I shall work better. I am very distracted here."

She is hesitant, perhaps suspicious, as she has every reason to be: I do not tend to play hooky from my work.

Yes, she can rent a car. All right. She has the sound of a woman who is in the dark being followed by a strange man. All right, she shall pack a picnic lunch. Can we perhaps take along Catalina and her family, whose apartment must be so hot in this season? No, decidedly we cannot. Tippy shall be delighted, I offer. Yes. She is at Monica's, a birthday party for one of the children, very nice. Still. We circle each other, breathing slowly and carefully, I feel we shall have need of *seconds*, do you understand what I mean? But while I may have a thousand friends after all these years, Sam appears to be no friend to Renata. There may be others and there may not be. Whom does she truly have but herself, her dearest enemy?

I should not have had a daughter. Nor should she have had another will to bend. Our family should have seen to its future in time and tied knots at all the entrances and exits. This defective line, like a plant that is all stem and leaves and nothing left for fruit or flower. No, perhaps I should have had *two* daughters. Then I would have known, would I not, that I could know nothing. One child tells you too much about yourself, or so you think; tells you more than can possibly be true. One child holds blame up to your face like a candle flame, to see you by. But two—dear god, now I see: look at two! I had thought one was too many but it was too few, look at Alejandro and this thieving twin, they negate each other; at least negate their mother's responsibility for them. Neither is the only necessary result. . . . Do you know what I am saying? I am saying that their characters would have fallen into the crack between. The evidence is contradictory. Renata is correct, she has hated her unborn brother and I have laughed her continually away, but she turns out to be correct in the end. It is he I would have loved. He would at very least have given me a second chance.

I remember this so well from school: that when General Cambronne was given the summons to surrender at Waterloo, the schoolbooks tell us that he replied, "The guard will die but will

not surrender." But do you know what was his sole (reported)
reply? Ah, she—Renata—has had her way indeed, at last has reduced me to a single word and one of her favorites if not mine,
the one she was born rehearsing. The general said, *"Merde,"* and
laid down his arms.

☙ ☙ ☙

At seven-thirty I am at her door. How bizarre. A woman in a
salmon-orange nightgown, ungirdled forever, gray hair unbraided,
stands knocking at the jamb of her own bedroom. Inside a young
woman who acts entirely like someone else's daughter stirs in her
mother's warm sheets, opens her eyes to a darkened room which
she undoubtedly shall never feel at home in. Why should she recognize it, there is a mirror above the long dresser, a wooden coat
of arms above the mirror shining with something at its top like a
pineapple, a hand grenade—bad copy of a Tudor design; photo-
graphs of eminent strangers in the corner above a Queen Anne
chair full of her tousled clothes. What are young women such as
Renata like when they arise? (My husband arose all grasping sex,
opened his pale eyes to find himself engorged with empty
thoughts and, I always thought, the simple need to urinate. How
he loved to violate my sleep.) Now how does this lithe young animal waken? Looking for company? I shall guess that she does not
always know who is beside her.

She flails in the sheets. How does she ever hear the child when
she wakens? There is such a peculiar bereft falling in my chest.
Bare to the waist, she rests. Her breasts disappear when she lies so.
A woman made in the medieval pattern to live no life of her own:
only to comb her weak blond hair and sing and follow men. She
has stood no chance with me.

I have felt this before—a dry need to cry with nothing to cry
for. Unculminating. Deep red. I have, as it were, smelled the feeling before, if you can follow. The jasmine I smelled with my very
first long menstrual periods, the pain I called the bloody flux. A

summer before an open window, not in Colmar, it was Paris, we were newly arrived from home, and the streets were wet. I was hot with a fever of cramping pain and I would not cry in a roomful of boy cousins. . . . And this is what the menstruation was for, was it not? This stranger asleep in my bed. Everyone is so sentimental about Rilke, his Greek boy in marble. That poem is like the threat of an unidentified accuser and to me it gives offense. I look at the marble white body of this woman and ask why—can someone persuade me precisely why—it is I who must change my life.

five

RENATA

The elevator sets down inch by inch in that parachute slow motion it has, a lot of time spent touching bottom. She emerges looking straight ahead, as though she's climbing to the gallows proudly. Without a single word we walk out, I in my coolest old Indian cotton, my mother dressed, I mean it, as though she were going to work—how sad, that she has no occasions on which to bend, say, in new directions. I suppose it's a cotton dress she's wearing, a kind of cord like a summer suit; but it's not a dress in which one could imagine sitting under a real tree. No wading for a woman in stockings.

I gesture to where we're double-parked. Maybe it saves us some awkwardness that Tippy, who came with me to get the car from Avis, is asleep all over the front seat. Wordlessly I open the back and Mother goes in still silent, the prisoner. And this is the way we leave the city. The car snakes in absolute silence along the highways, coming to all the joints, the choice points, and moving on. I can't say I'm tense; there's an almost chastening calm to our silence, I know Mother is thinking, thinking, probably cursing me under her breath, but I am trying to make myself remember across the long blank years to a time when both of us were pliable and able to take impressions, clay that hadn't hardened yet.

She is very precisely folding a large man's handkerchief in her lap. It becomes a tiny square. That's something she used to do

with me when I was little, she had the most intricate ways to tele-
scope fine papers by folding them. Then she'd shake out the folds
with a great flourish like a magician and there would be amazing
designs where I hadn't expected them. I'd try to do it and make a
tangle which she'd try to admire. "See, here is how you are to use
your nails," she would say and make an efficient edge like a newly
ironed seam. Well, she was trying; at her own good time trying.
We would walk through the park and look for succulents in the
grass. Puzzles and tricks on paper—I brought to school a method
for adding nines that made me famous for a day in arithmetic.
The teacher sent me to the board. There seemed to be some hope.
But she didn't have enough tricks and left to my own devices, I
never listened in that class.

Nut games. I remember those, at Passover, nut in the crack of
wall and floor, to be hit and moved and claimed for the "pot."
Mother doing the whole Passover service, both of us huddled
alone at our table like the survivors of a storm when I knew that
was the season of amplitude, time for the gathering of families.
But my grandfather was newly dead, my grandmother feeble, still
in Boston, and Mother was always too busy to take time off to go
there with me: her endless rasp of work burned up everything
green in a great circle around her, parched into my generation and
around back into her mother's. No time, no time for *bubba*, only
phone calls with the old lady incapable of hearing on the phone,
Mother shouting until the very act of speech would irritate her
into silence. I was always shocked, I had no way of knowing how a
grown woman might talk to her mother, what she might feel that
had nothing to do with love.

Now I drive without looking back at her but I'm aware of the
clench in which she sits, suppressing herself. The effort it takes
Gerda Stein to keep her mouth shut would animate a week of
conversation among ordinary people. The weight of her refusals,
like stones closed in her hand.

With a long wail, "Mommmmmmeeeee," Tippy is awake beside
me, stretching querulously. She puckers her chin trying to decide
whether to cry or not, then—she must feel the strength of her
grandmother's stifled presence too—she turns and smiles and
flings herself over the seat so that I get her foot at the side of my

head and nearly lose the steering wheel. I turn on the radio: country music and madrigals. I hum faintly to myself, trying to ignore them, to be alone; sing along with the piping voices as if there's a small audience inside my mouth.

In back they're being conspiratorial. Impossible secrets drift across to me. Mother prodding for real gold, even chips of it, venturing absurdly, "And when I am really, truly mad" (the troooly a very serious six-syllable word) "I stamp my feet, *so*, did you know that?"

But Tippy's going on about her princesses and won't be distracted. "I got a crown. *You* know *that?*"

"Where is it?"

"Home in my castle." I can see without seeing how her face breaks up into quarters at least, some for laughter, the others still, in the irreducible seriousness of it all. "It's gold with jewels all over but I leave it home all the time."

"Oh, you do not ever take it out and wear it?"

She's screwing up her face into a little parody of my mother thinking. Also she's kicking the seat behind me rhythmically. "Tippy," I'm forced to say, "please stop that."

She ignores me. "Sometimes I take it to my friends down the hall at the end. But no place else. And one time Mama stepped on it and cracked it along the whole side."

"It was an accident."

No one has a word for me, I suppose they want me back in my madrigals. My mother makes a grab for her, tickles all her warm places, makes her laugh a hiccupy slightly out-of-control laugh. Tippy must like her grandma today because she hasn't had to say no yet. "Do you know what you are, Grandma? You're a cantaloupe. A cant-a-loupe." She says the "loupe" as I've never heard it, in her mouth it's damp and dark.

"A cantaloupe, *Kind?!* A cantaloupe? How about a watermelon? No, a what is it, honeydew, is that a nice word to be? Honeydew." They're off again together, rocking. My mother has never been so boisterous; all for me. It's her proof of pulse, of vitality, for fear I'll exempt her from the living. The madrigals make me feel like I'm walking on a bath mat; terry cloth, yellow, soft little prickles. Yellowing moss . . . I watched Mother sleeping on a bus one time and said, "You look like your bones are made of iron." No, glass, it must have been glass because there was a sense of overvaluing in the remark, somewhere, of clutching at herself. Unseemly. Well, Lloyd's would have nothing to insure of her except her head, would they insure a fine-tuned information retrieval system, all the years of read words filed away in it, indexed, the pages filed, dozens and dozens of them on the head of a pin? Of me they'd insure only the part of proven value, that most efficient birth canal and corduroy road, that weeping broad and narrow way they all love better than they love my head, better than I love myself. Of Mother yes, only the head and the rest be damned. And whatever will Tippy have in a few years? Already she's one of those people who can separate two fingers up, space, two down. Her own person. She can't stand peanut butter; wool makes her sneeze; she likes her ears kissed. I fail her in my own special way, she will—how about this symmetry?—succeed me.

Tippy's shrieking with laughter in the back seat. I murmur, "Hey, take it easy back there, you'll start coughing and bring up your whole breakfast."

Tippy ignores the warning and the waves of giggles wash in and out. Giggling, that strong inhalation and sizzle of spit, is not something I've ever heard her do with her grandmother, who usually subdues things before she gets to that point. She's put on my purple flowered kerchief—I see that when she pokes her head wildly next to mine to grin—and goes on fumbling with the points. Grimly, Mother ties it for her and then tries to help her find her sandals. I wonder how long she can take the strain of this exaggerated gaiety before I get Tippy thrust back at me.

We're at the gate of Torora State Park. The ranger looks into the car and writes down how many of us there are. Tippy sticks out her tongue. The man thrusts his back, not smiling—amazing, long and red, it looks like a dog's hot sudden tongue and Tippy giggles convulsively, a little afraid.

A family has begun to pile out of the station wagon in front of our car, a scene from the circus. They come and come, each unbending, long legs, short legs, as they pull loose of the rear. I count eleven children and then the mother eases out, pale legs first. She's fairly young, fairly attractive, I guess, wearing a tight permanent and a hot pink sun dress. If she's the bearer of the stretch marks she deserves, she seems undaunted. Mother of the Year, well-ridden Guernsey cow, will she wear a bikini?

The man at the gate, leaning his arms on the window next to us, is making lewd notes on the scene, at which neither of us smiles encouragement. Finally Mother sits forward a bit and commands him, in her best belligerence, "You will please remove your arms from our window. You have an insulting mind, the mentality of a teen-ager." He looks amazed and straightens up abruptly. "You like some proof to tweak your pathetic little imagination," she says to his back as he retreats, "that a woman has been on her back for a man." Ah, the *ur*-feminist, are you, Mother. I applaud you with one hand.

We park the car. We've come two hours without a word. It has its own absurdity, so comic we ought to laugh and embrace and be done with this foolishness. But I'm not the grudge bearer today. What does she want to say to me, what news from the land of impartiality and restitution? My mother has disappeared into the depths below the back seat to look for her vast bag. The blighted *Times* Classified has come apart all over the place. Savagely she balls it up. She finds her shoes and pulls them onto her feet; they were off so that Tippy could demonstrate how good she's gotten at counting toes.

I lift Tippy out of the car. Her head is huge in my purple scarf, from the back she looks freakish, hypercephalic. Her feet are small as stones.

And so we stand and face each other on the parched gravel of the parking lot. My mother's mouth twitches irregularly and when she looks at me, full in the face with her lovely large heavy-lidded eyes, I feel a very strange, distant, disembodied pity. She has been failed. How else can I say it. I want to tell her I know, I too have failed and been failed and I want to say humbly and without protection, Mama, you're right. She seems terribly unrelated to me standing there, I feel as though, if I asked her what's the matter she'd take my hands, like a stranger, and tell me. This is hard to get right: not that I'm forgiving her our differences, or blaming myself for all the things she's caused me to be—only that in some elusive way, the grief in her, the pain that has actually silenced her, not me, and filled her up with this alien humility, pulls me away to a great distance, and I can almost turn and feel how her life must feel. What if she had been vulnerable all our lives, our life. . . .

But that's futile, isn't it, she's herself and therefore not often vulnerable. And I can't afford to be—the soldier who puts down his arms to stare into the eyes of his brother enemy—he gets a bayonet for his sympathy. There's no moral lesson here. Probably she was looking at me thinking, I shouldn't have expected anything better from you in the first place, how dare I be disappointed in you. And she's right, of course: I've made a profession of being unacceptable.

"We shall talk later," she says to me, nodding her head at all her foregone conclusions. "I have some things to say to you."

"I'd just as soon we not bother to talk at all," I tell her and to my astonishment I find my jaw quivering. "We have nothing to say, no negotiations. No compromises to make, why even bother? Why don't we just—sit under the same sky or something for a while? Let's go look at the waterfalls with Tippy, just—be quiet together." I look down in an embarrassment I can't explain. I feel as though I'm about to fall to pieces, shards of anger and regret and fear like slivers of broken mirror: seven times seven years bad luck.

Mother begins to answer but Tippy's pulling at my wrist. "All right," I tell her, "all right, all right, let's go see the rainbows." What good punctuation she can be. A dash in the conversation, and when you try to pick it up again, you can't remember what you were saying.

The view of the waterfall is down a cement pathway and even with my throatful of tears I can remember it with a lurch of wonder. Last time I was here, there were three or four, no, five, rainbows in the spray. It had turned out to be a weekend I was in the midst of breaking up with a man, oh who?—lover No. 6, 13, 28—someone called Anders who was Swiss and very soft-spoken and who played the flute. I brutalized him with my love, this was instead of my junior year of college, and he was fighting free. My mother loved him; maybe it was the Bach that poured out at his fingertips. So we came here to fight, to storm off into the woods alone and fling our sleeping bags down in opposite corners of the tent. But the first day, before all that, when we were looking up at the dense white fall, its wild spit and drizzle and the short arched rainbows just living in there perpetually, I had been so unfamiliarly, unbearably happy. . . . The way it all turned out, the coming back down, deflated, weary with stalking this enemy I loved, had felt more natural to me. I cried all the way home, the pain made a monkey out of me, but that was not as surprising and terrifying to me as the five unearned, undying rainbows.

"Mother, over here!" I call. She's down on one knee behind the far fender, tying Tippy's kerchief for the third time.

Mother unbends slowly and with a dignity so fierce it nearly makes me laugh. "Must one climb to see these waterfalls, Renata?" she asks me in precisely the tone she would use on a witness.

I do laugh. "No, maman, one—descends. One—ah—lowers oneself inch by inch beside the raging torrent. Come—it's a cinch."

So I walk slowly, breathing the washed air. Shaking my live hair, getting the dark rumble of the highway out of my ears. We aren't going to stay overnight. There's no tent in the trunk—can you imagine Gerda Stein in a sleeping bag, wearing bug spray, eating out of tin plates? She's like slum kids who wither when they get too far from concrete. I'd love to lie against the breathing side of the tent and watch car lights swell and dwindle on the walls, I'd float off on watery sleep on my air mattress alone. They wouldn't have me. (Then in the morning I'd feel a weight against my side and sure enough, there would be Tippy my love, pressed against me, afraid or too cold or too hot or too buggy and desperate, already crossing her legs tight, always desperate, to go pee.)

My mother is taking the steps slowly, as though she has just come out of a plaster cast. They are slippery, maybe you have to feel young and unbreakable to run down. She's calling back to Tippy to come see the rainbows. With great ostentation she does not look at me. Tippy is behind her, headed down the concrete path above the basin at the foot of the falls. She runs lightly as though she wears ballet shoes.

Well, there will be this waterish smell in the air for a whole day now, clean and pungent, and sharp smoke and red sparks turning in the air like Roman candles over all the dinner fires. I feel my chest swell my halter, feel the stiff fabric over my bare breasts. All your senses come unclogged here, like pores. Maybe it's time for Tippy and me to move to the country like everybody else. . . . You need to get exhausted and hungry, then have a thick rare steak, the hell with rice and veggies, and later, the way men like a good cigar, a nice strong sweaty man in a plaid woolen shirt. You need to make love in your clothes like a kid and then wear their smell the next day, that and the sharp fire smell. . . .

At one landing I stop and look down. My mother and Tippy are already down to the next turn. There are two falls really, the upper one so high and so strong it has polished some perfectly shaped saddles of rock. They look almost dry, the water beats over them so tightly, so smoothly. It snarls and hisses at the bottom and before it can straighten itself into a neat flow it is flung again, jagged and harsh, over a short chunky cliff, as though taken by surprise and pummeled to pieces once and for all. Humpty Dumpty foaming in a pool.

From above, I see Tippy taking the last small step down, her mouth open in the sudden rainy chill. The purple scarf, heavy as a flag, flaps a regular beat against her cheek.

"Hold her hand," I shout. My mother leans toward me, cupping her ear to show she is trying to hear, but the waterfall washes every sound out of the air. By now I'm pointing to my own hand with a furious thrusting finger—maybe it only looks like I'm asking for the time—"Get her *hand*, her *hand*."

I stop, the missed beat, to wonder what the yellow creepers are that have spilled over the path, that are being stepped on, oozing juice without color, slippery as blood. Gooseberries?

When I start down the path again, I look for my daughter's purple head, the borrowed grown-up babushka all around it, Tippy-turning-Renata. It takes a long moment to register, even to see it, a light-year passing. She was there and now she is not there.

My mother turns, her back is to me. She is alone.
She runs to safety on the grass.
There are no ledges down. I try to go but the rock face is sheer. The bastards. Am I supposed to jump? It's a straight line.

To the ranger my mother says, "I do not know. I do not know. Please not to ask again, it is impossible. I was not paying attention to know." She lies down on the grass, on the trampled creepers with her hands over her ears, elbows up, she lies like a large horse giving up, folding its unfoldable legs, and tries to sleep.

She is pulled up so violently by me—by my hand, I mean—that the ranger restrains me, holding my arm, looking at it anxiously as if it's an unpredictable animal. It is, in fact; it is not connected to me by any impulses I recognize.

No, I tell the ranger, rubbing my muscle slowly, angrily, round and round, no, it did not appear that this woman was trying to fling herself over the cliff. She would never do that. She preserves herself. This woman is my mother. She was here first. She was looking for my baby. She couldn't see anything even a second after it happened, all those bright colors, flags, vanished. But she wasn't going anywhere, no. Where in the world could she go?

My mother is a heap on the stone landing. Her head is retracted into her collar, her formal working-day go-to-court dress. Her skirt over her stockinged legs is pulled at an indiscreet angle over white thighs I hardly recognize. Bent over that way she is like something unnatural that might have grown beside the gooseberries, a huge gall. If they are gooseberries. She does not howl, as one might have predicted; or beat her breast in the tradition. She is quiet and hard and precise as a stone. Solidified. With her knees up and her arms around them she looks like a peasant in childbirth. I know that is not an appropriate thing to think. I should not forget how she always diminishes herself in anger, as though the force of her true feeling were so great she does not have to heighten it. Less is more. Is enough, at least. She trusts her powers. So, in sorrow or guilt, there too. I'll bet she didn't utter a sound having me.

The child, she tells the ranger in her measured voice, took one step back. One half step back, her mouth was open, asking, maybe smiling, into the sucking wind. She didn't fall over backward, feet up, head back. She disappeared. As if a trap door opened. As if the earth was pulled out from under her, so very simple: she was there one second, her curls, her purple, her yellow, her small red feet, and the next second—no sound, no protest!—she was gone.

"I do not believe it, things do not happen this way, I just shall not believe it," she goes on in her ordinary voice, parched of conviction. "I shall not believe she—ever was."

She does not believe in accident, in impotence, in anything but choosing. You see, I want to say, you see, *you see*. . . .

The ranger is not equipped to deal with the idiosyncrasies of accent she has preserved so quaintly all these years. He says, to no one, "I hope to hell that comes out clearer at the inquest, I couldn't get no more than two words of that."

My mother grabs his arm roughly. "Then you do not know how to listen to English, perfectly proper English," she says to him, finally excited.

"Whew, English!" the ranger says and pretends to mop his brow.

I know approximately what I am doing, it is so very easy to be calm. I am standing behind them, about to fly away, on the balls of my feet. I don't know where I think I'll run but I come very close. It's only chance that keeps me from disappearing into the woods and never coming back. I know how it is her voice has gone so blank. If I blink I'll wake up. We will go up to the top of the stone stairs and begin again. Some moments have no reality in your life, they're in your head. Why can't you choose the ones that will be real and count? Isn't it all in our heads? If I blink I'll go back to before. Why not? Why *not?*

The ranger holds Mother's arm stiffly with one hand, mine with the other. We look like we're about to do a folk dance with perfect classic symmetry. He says, "I got to get some more information. Can I trust you two here a minute? Do me a favor." Why does he say that? Do we look violent? Or does he think we should be? My features are bleached away in the blast of something like a bomb too far away to be heard. I feel like my eyebrows have been seared off, my nose, my collarbones sanded flat. She looks at me, unblinking, like a blind woman I've seen who always seems to me to be in a state of shock. There's something satisfying about it, as though the event for the shock has finally befallen. A long overdue rainstorm and then the bolt of lightning you've been waiting for.

Keeping his eye on us the ranger retrieves his book, what looks like his traffic ticket book, from a rock where it's gotten sodden with spray, and continues to make his plodding entries. I can never believe policemen aren't faking, the laborious way they enter the written world, like children. Tippy never learned to write: only T and W, I don't know why W.

"You got any more children?" he asks me.

The poor man, I think, he has sweated two great half circles on the back of his uniform. I feel apologetic. He is obviously a very nice man, of regular habits and simple expectations. We are shocking him. I feel a strange faint superiority—we are teaching him something—but when I cast around for it, like the punch line of a story I've forgotten, I can't imagine what it could be.

The ranger has received no answer.

"I mean, any other children—than this?" He waves one hand vaguely at the falls, then, looking horrified, as though it has betrayed him, he hides it behind his back. I try to see her face but I can't. What did she look like? I see a baby in a pink suit trying to crawl. That's all.

"Look," he begins, looking down, nearly pawing the ground with his toe like a shy boy about to ask a favor. "Look, you've got to—" He turns to me desperately. For a nice man he has wretchedly cold ice-blue eyes, very Nordic or German. I don't think they can see as clear through as they seem to. "You can't blame her, you better not have to live with that forever. I once— we lost a baby boy once, eight months old. We—" The man is overcome, the perfect stranger. He walks away quickly, showing us a broad back and a corn-beef-red neck. I want to tell him it's all right. Everyone has stories, I don't want their details, I just want to know everyone has them. There are too many details. Or no details. I reach out for him but he's gone to sit on the wet rock. A crowd has formed but there's nothing for them to see. Somewhere very far away I hear someone giving orders that seem to do with finding the body, people are hurrying as though it matters. Well, they matter, their sense, like my mother's, that things you do can help. They still believe that. Till something happens to teach them, they'll go on moving, moving fast. They'll think they're choosing where they go.

I turn back to her where she sits incongruously on the stone and open my mouth to shout something she needs to know—I wonder what it could be—but nothing comes out. It might be the news I've had for her all day and haven't been given an opening for, to tell her that Catalina Huerta is saved without her help. Is seeing visions. She told me yesterday while she washed the kitchen floor. Alejandro is coming to her regularly. His side is healed, he is happy and full of practical advice. She had been skeptical, what could she do with a vision but give it a very hard time, but now there is no doubt, he brought her the winning number last Friday —three hundred and 'fifty bucks with a guarantee from heaven. It had done me good to know that, it would do her good. But as I said, no words are coming out. My tongue like the rest of my face is burned away. *Tippy.*

Then, the whole top of her head beginning to move, slowly, laboriously rolling down her cheeks, my mother begins to cry.